AF505914

Transnational advocacy
on the ground

Manchester University Press

Transnational advocacy on the ground

Against corruption in Russia?

DIANA SCHMIDT-PFISTER

Manchester University Press

Manchester and New York

distributed in the United States exclusively by Palgrave Macmillan

Published by Manchester University Press
Oxford Road, Manchester M13 9NR, UK
and Room 400, 175 Fifth Avenue, New York, NY 10010, USA
www.manchesteruniversitypress.co.uk

Distributed in the United States exclusively by
Palgrave Macmillan, 175 Fifth Avenue, New York,
NY 10010, USA

Distributed in Canada exclusively by
UBC Press, University of British Columbia, 2029 West Mall,
Vancouver, BC, Canada V6T 1Z2

British Library Cataloguing-in-Publication Data
A catalogue record for this book is available from the British Library

Library of Congress Cataloging-in-Publication Data applied for

ISBN   978 0 7190 8468 3 hardback

First published 2010

Typeset
by Action Publishing Technology Ltd, Gloucester
Printed in Great Britain
by CPI Antony Rowe Ltd, Chippenham, Wiltshire

Contents

List of tables and figures

Preface

This book aims at examining the involvement of Russian civil society actors in transnational anti-corruption advocacy and therewith, more generally, at gaining a better understanding of the nature and implications of the interrelations between international, domestic and local actors in the context of advocacy related to a global cause. Accomplishing this aim has entailed a rather long and far-reaching research process. The idea for this research began in 2002 when I had just finalised a comprehensive study about the efforts to nominate the Siberian Lake Baikal as a UNESCO World Natural Heritage Site. Essentially, this presented an analysis of a particular transnational advocacy process having Russia, or more precisely a remote Siberian location, as its focus. But more generally, this study had once more underlined the importance of disentangling the case-specific relationships between the various actors involved. Earlier research had already suggested that domestic civil society organisations (CSOs) played a crucial role in most cases of transnational advocacy and global norm promotion. However, while focusing on the interrelations between the international and the domestic level, the resulting concepts of transnational advocacy seemed too imprecise concerning the role of CSOs today. Much of the debate on the role of civil society had remained biased normatively (civil society as the 'good ones') and conceptually (civil society as a leading force) as well as vague empirically. Having spent much time in Moscow and around Irkutsk and Buryatia (the two Russian regions embracing Lake Baikal) for interviews and observations, I felt that the roles of the various actors were less clear-cut and that the involvement of local civil society actors in particular was more ambivalent. Apart from these conceptual considerations, my study pointed to another issue in terms of content: the widespread concerns of Russian environmental activists that corruption was everywhere in Russia and was hampering their efforts to introduce international standards. At the same time, there seemed to be international concern about addressing this problem as well and there were possibilities to gain support through international and Western grant programmes. The negotiations of the United Nations Convention Against Corruption had only just started by that time. So I went deeper into these two aspects, the analytical puzzle of how to conceptualise the involvement of local (rather than domestic) civil society in transnational advocacy processes, and the empirical question of when and how transnational anti-corruption advocacy had arrived in Russia and how successful it might be. My doctoral research project, conducted at Queen's University Belfast (2003–6) thus presented a first attempt to contrast the empirical findings about anti-corruption advocacy with prominent theories about transnational advocacy networks (Schmidt 2006a). However, having become increasingly puzzled by the many discrepancies between given causal and normative assumptions and the empirical findings at hand, I finally realised that a more explorative and less predetermined analytical perspective was needed. Two more years followed during which I more carefully and more systematically traced the unfolding of transnational advocacy against corruption in Russia. I kept going back to the data, the many international documents and campaigns, country strategy papers and evaluation reports, surveys and indices, news pieces, websites, interview transcripts, and field notes. I also added new data, departing for a while from the Russian case and getting better insight into international anti-corruption advocacy in comparison with earlier advocacy in the environmental and human rights realms and into anti-corruption advocacy in the Eastern European region more generally. This process was facilitated by other collaborative projects in which I was involved at that time and which presented excellent room for subjecting my analysis of the Russian case to further comparative reflection and putting it into a wider perspective. Hence, rather than reproducing the main parts of my earlier doctoral study, this book presents a completely rewritten interpretation of the data at hand, supplemented by new data that allowed for a thorough assessment of transnational advocacy as a multi-faceted process. While I continued contrasting my findings with accepted notions of transnational advocacy networks, I found too many differences and contradictions that prevented me from simply modifying existing models with regard to this case. The contradictions were not merely related to the Russian case, but also to the process of anti-corruption advocacy in comparison with earlier global advocacy, especially in the environmental and human rights realms. I therefore felt that it was time to arrive at fresh theoretical conclusions on the basis of the rich empirical data basis at hand.

As a contribution to the series 'Perspectives on Democratic Practice', the book provides an exemplary discussion of anti-corruption advocacy as a global movement of a new generation. While, so far, there is no credible evidence that this movement has been successful in reducing corruption around the world, it presents an instructive case in terms of its comprehensive scope, professionalised structures, and the actor relationships entailed therewith. With its particular focus on the involvement of Russian civil society in that movement, this study sheds new light on the factors determining the inclusion and exclusion of civic actors on the ground.

Acknowledgements

The work presented here greatly benefited from the help of countless individuals and institutions. It is impossible to mention everybody. I want to express my thanks to the many commentators at conferences, seminars, and colloquiums where I presented preliminary arguments and selected findings, the many practitioners who agreed to be visited and interviewed, and the many other experts who readily answered detailed questions and provided additional material by email. I should here also acknowledge the influence of an earlier teacher, Prof. Dietrich Soyez, who directed my interest towards transnational advocacy and the role of civil society actors therein when I was a student of geography at the University of Cologne. I am particularly indebted to my former supervisor, David Phinnemore, for his critical, constructive, and extensive feedback on my PhD thesis, which laid the first groundwork for this book. I also wish to thank Prof. Stephen White who, as the external examiner of that thesis, engaged me in an in-depth discussion about the Russian case study that encouraged much of the follow-up research and the revisions I did for this book. Furthermore, I am much obliged to Valerie Bunce, Richard Sakwa and Luis de Sousa, Agnes and Patrick von Maravić, Thomas Pfister, Heiko Pleines, and Susanne Schatral for their instructive comments on earlier papers and partial drafts. Moreover, lots of Russian experts, activists, colleagues, and friends have contributed to the development of the ideas presented here and have continuously enlightened me on what would appear rather naive from a Russian point of view while seeming exciting from a Western perspective, and vice versa. Particular thanks are due to the team of Oleg Pachenkov and

Irina Olimpieva for sharing their views and findings on St. Petersburg and beyond, to Masha Lipman for inciting a major excursus into the general literature on Russian civil society, to Dmitry Vorobyev for introducing me to essential Russian authors in that field and for co-organising much of the field research undertaken in Irkutsk, as well as to the many individuals who have spared time, resources, and efforts in order to provide me with valuable information, materials and contacts within and beyond their networks. I am also grateful to Wyn Grant and Shirin Rai for encouraging and recommending the publication of this book within the series 'Perspectives on Democratic Practice' and, together with an anonymous referee, for their valuable comments on the manuscript. Not least, special thanks are due to Antonia Phinnemore for her careful proof reading of all the chapters, to Tony Mason at Manchester University Press for tolerating repeated delays in submitting the final version of the manuscript, and indeed to all the people at the Press who have helped to turn the latter into this final product.

In the course of the research and writing I have been hosted and assisted by numerous institutions that have provided hospitable and inspiring environments for writing, discussing and revising one or the other part of this book. I therefore wish to acknowledge the support of the Institute of Governance in Belfast, the Centre for Independent Social Research in St. Petersburg, the Centre for Independent Social Research and Education in Irkutsk, the Heinrich Böll Foundation's office in Moscow, the Research Centre for East European Studies and the Institute of Intercultural and International Studies at the University of Bremen, and the Centre of Excellence 'Cultural Foundations of Integration' at the University of Konstanz. The various field trips would not have been possible without the financial support provided by the Queen's University Belfast, the William & Betty MacQuitty endowment, the British Association for Slavonic and East European Studies, the European Cultural Foundation, and the German Research Foundation (DFG).

And many thanks to you, Thomas and Johannes.

List of abbreviations

ACN	Anti-Corruption Network for Transition Economies
BEEPS	Business Environment and Enterprise Performance Survey
BPI	Bribe Payers' Index
CoE	Council of Europe
CPI	Corruption Perception Index
CSO	Civil society organisation
EBRD	European Bank for Reconstruction and Development
EIB	European Investment Bank
EITI	Extractive Industries Transparency Initiative
EU	European Union
FATF	Financial Action Task Force
FSB	*Federal'naia sluzhba bezopasnosti Rossiiskoi Federatisi* Federal Security Service of the Russian Federation
GCB	Global Corruption Barometer
GONGO	Governmental nongovernmental organisation
GOPAC	Global Organisation of Parliamentarians Against Corruption
GRECO	Group of States against Corruption
GTZ	*Deutsche Gesellschaft für Technische Zusammenarbeit* German Association for Technical Assistance
IFI	International Financial Institution
IMF	International Monetary Fund
INDEM	Information Science for Democracy
INGO	International Nongovernmental Organisation
LDPR	Liberal Democratic Party of Russia

MERiT	*Ministerstvo ekonomicheskogo razvitiia i torgovli Rossiiskoi Federatsii*
	Ministry of Economic Development and Trade of the Russian Federation
MID	*Ministerstvo Inostrannykh Del Rossiiskoi Federatsii*
	Ministry of Foreign Affairs of the Russian Federation
MSI	Management Systems International
MVD	*Ministerstvo Vnutrennykh Del Rossiiskoi Federatsii*
	Ministry of the Interior of Russia
NAK	*National'nyi antikorruptsionnyi komitet*
	National Anti-corruption Committee
NGO	Nongovernmental organisation
OECD	Organisation for Economic Co-operation and Development
OLAF	European Anti-Fraud Office
OPORA	*Obshcherossiiskaia obshchestvennaia organizatsiia malogo i srednogo predprinimatel'stva*
	All-Russian civic small and medium business organisation
OSI	Open Society Institute
PGO	Prosecutor General's Office
RPI	Regional Press Institute
RSPP	*Rossiiskii Soiuz Promyshlennikov i Predprinimatelei*
	Russian Union of Industrialists and Entrepreneurs
SME	Small and medium-sized enterprises
SPAI	Stability Pact Anti-Corruption Initiative
TACIS	Technical Assistance to the Commonwealth of Independent States
TI	Transparency International
TraCCC	Transnational Crime and Corruption Center
U4	U4 Anti-Corruption Resource Centre (formerly Utstein Partnership)
UN	United Nations
UNCAC	United Nations Convention Against Corruption
UNDP	United Nations Development Programme
UNODC	United Nations Office on Drugs and Crime

USAID	United States Agency for International Development
VCIOM	*Vserossiiskii tsentr izucheniia obshchestvennogo mneniia* All-Russian Public Opinion Research Center
WTO	World Trade Organization

1

Transnational advocacy today

Transnational advocacy, that is, processes of principled and strategic mobilisation around a particular issue of international relevance, bringing together governmental and nongovernmental actors across international, domestic and local levels, is no longer a new phenomenon. In many issue areas, global networks, campaigns, and regimes that involve a multitude of nongovernmental and (inter-)governmental actors make international resources available to new actors in domestic struggles and are highly influential in international politics. Only about a decade ago, Margaret Keck and Kathryn Sikkink published one of the pioneering scholarly studies about the emergence and effectiveness of transnational advocacy networks. They suggested that transnational activism around human rights 'foreshadows transnational campaigns in a multiplicity of areas' (Keck and Sikkink 1998: ix). Building on their concept of the 'boomerang pattern', Thomas Risse and colleagues proposed a more dynamic model (known as the 'spiral model') as a 'truly universal' (Risse and Ropp 1999: 238) explanation of the causal mechanisms contained in other domestic socio-political processes of change (see also Risse and Ropp 1999: 273; Risse and Sikkink 1999: 6).[1] Innumerable studies have since then concentrated on the positive effects of combined pressure from above and below – through international and domestic nongovernmental agents – in various issue areas and on various target states. Today, the significance of such synergies and the role of civil society organisations (CSOs) as legitimate players in international and domestic politics have become widely acknowledged in the academic literature.[2]

However, transnational advocacy has become ever more complex in the new millennium. New issue areas have appeared on the international stage which may build on previously existing advocacy efforts in terms of structures, resources, actors and discourses.[3] There is an increasingly consolidating infrastructure for the exchange of information, resources, and services to be used by transnational advocacy in many fields. International organisations, private donors, CSOs, and other subcontractors have become ever more professionalised. This, however, may imply fundamental changes to the nature and impacts of transnational advocacy itself. Not least, in an age of sophisticated methods and technologies in gathering and globally disseminating information about certain socio-political aspects in any country and on a regular basis, it is time to reassess what this means for advocacy practices such as 'information politics' or 'leverage politics' (Keck and Sikkink 1998: 18–24). These are issues that have rarely been addressed within the literature on more recent transnational advocacy efforts.

This book thus presents an attempt to systematically trace and disentangle the highly complex patterns of interaction contained in recent transnational advocacy. It focuses on transnational advocacy against corruption as a rather young field of action and on the particular case of Russia during the Putin era as a rather challenging context for civil society involvement. Starting from the assumption that the study of global advocacy today requires conceptual perspectives other than those derived from studying forerunner global movements, it adopts a more explorative and inductive analytical perspective. It refrains from conventional conceptualisations of the state as a passive, reactive target and domestic CSOs as positive, oppositional, and pro-active forces, who 'seek the most effective means to rally opposition' (Risse and Sikkink 1999: 16), who 'want to tell the truth' (Risse 2000: 203), and who are, as 'principled activists', 'intensely self-conscious and self-reflective' (Keck and Sikkink 1998: 35) in their normative awareness. While the latter is a misplaced conception common to most of the work on civil society (Kopecký 2003: 2), analysis from such a dichotomising angle may prevent an unbiased assessment of the increasingly complex and potentially ambivalent relationships between the involved actors. If one would presume that ties between actors were explicit and visible, and that there was mutual agreement on roles, goals and targets (Keck and Sikkink 1998: 6), this would foreclose many aspects that may ideally just be explored by the empirical analysis. In particular the involvement of civil society actors in transnational advocacy remains a black box to be opened. Taking up on this gap in the literature on transnational advocacy, the following study asks how precisely synergies between domestic CSOs and international actors had unfolded in the given case and how the state had been addressed by these two actor categories. Importantly, this includes the inverse question: how are international and governmental actors relating to domestic civil society? In order to gain a better understanding of the actor relations, a thorough look is taken at the exchange of informational and material resources and services and at the roles of both domestic CSOs and the target state in inviting international networks and instruments into the country. Furthermore, the assessment of the actor relations includes the question: how are the various actors relating to the issue of common concern – corruption (in Russia)?

Anti-corruption advocacy

The global fight against corruption has become a crucial phenomenon in international (and in many cases national) politics. From an analytical perspective, anti-corruption advocacy at first seemed to present just another example of highly successful transnational norm promotion.[4] Within less than a decade, the initiatives of a handful of people, leading to the establishment of Transparency International (TI) as a global civil society organisation, had grown into a veritable international regime involving most leading international organisations, a number of international anti-corruption conventions, immense flows of financial and technical assistance, systematic global information-gathering and dissemination about corruption across countries, and major international conferences etc. (see Chapter 3 for more detail). Several researchers have traced the transformation of the problem of corruption from a domestic into a global concern (e.g. Glynn, Kobrin and Naim 1997; Naim 1995).

The emergence of the global anti-corruption regime during the 1990s was found to be comparable to that of environmental and human rights regimes in many respects, but 'unusual for its breadth and rapid emergence' (McCoy and Heckel 2001: 66).[5] However, the literatures about transnational anti-corruption efforts was also riddled with a number of questions and doubts. Anti-corruption strategies seemed 'beset by problems of transferability, sustainability, cost-effectiveness, sequencing and intent' (Williams 2000: xvii; see also Johnston 2005). Only a few programmes had been successfully implemented on the ground, and some even proved counterproductive.[6] The weighty aspect of Western financial assistance was critically commented upon as an 'anti-corruption industry' (Michael 2004a) or a 'projectization of anti-corruption' that converted the moral campaign issue 'into grant categories and technical assistance contracts' (Sampson 2005: 108, 109). As such, anti-corruption mobilisation appeared to be globalised from its inception, beginning at the top and then penetrating locally (Sampson 2005: 106). Moreover, one of the main awareness-raising and international shaming tools, the cross-country Corruption Perception Index (CPI), regularly published by TI since the mid-1990s, had become criticised for its imprecision in measuring corruption and its failure to contribute to the implementation of international anti-corruption treaties (e.g. Abramo 2005; Galtung 2006). It was also frequently noted that the centrality of values which had characterised traditional transnational activism was supplemented or even outweighed by obvious material concerns (Hotchkiss 1998; Marquette 2004: 425). Not least, authors remain puzzled about the contradictory correlations between the levels of (perceived) corruption and anti-corruption efforts in a given country. These various issues only reinforce the argument that anti-corruption efforts call for a more attentive analysis in their own right.

Clearly, anti-corruption advocacy presented a global movement of a new generation. The possibility of 'piggybacking' anti-corruption efforts upon pre-existing structures, discourses and actor constellations (Schmidt 2007a) presented an important historical factor in explaining the fast emergence of the regime. However, this very condition may have entailed other aspects inhibiting equally resounding successes in the actual implementation of assistance programmes and international instruments. How are the various actors on this basis interrelating to each other in their efforts to promote institutions, practices, and values in a given domestic context (or in a number of countries at once)? Regarding the domestic changes effected by external anti-corruption advocacy, many recent studies have stopped at showing *that* anti-corruption laws have been adopted, anti-corruption institutions have been installed, anti-corruption training programmes realised etc. and *that* a range of international, governmental, and nongovernmental actors had been involved in this process. However, there have been few thorough analyses of *how* these various actors actually related to each other, how they relate to corruption, and how information and resources circulated within their relations to each other.[7] These are important issues that require further empirical analysis.

Eastern Europe presented a region that had received particular attention on the part of external anti-corruption promoters and where the effect of tightly coupling anti-corruption promotion to the existing practices of democracy promotion was most pronounced.[8] Also with regard to this region, a number of concerns about the effectiveness of anti-corruption efforts were raised by analysts. With the benefit of hindsight, anti-corruption promotion on the part of the European Union (EU) towards post-Communist accession countries, for example, had produced mixed results. Although, with the second round of EU eastern enlargement in 2007, EU anti-corruption requirements had become more demanding, they still appeared more as a ritual fulfilling a symbolic function (Ivanov 2010). Moreover, in post-Soviet countries where democratisation failed to take root, such as Ukraine, Belarus, or Russia, the anti-corruption cause had been instrumentalised by governments against their political opponents (Coulloudon 2002; Krastev 2004: xiv; Savintseva and Stykow 2005: 200). In general, external anti-corruption promotion in Eastern European countries had involved the direct provision of Western financial assistance to local CSOs and advocacy coalitions, yet in some countries the limited success of civic, donor-funded anti-corruption projects fell into a context of low trust in democratic institutions (on south-eastern Europe, see Tisne and Smilov 2004). Furthermore, concerns have been raised that foreign-funded initiatives have not only supported anti-corruption mechanisms but also the development of 'donor-driven civil societies' with weak local roots and possibly even additional incentives for mismanagement and corruption (Heinrich 2003: 273).

Regarding Russia, as mentioned, concerns have been raised about the instrumentalisation of governmental anti-corruption efforts against political opponents. With regard to official anti-corruption efforts in Soviet Russia and during the first post-Soviet decade, authors further pointed to the inherent risk of delegitimising the state (Coulloudon 2002; Holmes 1993). With regard to civil society engagement, the historically rooted reluctance to engage in whistleblowing and disclosure of information about corruption was underlined (Martirossian 2004). More recent contributions on anti-corruption efforts during the Putin era, in turn, referred to various positive examples of civic engagement but a generally limited role of civic actors in that field (Demidov 2005; Savintseva and Stykow 2005). However, the complex interplay between international and domestic anti-corruption advocacy in this political context has not been studied to date. Russia makes for a particularly interesting case though. The onset of Putin's presidency marked a particular moment, given that this country's image abroad was typically associated with attributes like economic crime, Mafia activity and bureaucratic corruption during the 1990s. When Putin became President in 2000, he declared anti-corruption as one of his reform priorities and thus raised high hopes among international actors that corruption problems were to be addressed under his leadership. Throughout the Putin era (January 2000–May 2008), the Russian government did indeed show increasing commitment to international anti-corruption collaboration. At the same time, Russia became increasingly authoritarian and 'anti-Western' under the Putin administration and international norm promotion in general remained less successful.

In addition, the literature on Russian CSOs in general has underlined the existential dependence of the latter on foreign financial assistance (especially Henderson 2003; McIntosh Sundstrom 2006). In this context, domestic organisations not only became increasingly professionalised in interacting with foreign donors, but they were also competing amongst each other for resources and privileges, especially when joining a common activity field, and were not rarely using foreign assistance opportunistically for securing their own survival. Henderson (2003) further noted that these financial dependencies entailed asymmetrical or hegemonic relations between Western donors and local recipients that may obviously hamper common advocacy efforts. Moreover, under the conditions of increasing authoritarianism during the Putin era, the relationships between the state and CSOs underwent drastic changes, with many Russian CSOs seeking to avoid any interaction with state authorities, some seeking more collaborative relationships rather than openly pressuring the state, and the latter inserting more and more governmental nongovernmental organisations (GONGOs) into the civic sphere.[9] Taking account of these context-specific issues, it should thus be most interesting to analyse how the tripartite relations between external, domestic civil society, and governmental actors were unfolding as part of transnational anti-corruption advocacy in Russia.

A new analytical framework

The previous sections have raised various questions that need addressing when studying transnational advocacy today. The analysis presented in this book will focus particularly on the involvement of domestic civil society actors in anti-corruption advocacy in Russia during the Putin era. Following an explorative research design based on a Grounded Theory methodology, it has arrived at case-specific theoretical conclusions as well as more general conclusions about how best to study transnational advocacy in various fields and contexts. It is hoped that both the specific and general arguments may inspire future studies about transnational advocacy in general, about transnational anti-corruption advocacy elsewhere, or about other transnational advocacy efforts in Russia. The answers to the case-specific questions will only be discussed in the concluding chapter. At this point I am proposing a new analytical framework which, as a heuristic tool, seeks to encourage a more searching and less pre-modelled analysis of transnational advocacy processes.

Given the increasing complexity of transnational advocacy and the high likelihood that a certain issue area may be taken up by a range of structures, actors and discourses that have been active in other areas, a wider analytical framework is needed which aims at exploring an advocacy process as such rather than (or before) explaining its successfulness. When studying transnational advocacy, the overall conception of a tripartite, transnational actor constellation around a particular issue and targeting a particular state remains helpful. However, preset models about the modus of interaction between these actor categories seem less useful when moving on to analysing advocacy around new issues and within contexts other than those previously considered. In each given case fresh attention needs to be paid to the ways in which the various actors relate to the advocacy issue *and* to each other. Such an actor-centred view is particularly fruitful when combined with a process-tracing method (George and Bennett 2005) that enables the researcher to better distinguish general causal patterns from coincidental factors or case-specific contingencies explaining the outcome of the case studied.

It is proposed to proceed in four main steps (see Table 1): first, the various actors and structures involved in the given advocacy process need to be identified. While the targeted government(s) may be obvious, a number of international and domestic nongovernmental actors are probably engaged more or less directly in that process. But also with regard to the state, various governmental units and political leaders may take up on the promoted issue and may relate to its various promoters in different ways. Second, once the actor constellations are roughly sketched, the task remains to more precisely determine the nature, scope and implications of the relationships between the various actors involved. This requires another and more thorough analysis of their respective agendas (what they are postulating) and actions (what they are actually doing) in relation to the issue at stake and to each other. While the differentiation between rhetoric and action may not always be an easy task, it is an essential one that should prevent researchers from drawing premature conclusions that confuse ideal or strategic statements with actual developments. Third, it is important to consider how the respective agendas and actions, and thus possibly the actor relations, are changing over time. In order to do so, the data should again be re-assessed with due attention to the precise timing of statements, actions, or events. Finally, the wider international, domestic, and local contexts have to be accounted for if one wants to distinguish certain dynamics that are particular to the issue area, country, project etc. analysed from dynamics that are part of the more general environment within which the case studied is embedded.

Table 1 *Tracing processes of transnational advocacy: four steps*

I	II	III	IV
	Empirical research		*Theory building*
Actors and structures	**Actor relationships**	**Change over time**	**Causalities and contingencies**
Roughly: Actor constellation	*More precisely:* Actors' agendas and actions in relation to the advocacy issue and to each other	*More precisely:* The timing of agendas, actions, interactions	*Differentiation:* Contextual dynamics Case-specific dynamics

How this rough analytical scheme is operationalised eventually depends on the particular case studied as much as on the particular research interest of the analyst. The following chapter provides a more detailed methodological discussion of the particular approach adopted for the case study at hand. While the above-outlined framework would not generally foreclose testing theoretical arguments, I have myself adopted a grounded theory approach that puts much emphasis on a continuous dialogue between empirical research and the development of theoretical arguments (Glaser and Strauss 1967; Strauss and Corbin 1998). As mentioned in the preface, this option was chosen after I had for a long time been preoccupied with the many mismatches between existing models about transnational advocacy and the case of anti-corruption advocacy in Russia.[10] The analysis presented here is thus more sympathetic with Moore's (1951: 4) argument:

> I have come to the conclusion that it is advisable to plunge into the data with only the simplest and most flexible hypotheses,

together with some ideas about the ways in which one might examine them.

Methodologically, I found it essential to move beyond a study of documents and include a multi-sited ethnographic approach based on a large number of interviews as well as participant observation among Russian CSOs, in order to more thoroughly assess the self-perceptions and mutual perceptions especially of the international and domestic nongovernmental anti-corruption proponents. Moreover, since the roles and involvement of the latter has been in the foreground, an in-case comparative study of civic anti-corruption engagement in three different Russian cities has been conducted (Moscow, St. Petersburg, Irkutsk).

Organisation of the book

Chapter 2 elaborates on the methodological approach adopted for the following case study. Besides outlining the ways in which the data were gathered and interpreted, it refers to various challenges encountered in the course of the research process. Chapter 3 presents an overview of the development of transnational anti-corruption advocacy both in general and with regard to Eastern Europe. From a macro-perspective, it introduces the main actors involved and their (changing) approaches. It further asks how two key aspects have been addressed as part of these activities: corruption as the common concern and civil society involvement as a most frequently emphasised means or condition for counteracting this problem. Chapter 4 portrays in more detail the relevant actors and their various activities in Russia. It casts a stronger focus on the changing agendas and actions during the time of Putin's presidency (2000–8). In this light, the following two chapters then direct the focus towards Russia's domestic level. Chapter 5 starts with governmental anti-corruption initiatives throughout the Putin era. Furthermore, Chapters 4 and 5 reconsider how international actors and the Russian government have been relating to corruption as well as to Russian civil society. Chapter 6 adds a thorough analysis of the remaining key dimension pertaining to transnational advocacy 'on the ground': civic anti-corruption efforts in Russia during the Putin era. By presenting three local case studies, it shows how the same international and domestic contexts come to bear differently in different local contexts within the same target state. Finally, Chapter 7 zooms out again and considers the full picture of anti-corruption advocacy in Russia. It elaborates on the nature, scope and impacts of the relationships between the actors at all three levels of analysis with regard to the core question of civil society involvement as well as the question of successfulness of international and domestic anti-corruption promoters in pushing the state towards accepting and implementing international standards. It concludes with a wider perspective on anti-corruption advocacy in Russia and in general by outlining how this differs from earlier global movements.

Notes

1 The boomerang pattern and the spiral model refer to a situation where channels between a state and its domestic nongovernmental groups are blocked so that the latter bypass their state and directly search out international allies to help them to put pressure on their state to behave according to international norms (Keck and Sikkink 1998: 12; Risse and Sikkink 1999: 18). However, even Sikkink (2005: 154) herself later underlined that patterns of international–domestic interactions do not fit the boomerang or spiral where activists do not seek out international allies because of domestic repression.

2 Civil society is understood here as the organised sphere of civic engagement outside the spheres of the state, the economy, or private households. The term nongovermental organisation (NGO) is used only where precisely this form of organisation, as a legal entity, is referred to. Otherwise, the more encompassing terms civil society organisations (CSOs) or civic groups are used as these subsume a wider range of legally possible forms of organisations as well as more informal formations.

3 Already Keck and Sikkink acknowledged that there was an increasing exchange within and among networks around different issue areas, so that experiences, individuals and funding all moved back and forth among them (Keck and Sikkink 1998: 9).

4 For a more comprehensive discussion of the literature on corruption and anti-corruption efforts, with a particular emphasis on Eastern Europe and shifting interpretations over time, see Schmidt (2007b).

5 Following the analysis presented by McCoy and Heckel, the UN Convention Against Corruption (UNCAC) appeared to just confirm that argument: soon after the need for the UNCAC as an international legal instrument was officially recognised in December 2000 (resolution 55/61 of the General Assembly), the UNCAC had been opened for signature in December 2003 and came into force on 15 December 2005. In

contrast, the negotiation and adoption of the first international treaties in the realm of human rights took several decades: see for example Risse and Sikkink (1999).

6 This was not a totally new observation. In their case study of domestic and local anti-corruption efforts in the USA and New York City, Anechiarico and Jacobs (1996) had already pointed to the unintended counter-effects of over-regulation and less efficient government.

7 A recent volume reconsidering the roles of governments, NGOs and specialised anti-corruption agencies, edited by de Sousa, Hindess Larmour and (2009) presents a promising step into this direction.

8 In this book, the term *Eastern Europe* is used when referring to the European post-Communist and post-Soviet countries, including the successor states of the former Socialist Republic of Yugoslavia, Czech Republic, Hungary, Poland, Slovakia, Slovenia, Estonia, Latvia, Lithuania (also referred to as Central and Eastern Europe; the latter three also referred to as the Baltic states), Bosnia and Herzegovina, Bulgaria, Croatia, Republic of Macedonia, Romania, Serbia (also referred to as south-east Europe), Belarus, Moldova, Ukraine, Russia, Armenia, Azerbaijan, Georgia, Kazakhstan, the Kyrgyz Republic, Tajikistan, Turkmenistan, Uzbekistan (also referred to as post-Soviet countries). The Baltic countries, which are also post-Soviet countries, are referred to as an extra category given their distinct path of development since the early 1990s.

9 For a more detailed review of the literature on Russian civil society, see Schmidt-Pfister (2008), in particular pp. 49–54 on 'transnationalizing civil society' and pp. 46–9 on 'civil society as "third sector"'.

10 See Schmidt (2006a) for the resulting extensive discussion of these mismatches which has, although enhancing my understanding of earlier advocacy processes, deflected me from immersing myself into the empirical data.

2

Methodological considerations

An analysis of transnational anti-corruption efforts differs substantially from analysing corruption itself. This applies not only to the theoretical framework but also to the data and their interpretation.[1] Before presenting the findings resulting from the study of anti-corruption advocacy in Russia, this chapter discusses the ways in which I have approached this case and the particular benefits and challenges entailed therewith. By focusing on the Putin era (January 2000–May 2008), the time frame of the empirical study spans a most revealing period throughout which anti-corruption advocacy from both above and below increased significantly in Russia. At the same time, the Russian state had become more assertive towards international actors, more suspicious of Western efforts of norm promotion, and more repressive towards domestic civil society actors. From a cursory perspective, or even from a Russia studies perspective, one might thus expect this to be a less successful case of anti-corruption advocacy. However, a thorough process-tracing revealed that in this particular issue area, transnational advocacy was eventually rather successful. Many of the goals and results envisioned by international actors, Russian CSOs, or politicians had not materialised within a few years. Following the course of the developments under the Putin administration over the whole period, my study has arrived at a comprehensive and clear picture of incremental change which makes explicit the cumulative weight of several measures undertaken by the various external and domestic actors.

Furthermore, from a conventional perspective of transnational advocacy studies, Russia would have been considered as one single unit targeted by domestic civil society (understood as a unit too) and international actors. Inspired by Russia studies and their emphasis on the growing economic, socio-cultural and political disparities between the more than 80 Russian regions in the course of the post-Soviet transformation, I sought to move beyond this 'container-case' view and to investigate the involvement of civil society actors in different cities within the same target country.[2] Apparently, civic advocacy potentials also varied across the country, with Moscow-based groups being better connected to central authorities and international partners than those acting at great distances from Moscow. Regarding transnational campaigns involving local civil society, recent studies on various regions and localities have only demonstrated the need for more a coherent comparative inquiry and for fresh empirical research about potential changes under the Putin administration. For example, a recent volume on Russian civil society (Evans, Henry and Sundstrom 2006) contains chapters that creditably move beyond Moscow by studying various civil society actors in various cities. But, standing detached from each other and referring to different issue areas, these chapters cannot offer any systematic comparative insights. A first comprehensive and thoroughly comparative study on foreign assistance to Russian civil society has been presented by Lisa McIntosh Sundstrom (2006). However, both publications are based on field research before 2000.

Moreover, according to Russian International Relations scholars, global impacts upon the Russian regions especially present an important issue for future research with many aspects having remained unexplored or even unidentified (Il'yin 2005: 122). Also regarding anti-corruption efforts in particular, previous studies suggest that, while the position articulated by the President is particularly crucial in Russia, domestic efforts to combat corruption and crime would eventually depend on 'how the game is played out on the regional and local level' (Volkov 2002: 185). However, again, the locally comparative approach adopted for this study leads to different conclusions: whereas anti-corruption efforts at the local level have shown only temporary successes, both governmental and civic anti-corruption advocacy was eventually heavily centralised in Moscow during the Putin era.

With Putin staying on as Russia's Prime Minister, the Putin era can be considered as being over only in the most formal sense. The book may thus present a valuable contribution to Russia studies as it deals with a momentous chapter in Russia's most recent history. Importantly, it provides not only a snapshot discussion of a certain event during that time, but contains a thorough analysis of an ongoing process spanning the whole period of Putin's presidency. For the latter reason, this book also offers an important case study in the field of anti-corruption research. The chosen case also marks a time frame when global anti-corruption promotion experienced a first remarkable slowdown. Aspects like civil society involvement and the particular difficulties of Western-assisted anti-corruption promotion in Eastern Europe had been at the centre of new questions and doubts (Michael 2004b; Schmidt 2007b; Tisne and Smilov 2004). Despite a new anti-corruption enthusiasm prevailing at the international level since the entry into force of the United Nations Convention Against Corruption (UNCAC) in 2005, the analysis presented here underlines the persisting relevance of these questions. Finally, and not least, while studies on the transformation of Russian governance under President Putin and studies on transnational anti-corruption efforts have been working very much in parallel, this book presents a major attempt to bring these two fields of study together.

Data collection

> One cannot go in and say, 'Tell me your grammar.' Even if people have been 'taught' their grammar, [one] must cautiously view their statements as another kind of data. (Agar 1980: 237)

> [T]o rely on what people say about what they believe and do, without also observing what they do, is to neglect the complex relationship between attitudes and behaviour. (Hammersley 1990: 597)

In order to do justice to the complex dynamics involved in the issue of changing actor relationships in the course of transnational advocacy and to the multi-level character of the study, an eclectic set of data has been used and much triangulation had to be undertaken in order to eventually arrive at a meaningful overall picture.

With regard to all levels of analysis, I have continuously traced official documents, publications, public statements, grey literature, Internet portals and the news. Besides many contextual insights, I was particularly interested in retrieving information about the changing roles of and relationships between the various actors involved in anti-corruption promotion in Russia and Eastern Europe more generally. At times, this has been a veritable Sisyphean task since these sources tended to be less explicit about actual interactions and relations. They were usually revealing about the self-perception of the various authors or people cited and the perception of other actors from their perspective. For example, the involvement of civil society in anti-corruption efforts was frequently stated among the objectives of international actors and among the recommendations made by international actors to the Russian (and other) government(s). But idealised or assumed roles were not my sole interest. Moreover, while using secondary sources such as existing studies about anti-corruption efforts or transnational advocacy and civil society involvement in Russia, I had to carefully consider whether authors have been participants or observers of the projects presented. Many publications in this field have taken the form of action research, commissioned or at least sponsored by various donors with a stake in the issue, and have thus contained rather biased (often overly optimistic) views.

Overall, all kinds of documents, websites, news etc. presented important sources for retrieving many historical and technical facts. Amongst others, it was evident that a number of civic anti-corruption projects had been conducted across Russia and that, eventually, domestic CSOs had been involved in collaborative initiatives between the Russian state and international actors. However, crucial information about informal and behind-the-scenes relations or the operational conditions of groups and individuals was not recorded in such documents. In order to gain a better understanding of the actual patterns of interaction, especially between international and Russian civil society actors, I had to talk to many people who had been involved in this venture. Repeated – and in Russia rather extended – periods of field research were thus undertaken between 2003 and 2007 as a main way to gain insight into the particular pattern of anti-corruption advocacy from both above and below.

Regarding civic participation in transnational advocacy 'on the ground', that is, at the local level, I had selected three regional capitals which provided different preconditions for civic anti-corruption initiatives. Moscow, St. Petersburg and Irkutsk were quite similar in terms of a relatively high concentration of activists involved in anti-corruption projects. Yet the cities were different regarding the nature of the involvement: Moscow presented the locus of TI-Russia and some other civic anti-corruption groups. In St. Petersburg, various groups had taken up anti-corruption projects in addition to their ongoing work and usually with foreign funding. Irkutsk, in turn, presented one of the target regions of the Anti-Corruption Coalition template promoted and supported by the United States Agency for International Development (USAID). The analysis at the local level thus explored how these civic anti-corruption activities differed from each other in their approaches and effectiveness, whether they were interconnected, and how the encountered differences were related to the interactions between local actors, central and local authorities, and international actors. Overall, I spent about nine months in these three cities and I conducted about 60 interviews as well as numerous background conversations with representatives of Russian CSOs, professional associations or local firms, and with individual activists and journalists.[3] I also used more than 20 events and occasions for participant observation, including roundtables, press conferences, informal and formal meetings, public and closed meetings, small seminars, or international conferences.

In addition, I conducted a significant number of interviews with foreign and Russian experts on anti-corruption and/or civil society assistance who were working in international and foreign offices in Moscow and St. Petersburg (30 interviews) or at key nodes of transnational anti-corruption promotion outside Russia. I visited the headquarters of the most relevant international actors in Berlin, Brussels, Strasbourg, and Washington, DC in order to talk to representatives of international organisations, foreign donor organisations and think tanks (25 interviews). As these research trips were shorter, the opportunities to collect data through participant observation were limited to only six events, such as conferences or in-house seminars held or visited by some of the interviewees. Of course, it would have been most interesting to supplement this data basis with interviews at the Russian governmental level. Yet this was impossible due to constraints in the time and resources I could spend on field research in Russia during these years, all the more since the arrangement of such interviews would have required additional, careful and extensive efforts to establish the relevant channels of access to this dimension of the field.

I had to promise anonymity to most informants, whilst some would have liked to see their personal views published. In order to avoid an unbalanced representation of individual views, I have disassociated the names, places and precise affiliations of all interviewees from the evidence provided in the following chapters. From the actor-centred perspective adopted here, it has not always been possible or sensible to fully anonymise the interview data. In many instances, an interviewee's affiliation with a certain organisation thus remains obvious, but not his or her specific department, unit, office location, or status within the organisation. Further-more, from the process-tracing perspective, I considered it important to state the year in which the interview was conducted.

Interviews and personal conversations with activists and experts have been a most useful means for gathering in-depth information from the view of participants about the various actors' expectations, activities, experiences, and contextualised interpretations of key concepts or events. By visiting several organisations at least twice and, as far as possible, conducting two interviews with certain individuals, I have been able to record changes in these respects. The interviews have been semi-structured, i.e. guided by a set of open-ended questions that allowed for narrative answers about anti-corruption initiatives, civic engagement (in Russia and as part of transnational anti-corruption advocacy), and relationships with other actors. This type of questioning proved well-suited for retrieving much valuable information that I would otherwise not have asked for, or that may not have been provided in response to a direct question, especially concerning relationships with other (groups of) people. But semi-structured interviews may also be a risky strategy, in particular when the respondents are high-ranking, busy international officials who have, at best, scheduled not more than an hour for such a meeting. If somebody answers the first few questions at length, there may not be much room left for the remaining questions on the list or for taking up on one or the other important aspect. In Russia, in contrast, most senior respondents were not used to being interviewed about their professional life, especially by a Western young woman. The prime challenges here were to first build sufficient trust through a more casual conversation (sometimes over lots of tea, coffee and cigarettes) and at some point to successfully redirect the attention towards the issues on my questionnaire. It was then often impossible to bring the voice recorder into play. Moreover, especially in the Russian context, gaining access to interviewees proved to be a very time-consuming task. Hardly any of these interviews had been arranged in advance and by email. I had to be in town for several weeks and had to spend much time calling people up and arranging contacts through mediators.

By personally visiting the interviewees in their offices, I was further able to gather material produced by various organisations (books, leaflets, posters, videos) as well as unpublished documents (draft proposals for legal reforms, protocols of meetings, internal project reports, letters etc.). None of these would have been available elsewhere or sent by email or mail.[4] Beyond that, I could gain invaluable insights into people's natural working environments and the very conditions under which they were pursuing their efforts to fight against corruption or to foster civil society engagement in Russia more generally. Perhaps needless to say, there are blatant disparities between the modern, well-equipped, often security guarded offices of foreign representatives outside Russia and in Moscow and the rough-and-ready quarters of Russian CSOs, especially outside Moscow. The latter were mostly difficult to locate, often set up in tumbledown buildings or former tenement blocks, and scattered throughout the city. Moreover, having lived with Russian friends, friends of friends, or colleagues rather than in hotels, and having been based at various offices of Russian CSOs or research centres during that time, I developed much knowledge from casual conversation. Still, I was aware that I could not solely rely on people's explanations of their actions and motivations.

Participant observation during meetings and events and during the daily work of some organisations was most instructive regarding certain controversies between Western and Russian representatives, between experts, activists, entrepreneurs and officials, or between Russian experts and activists amongst each other. In contrast to interviews, the participants soon forgot about or got used to my presence while becoming immersed in the discussions amongst themselves. These discussions often revealed issues which I had previously not thought about, and would certainly not have asked about in interviews, but which presented some of the most enlightening tesserae to complete a meaningful picture. Even where the discussion itself went astray, there was much to be learned from observing routines, such as common styles of interaction and communication, or less explicit tensions between diverging expectations unobtrusively, including the possibility of openly taking notes.[5] Furthermore, I could gain insights into personal views of some interviewees that were different or more pronounced in comparison with their more careful statements during the interview. But then, there was even more time needed than in the case of interviews to get access especially to closed meetings, that is, to first win the trust of gatekeepers who would dare to bring somebody along to a debate about political and sensitive issues.

Data interpretation

Based on the analytical approach outlined in Chapter 1, I have gathered and evaluated the data in four main steps: identifying actors; determining actor relationships; tracing change over time; and demarcating particular and general contingencies and causalities.

It may be important to note that neither data gathering nor interpretation have been strictly separate tasks, nor have the four steps presented rigorously discrete phases during the research process. Rather, by adopting a grounded theory perspective (Glaser and Strauss 1967; Strauss and Corbin 1998) as well as a process-tracing methodology (George and Bennett 2005), I was continuously moving back and forth between collecting empirical information about particular events, actors or contextual aspects and interpreting these with regard to the larger picture of the whole process that I was about to elaborate.

First, at all levels of action, I sought to identify the various actors involved in transnational anti-corruption activities in Russia. This has been an ongoing task, not only because new actors kept emerging in this field. The establishment of specific anti-corruption institutions or coalitions has been a core concern to external anti-corruption promoters. Also, especially at the local level, some relevant organisations or individuals were difficult to track down. With regard to international organisations, this analytical step included the identification of different units responsible for promoting anti-corruption measures (in general and in Russia) and for promoting civil society engagement (in Eastern Europe and in Russia). As a result, a rough map was established of the actor constellations in the given case.

Second, I went back to the information I had gathered about these various actors in order to more precisely determine the nature, scope and implications of their relationships. This included a more detailed analysis of the various actors' understandings of corruption, of appropriate anti-corruption measures, and of the roles of civil society actors in Russia. This step involved the task of distinguishing between rhetorical commitments to collaboration and exchange (as postulated in many programmes or project outlines, country strategy papers, or public speeches of politicians) and actual interaction (as illuminated mainly through personal interviews and participant observation). In this regard, it should be underlined that documents like indices or surveys about corruption which had been sponsored or published by any of the actors, have been mainly looked at as objects determining the interrelations between these and other actors rather than as sources of hard facts. When citing CPI data, for example, I did not mean to refer to the actual level of corruption in Russia but rather to the ways of how these data had been put to use or perceived by the various agents studied. Similarly, many material artefacts that I have gathered during the field research presented valuable indicators about the production and dissemination of information among the involved actors.

Third, once this elementary database had been established,

a more thorough assessment of the collected data with regard to change over time became possible. Following a process-tracing method, this analytical step consisted in restoring the course of action taken by the various actors and the unfolding of their relationships with much sensitivity to the timing of the statements, actions or events. I had refined the process-tracing method for this research by first establishing a chronological account at each level of action while sticking as closely to the data as possible. Essentially, the results of this task are presented in Chapters 3, 4 (international / foreign actors), 5 (Russian government), and 6 (Russian CSOs). For the sake of readability, processed versions of the chronologies at each analytical level are provided in this book. In each chapter, the discussion proceeds actor-by-actor or is structured along relevant themes while maintaining a chrono-logical order in the subsections or paragraphs. Subsequently, the developments were re-examined by superimposing these parallel accounts in order to get a better understanding of what has been happening at the junctions. By reconsidering the changing agendas and actions of the various actors at all three levels during that time, I could eventually illuminate how and why certain actors managed to develop closer rela-tionships, whereas tensions emerged or relationships had been cancelled between other actors.

Finally, another re-assessment of the whole process remained due in order to distinguish particular, case-specific from more general developments. Before more abstract conclusions could be reached, I had to reconsider which developments were determined by the particular dynamics making up the given case – i.e. the particular advocacy field (anti-corruption) in this particular target country (Russia) at this particular time (Putin era) – and to what extent the case was embedded in wider contextual developments (e.g. transnational anti-corruption advocacy in Eastern Europe or civil society development in Russia in general).

The enormous heuristic value of this multi-step approach leading towards a multi-level process tracing became evident only when the research was already under way. As mentioned in the preface, I had been following up on the case study of transnational anti-corruption advocacy in Russia for a long time, not least because it failed to fit conventional theories about successful advocacy in too many respects. The advocacy process I was looking at presented a thick conglomerate of seemingly simultaneously occurring actions, events and longer-term developments. Only by intensely re-examining this deviant case with great attention to timing and over a longer-term horizon, was I able to identify concurrences or sequences and the cumulative, at times indirect, synergies emerging from certain actions or events.[6] The thorough process tracing proved well suited for a more explorative approach that sought to scrutinise any conventional conceptual bias (in this case, for example, civil society as the leading force and as the categorically good one). It proved important to identify which actions had been pro-actively initiated by which actors and who had been responding to certain measures. Otherwise I would have arrived at rather premature and certainly different conclusions about key developments such as, for example, the failure of Western-assisted civic anti-corruption projects in the Russian regions or the emergence of the GONGO *Protiv Korruptsii* which, whilst openly criticising the Russian NGO Information Science for Democracy (INDEM) as well as the use of foreign funding, collaborated with the Council of Europe (along with TI-Russia, a close partner of INDEM).

An ethnographic approach to studying transnational advocacy

Shadowy activities such as corruption, patronage or favouritism have always attracted ethnographic research. Studies on anti-corruption efforts, however, have tended to deal with corruption as an unambiguous and measurable variable while focusing on policies and legislatures designed to address the problem. Yet the complex patterns of interaction involved in the processes of promoting anti-corruption measures across countries, and especially the actual involvement of civil society actors within certain countries, have remained hidden from the largely macro-analytical perspectives. As a rare exception, anthropologist Steven Sampson (2005, 2009) has demonstrated the usefulness of an ethnographic perspective when studying the rhetoric, ideas and actions during international anti-corruption campaigns in post-Communist contexts.

As outlined above, the adoption of an ethnographic approach which heavily built on field research and participant observation as means for data collection and interpretation, based on a holistic and reflective perspective, proved particularly fruitful for gaining a clearer picture of transnational anti-corruption advocacy in Russia. Similarly, recent anthropological research has demonstrated that connections between global politics and domestic change as well as transnational engagement are readily accessible through ethnographic methods (e.g. Burawoy 2000; Greenhouse 2002; Warren 2002). While seeking a fuller understanding of the interplay between transnational effects and domestic politics, such ethnographic research endeavours 'a more finely grained picture of multiple centres of politics and social interests ... and a more fluid sense of transnationalism and international connections' (Warren 2002: 381). Emphasising that transnational processes are interwoven with people's everyday practices, these studies maintain that our knowledge of such processes must be grounded in local and concrete experiences. In particular transformation countries should not be addressed as gross units, but with regard to the people inhabiting these states and their efforts to position themselves within highly unpredictable socio-political circumstances. State–civil society relations in such countries call for an elaborated analysis since 'the absence of effective mediating institutions or established routines (even within state agencies) is marked by highly improvisational manoeuvres on the part of state actors as well as among those whose situations put them at the margins (often quite central margins) between public and private sectors' (Greenhouse 2002: 2).

Importantly, an ethnographic approach to transnational advocacy requires a 'multi-sited ethnography' (Marcus 1995) that moves beyond the conventional single-site location of field research to multiple sites that cross-cut dichotomies such as the local and the global and include transnational ties as part of the research object (Burawoy 2000: 4). In other words, such research explores how the social relations in which the subjects of study are involved are stretching the boundaries of the field across various local sites. Usually, an inside description and understanding of daily routines and changing practices and of actors' relationships is made possible by spending a considerable amount of time within a social setting and gathering data through participant observation (e.g. Brewer 2000: 59). Or, as Goffman (1989: 125) notes on ethnography:

> It's one [method] of getting data, it seems to me, by subjecting yourself, your own body and your own personality, and your own social situation, to the set of contingencies that play upon a set of individuals, so that you can physically and ecologically penetrate their circle of response to their social situation, or their work situation, or their ethnic situation, or whatever. So that you are close to them while they are responding to what life does to them.

For a multi-sited ethnography this means that the field research at the different sites will inevitably be of a variable intensity and quality. Nevertheless, the important contribution of such an approach is to 'bring these sites into the same framework of study and to posit their relationships on the basis of first-hand ethnographic research' (Marcus 1995: 100). In this regard, the study presented here could reveal an imbalanced involvement and at times unintended exclusion of civil society actors across various locations inside Russia in the collaborative anti-corruption efforts that have unfolded between international organisations and the Russian government. It has revealed synergies and tensions at the junctions of international, governmental, and domestic civic engagement that would not have been discernible from merely studying strategy papers, project reports, legal drafts, news, etc. It has further shown that the potency of transnational advocacy at each level of action still very much depends on the presence of some highly motivated individuals. This has already been documented in earlier studies on the emergence and diffusion of global norms and advocacy issues (e.g. Finnemore and Sikkink 1998; McAdam and Rucht 1993; Nadelmann 1990). One may assume that, once transnational advocacy becomes more and more structured and professionalised (with a high turnover in expert staff especially within international organisations), this may leave less room for individual pro-active engagement. This study of transnational anti-corruption advocacy, however, does not verify this assumption.

Furthermore, an ethnographic perspective ideally entails a highly reflective awareness of the role of the researcher in the knowledge produced and in the process of analysis. In this vein, some notes will be added about the particular challenges encountered during this research.

Challenges involved in this research

The value added of close-up and continuous data gathering combined with ongoing as well as retrospective theoretical reflection may seem rather obvious. Yet with regard to the case at hand, this research process also harboured various methodological challenges. The remaining sections briefly refer to two kinds of difficulties that may be of more general relevance: following up on a process of transnational advocacy over time and across levels (and units) of action; and studying sensitive issues.

Studying complex issues

As outlined above, I paid great attention to studying transnational advocacy over time and across levels of action. The four-step approach I had taken meant that I had been returning to the data again and again in order to retrieve additional information about the relationship between certain actors or about the timing, scope, background or other details related to certain initiatives or events. While I could use the advantage that I had talked to numerous persons involved and that many of them could be contacted by email for some follow-up questions, there were still many organisations, departments or individuals involved with whom I had not been in personal contact. In the given case, most actors under consideration maintained their own websites and particular websites had been established for some key events or campaigns. However, in contrast to 'real' documents, websites and their contents tend to be in flux. Project-related websites had been given up once a project had ended. Domains and URLs kept changing. The manageability of electronic project databases of most donor organisations was of varying quality and many did not reach far back in time. Some organisations regularly updated their websites with regard to their changing strategies, assumptions, and positions; others did not. The latter changes are most interesting for a researcher who seeks to study unfolding patterns of interaction. But it is almost impossible to consistently follow up on them. Overall, these problems are probably unavoidable. Also field research has to deal with the permanent challenge that former access points may close down while others may be opening up. Social researchers will always face the challenge of incomplete data bases. In this regard, the constant contrasting of information retrieved from various sources and about various levels of action has proved particularly helpful.

Moreover, while studying transnational advocacy, researchers have to account for the agendas and actions of international actors as well as the governments and domestic civil society actors in the countries concerned. As noted above, when also adopting an ethnographic perspective, this entails the major difficulty that field research can hardly be conducted with the same intensity at all these levels of analysis. For my own study, I sought to make this multi-level study manageable by concentrating on one country and on one particular aspect, namely how pressure is exerted onto the country's government 'from above and below'. More precisely, I was interested in the particular role of domestic civil society therein. Interviews and field research were therefore conducted at the international and local levels, with the most intense field research being concentrated at the locus of civic action inside Russia.

As outlined in the previous chapter, a key characteristic of anti-corruption advocacy is that the issue of corruption had been taken up by numerous pre-existing actors and institutions, both at the international, governmental and local level. This aspect introduced the additional methodological challenge that information about concrete anti-corruption programmes, budgets or projects was often difficult to locate since these were hidden under wider programmatic headings or maintained by various departments within one single organisation. Moreover, while much is known today about the key anti-corruption promoters at the international level, in Russia it was less obvious which governmental departments and which CSOs were dealing with corruption-related issues. The identification of actors, programmes and activities thus presented an ongoing task rather than a discrete, first analytical step. This implied that with each new actor or activity I had learnt about, I had to return to the tasks of inserting these into the given picture of actor constellations, relationships and processes, thus readjusting the latter with regard to the added pieces of information.

Studying sensitive issues

> Do you know how dangerous this is what you are doing? I'm surprised that you have not been removed by a car accident yet.

This comment was made by one of the interviewees after I had briefly introduced my research activities.[7] It perfectly illustrates a typical misunderstanding that I encountered throughout this research. I was not, as conversational partners tended to assume, interested in investigating corruption in Russia. Rather, I was aiming at a better understanding of the approaches chosen by those actors inside and outside Russia who sought to counteract corruption and how these various actors related to each other. I have thus not primarily faced the typical communicative challenges or even dangers when asking direct questions about allegedly immoral or illegal practices such as bribing or intriguing, or when observing corrupt acts.[8] The most sensitive issue I had to deal with proved to be the core question of how Russian civil society actors were involved in transnational anti-corruption advocacy.

On the basis of previous research on environmental protection in Russia, I had expected that CSOs and activists were easily accessible as they were particularly eager to make their opinions and objectives public, especially to foreign researchers. However, as the political climate in Russia was changing rapidly during the course of my study, the situation of Russian CSOs had changed too. After more than ten years of Western assistance to civil society development and democratisation, the government started to perceive domestic CSOs as a potentially influential voice. Using more or less subtle means, the Putin administration sought to disturb, co-opt, or silence much activism related to political matters. Also some of my former interviewees and contacts had experienced setbacks, ranging from arbitrary inspections and raided offices to investigations by the Federal Security Service (FSB) and even arrests. Nevertheless, representatives of most Russian CSOs remained accessible for interviews. By that time, I had been out in the field already for several years and had been able to develop the necessary rapport and trust of some key gatekeepers and informants. But most interviewees notably became more careful when talking about one of my main research interests – their relationships with other actors, including Russian authorities, foreign partners or other Russian CSOs.

For many of the Russian CSOs that I visited, except for some human rights and environmental groups and the core Moscow anti-corruption organisations, relations with any state authorities were not a major issue. Within the more restrictive political environment, many CSOs sought to work at a greater distance from the state while concentrating on social service provision at the local level. Politics did not play any major role in their daily activities, and there was not much to say about it. For Moscow-based organisations, which were more oriented towards federal politics, the political changes during the 2000s were more perceptible. Some sought to distance themselves from politics, some to enhance their relationships with key individuals or institutions inside the political system, and the search for new strategies entailed new cleavages amongst various groups. Other CSOs in the regions, which were interested in pushing local reforms and thus in actively influencing their local administrations, fully experienced disturbances only with the insertion of Kremlin-close regional governors by the mid-2000s. But also relations with Western partners had become a sensitive issue. In addition to the problem that Russian CSOs were in constant competition amongst each other for foreign funding, governmental rhetoric and action against Western funding made most interviewees careful not to disclose too much detail about their funding sources. While they were themselves advocating the rule of law in Russia, they were reluctant to talk about their strategies to circumvent the law for the sake of getting access to foreign financial support. Inquiring into the details of these developments became more difficult during interviews. Moreover, some new groups working closer to the government had emerged, especially in Moscow, whom I sought to consult. Their representatives were rather sceptical about my research. They remained highly reserved about their precise relationships with other actors and about their working environments. For example, they usually proposed meetings in neutral places such as bars somewhere close to their offices.

During the realisation of the empirical research, I was thus less concerned about my personal safety than about mastering the increasingly delicate balancing act between maintaining access to many different organisations within Russia over a longer period and trying not to interfere with existing or emerging factions. Doing field research implies stepping into existing social relationships, and I knew that just minor blunders could jeopardise not only the quality of my data but also the actual work of my informants. Following Lofland and Lofland (1995: 58), I tried to handle this challenge by making clear my research interest in anti-corruption groups as an analytical category. Although it was not always possible to convey that I was interested in a rather abstract idea of social relations and the transnational promotion of ideas, most informants understood and accepted that I did not aim to become involved in or actually solve an array of locally existing problems. Moreover, in order to avoid problems on one front or the other, I refrained from employing any covert research methods in situations when I could draw on participant observation.[9] Finally, a high awareness of the timing of events was crucial also for realising the field research, since the steady course of events always included contingencies which proved conducive or prejudicial to the quality of information I could retrieve during interviews (e.g. certain scandals or affairs, governmental measures, locally launched projects and campaigns, or even the presence of other researchers).

Notes

1 This sounds plausible. However, during numerous presentations at conferences and conversations with other scholars I noticed that the need for a different theoretical and methodological basis was usually not acknowledged.

2 According to the Russian Constitution of 1993, the Russian Federation consisted of 89 federal subjects (regions and autonomous districts). The actual number has been slightly reduced since 2005, as some of the regions were merged in the course of the federal reform under President Putin.

3 'Proper interviews' were announced and arranged as such (34 interviews in Moscow, 16 interviews in St. Petersburg, and 18 interviews in Irkutsk). In contrast to the many spontaneous – and usually not less illuminating – conversations with relevant experts (both Russian and foreign), a particular date and time was arranged for an interview and I

usually visited the interviewees in their offices. Some interviews were recorded; in all other cases I was able to openly take notes during the interview.

4 Also requests for additional information or documentation after leaving the field often failed, even where this possibility was explicitly announced during an interview.

5 In many other situations and during informal conversations, it would have been awkward to write down important details. On note-taking in field research, see e.g. Goffman (1989) and Brewer (2000: 87).

6 See also George and Bennett (2005) on the inductive value of process tracing, especially when thoroughly studying one deviant case that does not match existing theories.

7 Representative of a European donor organisation, 2005.

8 On the dangerous aspects of research on corruption, see Shore and Haller (2005: 16).

9 On more or less desirable transparency of the research and on planning overt or covert modes of inquiry, see Lee (1995; 1999), Creswell (2003) or Hornsby-Smith (1993).

3

Global anti-corruption promotion and Eastern Europe

Before turning to the Russian case study, this chapter sketches a wider contextual picture of the emergence and character of the global anti-corruption regime and how Eastern Europe has become embraced by this regime. It further asks how two key aspects have been addressed as part of these activities: corruption as the common concern and civil society involvement as a most frequently emphasised means or condition for counteracting this problem. The insights gained therewith allow for a better understanding of the general dynamics entailed in this rather young and increasingly powerful advocacy area. For the following analysis of the Russian case, they provide important background information about the state of external anti-corruption promotion in Eastern Europe by the onset of and during the Putin era (since 2000), the time frame which will be the main focus in the following chapters.

A global anti-corruption regime

The emergence of a truly global anti-corruption regime only began during the 1990s. While there had been major campaigns against corruption earlier on, this time marked a transition from understanding corruption as a domestic political problem to regarding it as a global political issue that should be tackled by transnational counter-initiatives (Glynn, Kobrin and Naim 1997; Naim 1995).[1] The leading role of civil society in triggering this process has often been underlined. Yet strictly speaking, this role has been most actively played by major transnationally operating nongovernmental organisations, such as Transparency International, the International Chamber of Commerce or the American Bar Association. Among these organisations, TI presents the most specialised and perhaps the most influential civic anti-corruption advocacy organisation. TI was founded as an NGO in 1993 with the particular mandate of fighting corruption. Overall, it has substantially contributed to bringing corruption onto the international agenda, starting from the pioneering work of breaking a taboo, especially among international aid organisations, up to continuous awareness-raising and lobbying for the international anti-corruption conventions. Under the direction of its Berlin-based Secretariat (TI-S), TI has set up a global network of 'National Chapters'. With one Chapter per country, this network had expanded to more than 60 Chapters after 4 years and about 90 Chapters by 2009. TI Chapters are domestically registered and relatively autonomous nongovernmental organisations (NGOs) and at the same time through a franchising system formally tied to the global TI movement. In order to strengthen the organisational structure, cohesion and internal integrity of this movement, a formal accreditation procedure was introduced in 2003, during which national organisations gradually move up to the status of a National Chapter.[2] Not least due to the personal background of some of its founders, who came from World Bank and Commonwealth Secretariat contexts, the TI-S could from the very beginning establish close links to international financial institutions (IFIs), international organisations, national governments, and multinational corporations.[3] Initially, the OECD (Organisation for Economic Co-operation and Development), the International Monetary Fund (IMF) and the World Bank appeared as the 'leading anti-corruption crusaders' (Williams and Theobald 2000). Not surprisingly, the emergence of the global anti-corruption regime during the 1990s was therefore exceptionally powerful and fast (McCoy and Heckel 2001: 66).

Within less than two decades, a comprehensive anti-corruption regime was put into place that included the establishment of various regional and sectoral agreements or networks under the auspices of major international organisations – such as the Working Group Against Bribery at the OECD, the Anti-Corruption Network for Transition

Economies (ACN) as a regional outreach programme of that Working Group, or the Group of States against Corruption (GRECO) at the Council of Europe (CoE) – the incorporation of an anti-corruption focus into existing sectoral or regional initiatives (e.g. into the United Nations Global Compact or the Stability Pact for South Eastern Europe), and the adoption of international anti-corruption conventions by the OECD, the United Nations (UN), and regional organisations such as the Organization of American States, the Council of Europe, and the EU.[4] Other transnationally operating initiatives of various kinds emerged during the early 2000s, such as the Global Organisation of Parliamentarians Against Corruption (GOPAC), the U4 Anti-Corruption Resource Centre for donors, the Publish What You Pay coalition, or the Extractive Industries Transparency Initiative (EITI) (see condensed chronological overview in Table 2). This regime was further bolstered by a growing number of tools for exchanging information on a global and regular basis as well as technical and financial assistance programmes supporting anti-corruption efforts in numerous countries.

To date, the evolution of the global anti-corruption regime has remained highly dynamic as new actors and initiatives have kept emerging and existing actors have kept revising their anti-corruption strategies. It is important to note that, while anti-corruption has been incorporated as an add-on theme into pre-existing international and transnational activities, hardly any original anti-corruption organisations have emerged at the international level. Since the early 2000s, the reach of this regime has further expanded while some international actors adopted explicit mainstreaming strategies in order to tackle corruption as a cross-cutting issue with relevance to almost all other areas of their engagement.[5] Since the mid-2000s, the regime has been deepened while most of the international actors adopted anti-corruption and ethics policies also with regard to their internal governance and started to better coordinate their global anti-corruption efforts between themselves.[6] Moreover, global anti-corruption promotion gained new momentum with the entering into force of the CoE Criminal and Civil Law Conventions on Corruption in 2002/2003 and of the UNCAC in 2005. Yet this also implied a crucial shift from broader agenda-setting, awareness-raising and capacity-

Table 2 *Emerging structures of the international anti-corruption regime*

Year	Network or treaty established
1993	TI
1994	OECD Working Group on Bribery
1996	Inter-American Convention Against Corruption (adopted)
1996	UN Declaration against Corruption and Bribery in International Commercial Transactions
1997	OECD Anti-Bribery Convention (adopted)
1997	Inter-American Convention Against Corruption (in force)
1997	EU Convention on the Fight Against Corruption Involving Officials of the European Communities (adopted)
1998	ACN (OECD)
1999	CoE Criminal Law Convention on Corruption (adopted)
1999	CoE Civil Law Convention on Corruption (adopted)
1999	Asian Development Bank/OECD Anti-Corruption Initiative for Asia-Pacific
1999	OECD Anti-Bribery Convention (in force)
1999	GRECO (CoE)
2000	Stability Pact Anti-Corruption Initiative (SPAI)
2002	CoE Criminal Law Convention on Corruption (in force)
2002	Global Organisation of Parliamentarians Against Corruption (GOPAC)
2002	U4 Anti-Corruption Resource Centre for development agencies
2002	Publish What You Pay (PWYP) coalition
2003	CoE Civil Law Convention on Corruption (in force)
2003	Additional Protocol to the Criminal Law Convention on Corruption (adopted)
2003	Istanbul Action Plan (Sub-Regional Anti-Corruption Action Plan for 6 post-Soviet countries)
2003	Extractive Industries Transparency Initiative (EITI)
2003	UNCAC (adopted)
2004	UN Global Compact added anti-corruption as the 10th principle
2005	Additional Protocol to the Criminal Law Convention on Corruption (in force)
2005	EU Convention on the Fight Against Corruption Involving Officials of the European Communities (in force)
2005	UNCAC (in force)

Note: Table refers only to those international conventions and networks that explicitly address the issue of corruption.

building towards promoting a more confined set of (mainly legislative) measures to prevent and criminalise corruption in the participating states and to foster international collaboration in prosecutorial matters.[7] In addition, supranational monitoring and country-to-country peer review systems for assessing the domestic implementation of these international treaties came to the fore. These tendencies may also have implied a stronger focus on interaction with governments rather than civil society.

In general, global anti-corruption promotion has been pursued along three main avenues: through diagnostics and information-gathering; technical and financial assistance; and international cooperation through specific anti-corruption networks and conventions. Of course, these are not discrete categories. Most international actors have incorporated all these elements into their strategies and there have been interrelations such as much financial assistance being provided to diagnostic projects and to the implementation of international anti-corruption conventions, or particular forms of monitoring and information-gathering being developed in the context of these conventions. Analytically, however, the distinction is useful in order to elaborate more generally on the changing practices of information politics and leverage politics in this area. With regard to Eastern Europe, the following sections thus show that transnational anti-corruption promotion has been less situational and campaign-like. Rather, being based on pre-existing routines of international collaboration, it has been quite structured and technical from the very beginning.

External anti-corruption promotion in Eastern Europe

Eastern Europe, however vaguely defined, has become a particular target region for international anti-corruption efforts in two, not necessarily opposing respects. These countries displayed comparatively high levels of corruption, but the end of the Cold War and collapse of Communism were also optimistically associated with eroded support for kleptocratic regimes. Accordingly, prospects of democratisation have been linked to prospects of anti-corruption in this region. At the same time, concerns have been raised about new opportunities for corruption that emerged with the rapid privatisation programmes and the extensive transformations. In this region, the emerging global anti-corruption regime could directly build upon the structures and practices of democracy promotion that had been established since the early 1990s. Most international organisations and donor agencies had launched particular regional programmes for Europe and central Asia, for sub-regions such as the Balkans or CIS-countries, or even for individual Eastern European countries before also adopting anti-corruption strategies. The following sections discuss in more detail how anti-corruption measures have been promoted through information-gathering, assistance, and international collaboration and how the Eastern European countries have been targeted therewith.

Diagnostics and information-gathering

Assessments and measurements of the levels of corruption across countries have become integral parts of global anti-corruption promotion. The IFIs and most international organisations have been pursuing active information-gathering strategies that included various forms of country reports about the corruption situation and anti-corruption efforts in certain countries as well as (cross-country) quantitative measurements of corruption. These various data should not only inform the international actors themselves while designing their strategies but were also considered as strategic means to actively influence the policy-making in the countries considered. For example, shortly after the launch of the CPI, TI leaders referred to this index as a powerful tool for raising public awareness and for pushing governments to undertake reforms (TI 1997). The World Bank contended that its surveys and country reports have assisted the countries in building action plans and promoting broad participation; have empowered citizens, enterprises and governmental reformers; and have helped to depoliticise the debate about corruption.[8] Similarly, the OECD underlined the practical impact of the monitoring process: 'Countries have introduced legislative amendments to strengthen their anti-bribery laws. Pressure is on to step up enforcement of these laws.'[9] As outlined in the following, Eastern European countries have not only been part of global assessments, but also subject to a multitude of efforts to gather corruption-related information at regional, country-specific, or sectoral levels.

During the 1990s, reports about the corruption situation in a particular Eastern European country had been issued in a rather arbitrary fashion. The issue of corruption was often included as one among several aspects in other, closely related assessments. Two out of the many examples are the OECD Regulatory Reform Programme, which included comprehensive reviews of reforms since 1997, and the Non-Cooperative Countries and Territories (NCCTs) exercise initiated by the Financial Action Task Force (FATF) in 1998 and focusing on international anti-money-laundering standards. These assessments resulted in a series of country reports touching upon corruption and related aspects. The OECD evaluations comprised OECD member countries (including the Czech Republic, Hungary, Poland and Slovakia) and some non-member countries (including the Baltic and Balkan states and the post-Soviet countries); the FATF evaluation considered a sample of 47 rather suspicious jurisdictions, for the most part offshore financial centres, as well as the Eastern European OECD member countries plus Russia and Ukraine.[10] In the context of the EU eastern enlargements (in 2004 and 2007), the European candidate and new member countries, and later on also the new neighbouring countries, had become a particular focus of systematic and comprehensive country reviews. The corruption situation and anti-corruption policies in these countries presented a special theme covered in the resulting country reports.[11]

In the context of anti-corruption conventions, monitoring regimes were established at OECD, CoE and UN level as a more focused form of gathering corruption-related information about the participating countries. The mandate of the OECD Working Group on Bribery had been amended in 1997 to include systematic country monitoring of the implementation of the OECD Anti-Bribery Convention and the Revised Recommendation on Combating Bribery in International Business Transactions (OECD 1997). Similarly, GRECO was established in 1999 by the CoE in order to monitor the compliance of its member states with the organisation's anti-corruption standards. Both institutions have effected rigorous and formal country-to-country peer review mechanisms since 1999 (OECD) and 2000 (GRECO).[12] Country assessments within these frameworks are based on information gathered through standardised questionnaires, on-site visits of evaluation teams, and self-reporting on the part of the assessed countries. Proceeding in several steps, the evaluations result in country reports containing clear recommendations to the government of the country under consideration. These are followed by compliance or progress reports after two or three years in order to evaluate the implementation of these recommendations (GRECO) or of a country's anti-bribery legislation (OECD). GRECO evaluations have equally considered all 46 GRECO member states, including the USA, 25 Western European and 20 Eastern European and central Asian countries. Three separate evaluation rounds (2000–2; 2003–6; since 2007) have focused on selected sets of GRECO's 20 Guiding Principles against Corruption. On the grounds that higher levels of corruption could be observed in the Eastern European countries, these were usually asked to set up a specific Anti-Corruption Strategy, accompanied by a timetable or action plan. GRECO has considered these documents as a valuable means for exerting pressure on the governments to, at least, officially demonstrate an interest in actively addressing corruption.[13] Indeed, it has been found that most Eastern European countries, while scoring lower in the CPI, have shown more stringent implementation of the GRECO recommendations than the Western countries (Wolf 2010). Indicating awareness of the sensitivity of these matters, GRECO country monitoring reports are negotiated in plenary meetings before being adopted and are made public only if the authorities of the assessed country express their agreement. OECD evaluations have considered all 38 countries that have ratified the OECD Anti-Bribery convention, including only seven Eastern European countries (Bulgaria, Czech Republic, Estonia, Hungary, Poland, Slovak Republic, Slovenia). At the OECD level, a separate review and monitoring mechanism was established within the framework of the ACN for those post-Soviet countries that had endorsed another anti-corruption document, the Istanbul Action Plan of 2003 (Armenia, Azerbaijan, Georgia, Kazakhstan, the Kyrgyz Republic,

Russia, Tajikistan, Ukraine). For these countries, this meant another review of the institutional and legal framework for fighting corruption (based on self-assessment reports), the implementation of certain recommendations made by experts from ACN and OECD countries, and since 2004 on-site visits by teams of experts in order to monitor the progress made in implementing the recommendations. Among the eight participating countries, only Russia failed to submit appropriate self-assessment reports and to submit itself to the monitoring procedure.[14] At the UN level, in contrast, a self-assessment checklist and computer-based assessment system have been in place since 2007 as a mechanism for reviewing the implementation of the UNCAC. The realisation of this approach is thus still in its early stages and resonance among the state parties to this convention (including 26 Eastern European countries) remains to be seen.[15]

In addition to country reports in the framework of particular multilateral programmes or agreements, which usually referred to information gained from official sources and documents, numerous surveys among citizens, entrepreneurs and experts as well as scholarly studies about the corruption situation across countries have become internationally available. Various donors and other organisations have supported such analytical work about particular countries and sectors. For example, USAID supported surveys about corruption in particular regions inside Eastern European countries in the context of Anti-Corruption Coalition building projects (Bulgaria, Russia, Ukraine) as well as pilot studies about corruption in particular sectors in several Eastern European countries (Bulgaria, Georgia, Romania, Russia) that combined qualitative analysis and surveys of local authorities and businesses (USAID 2005a). The local offices of the Soros Foundations Network/Open Society Institute (OSI) and other organisations, such as for example Tiri or the Transnational Crime and Corruption Center (TraCCC), had supported numerous studies about corruption, crime and related issues conducted by organisations active across the region.[16] Opinion surveys in particular have in some countries created strong reactions on the part of the domestic media and governments (on southeastern Europe, see Tisne and Smilov 2004).

The World Bank, besides financing corruption-related

surveys in many countries, has also maintained its own units to carry out global and regional analyses. Most notably, the Bank has since 1999 conducted the Business Environment and Enterprise Performance Survey (BEEPS) in cooperation with the European Bank for Reconstruction and Development (EBRD) in order to assess the conditions for business development in 27 Eastern European countries (plus Turkey). On this basis, the World Bank published a series of comparative cross-country 'Anti-Corruption in Transition' reports presenting the corruption-related findings in these countries (Anderson and Gray 2006; Gray, Hellman and Ryterman 2004; World Bank 2000a). The datasets were also provided online in order 'to encourage continuing research and input into policy dialogue with countries in central and eastern Europe and the Commonwealth of Independent States'.[17] It remains difficult to judge, however, to what extent they were actually put to use within the analysed countries. In contrast, another form of data gathering and dissemination has clearly gained wider prominence: corruption-related cross-country indices.

The CPI, published by TI since 1995, and the 'Control of Corruption' section contained in the Worldwide Governance Indicators published by the World Bank since 1996 have become the most prominent measurements of perceived corruption across countries. These aggregate indicators are based on many different surveys undertaken by different organisations and comprise countries around the globe. TI has further published a Bribe Payers' Index (BPI) since 1999, which assesses the leading industrial nations (including Russia) according to the likelihood that their firms would pay or offer bribes abroad, and the Global Corruption Barometer (GCB) since 2003, a survey of general popular attitudes towards and popular experiences of corruption. Both assessments also provide a picture of corruption in different sectors.[18] In addition, measurements of corruption in post-Communist countries in particular have been published as part of the Nations in Transit surveys issued by Freedom House since 1999.[19] All these surveys have been conducted regularly (for the most part annually) and have resulted in quantitative statements about corruption in each country or a particular geographical region, most commonly presented as a calculated score and used for ranking the assessed countries.[20] As part of the global rankings, Eastern European and particularly the post-Soviet and south-east European countries usually appeared as problematic compared to Western (European) countries. Such instruments for measuring corruption were eagerly taken up by expert and scholarly communities and the media, as the quantification allowed the assessment of a complex issue to be turned into handy datasets to be readily used for comparisons. They have also faced much criticism, on the part of lowly-ranked governments who felt offended, but also on the part of scholars with regard to methodological concerns (e.g. Abramo 2005; Galtung 2006). In response, the authors of the CPI started to provide accompanying methodology papers for each index from 1999 and to explicitly acknowledge the 'unavoidable level of imprecision' (Lambsdorff 2001) included in measurements of perception since 2001. The authors of the Worldwide Governance Indicators responded in detail to more recent scholarly critiques (Kaufmann, Kraay and Mastruzzi 2007d, 2007c, 2007b). In the media, however, the CPI in particular has remained a most widely cited source. This was not least promoted by TI's own media campaigns and the practice of providing separate press releases for each CPI (since 1997) which point to the most striking developments.

Lending, financial assistance and technical assistance

Since the late 1990s, IFIs, international organisations, bilateral aid organisations, and other Western donors have provided various forms of technical and financial assistance for anti-corruption measures to governments and, albeit on a much lower scale, to the private and civil society sectors. In Eastern Europe, such assistance could build on pre-existing donor–recipient constellations and practices that had evolved with the democracy promotion efforts throughout the 1990s. Exact figures for the volumes of this assistance are impossible to determine. Some donors launched specific anti-corruption programmes, some supported anti-corruption measures under other programmes supporting economic reform and democratic governance, and most of the donors further maintained particular programmes for promoting such reforms in Eastern Europe. In practice, concrete anti-corruption assistance was thus provided within various frameworks, and the scope of anti-corruption assistance has been continuously broadened. The scattering of anti-corruption assistance across many fields and programmes has opened up a particularly wide range of vantage points for external financial and technical assistance in this field, but it also seemed to hinder coordination among the numerous international actors and initiatives.

The major IFIs started to make their public and private sector lending practices conditional upon the occurence of corruption problems and anti-corruption efforts in recipient countries from 1996/1997. Yet this was more an issue in developing countries. In Eastern Europe, it has been more important that the IFIs have also provided technical and financial assistance to support various anti-corruption measures. The World Bank, for example, first considered corruption affecting its own projects in a country and a government's achievement of development objectives (World Bank 1997). In 2000, it officially made 'anti-corruption in transition economies' one of its main strategies (World Bank 2000b: 61; 2000a). By 2007, it came up with a revised anti-corruption strategy that underscored the importance of country-specific approaches (World Bank 2008). The IMF first focused on corruption related to fiscal and financial sector management and then on governance more generally. Since 2000, the IMF has expanded its technical assistance and surveillance into the area of anti-money-laundering and, following the events of 11 September 2001, into the area of combating the financing of terrorism (IMF 1997).[21] The EBRD, since 1991 the main supporter of reforms in Eastern European and central Asian countries through investment in the private sector, has adopted a focus on good corporate governance and ethical standards in business operations in order to combat corruption and fraud in its own operations and more generally since the late 1990s. Together with the World Bank, it has also been a major supporter of administrative reform at the local and municipal levels. The EBRD's strategy encompassed awareness-raising and financial and technical assistance, and did not provide for a formal sanctioning process regarding corruption in its own private sector operations (EBRD 2006).

At the UN level, a United Nations Assembly resolution

was adopted in 1997 which requested assistance for member states in anti-corruption strategies – thus practically on a global scale. In particular the longer-standing United Nations Development Programme (UNDP, since 1965), a grant-making organisation providing and coordinating technical and financial assistance to governments for institutional and legal reform projects, and the United Nations Office on Drugs and Crime (UNODC), established in 1997 and mandated to assist member states in their struggle against illicit drugs, crime and terrorism, took a special interest in the issue. While providing unconditional support, the UNDP understood anti-corruption efforts as key to achieving the main objectives formulated by its mandate to fight poverty and to support the achievement of the Millennium Development Goals. Anti-corruption assistance has been provided under the UNDP's Democratic Governance theme and was initially focused on awareness-raising, diagnostics and policy advice (1998–2003). Since 2004, it has further supported the building of coalitions, the capacity of independent anti-corruption commissions, the development of regulatory frameworks, the improvement of financial management, and the strengthening of the media and civil society as oversight institutions (UNDP 1997, 2004). UNODC became a major promoter of the UNCAC, especially since this convention entered into force in 2003. It launched a more specific Global Programme against Corruption in order to assist states in implementing the provisions of the UNCAC. This programme has been realised through a particular UNODC Anti-Corruption Unit, in collaboration with other UN agencies and through the UNODC network of field offices (including offices in Bulgaria – with six satellite offices in south-eastern Europe, in Vilnius for the three Baltic states, in Uzbekistan for central Asia, and in Moscow for Russia and Belarus). It contained technical assistance, research and analytical work, and strategies for public awareness raising. As part of the latter focus, UNODC has used the International Anti-Corruption Day (9 December, since 2003) for comprehensive campaigns, for example through the provision of radio and video spots, posters and leaflets in various languages.[22]

At a European regional level, Eastern European countries have become a focus for anti-corruption assistance programmes that are financed by the EU and various bilateral donors and implemented by the CoE. As a first initiative, the Octopus I+II programmes (1996–2000) maintained a combined focus on the fight against corruption and against organised crime in transition countries. These programmes enabled experts from the target countries (ministers, judges, law enforcement officers) to participate in seminars and study visits to EU member states. On this basis, the participants were encouraged to draft recommendations for corruption and crime-related policy and legal reforms in their countries. Since then, more focused programmes have been implemented to support certain anti-corruption measures in particular Eastern European countries, such as the PACO project in Moldova (2005), the RUCOLA projects in Russia (2005–7), the UPAC project in Ukraine (2006–9), or the GEPAC project in Georgia (since 2008).[23]

In addition, a number of bilateral aid agencies and private foundations have provided anti-corruption assistance since the late 1990s. In Eastern Europe, USAID has played a major role as it has supported a large number of anti-corruption projects explicitly within its 'Democracy and Governance' framework as well as under many other programmes, including those targeted at Eastern Europe and at civil society actors. The Canadian International Development Agency (CIDA), which has also been active in all Eastern European countries, has assisted anti-corruption initiatives more indirectly through supporting other multilateral or international initiatives (e.g. implemented by GOPAC, OSCE, UN or the World Bank). Among the European aid agencies, the *Deutsche Gesellschaft für Technische Zusammenarbeit* (GTZ) has become a main supporter of good governance and anti-corruption measures across Eastern Europe and central Asia. The Swedish International Development Cooperation Agency (SIDA) and the UK Department for International Development (DFID) maintained a stronger focus on corruption in post-Soviet and south-east European countries, with the former assisting countries directly and the latter again through other supranational initiatives (e.g. the U4, EU, EBRD, UN or World Bank). While most of these donors are primarily working with governments and local administrations, they have also offered small grant programmes for supporting civic anti-corruption projects. Furthermore, private foundations such as the Eurasia Foundation and the Soros Foundations Network have actively supported anti-corruption projects undertaken by civil society actors and have sought to more generally support the strengthening of such actors as essential oversight and advocacy institutions in the fledging democracies across the region.[24]

International anti-corruption networks and conventions

International anti-corruption networks and treaties present a more recent and apparently powerful avenue of external anti-corruption promotion in Eastern Europe. An increasing number of countries across the region have become involved in the TI network at the civil society level and in the inter-governmental networks and conventions at the OECD, CoE and UN levels since the late 1990s and especially during the 2000s.

As mentioned above, TI presents the most original global network specifically devoted to anti-corruption advocacy. Understanding itself as 'the global civil society organisation leading the fight against corruption',[25] it sought to expand its reach through National Chapters which are supposed to implement country-specific programmes while also pursuing agreed global and regional strategies. In addition to a common organisational framework, TI has defined five thematic priorities for the whole movement: corruption in politics, corruption in public contracting, corruption in the private sector, international anti-corruption conventions, and poverty and development.[26] In addition, regional depart-ments at the TI-S have sought to develop strategies and campaigns that respond to regionally distinct patterns of corruption. Among those, the 'Europe and Central Asia Department' has grown into the largest unit, working with Chapters and contact groups in 42 countries by 2009. It has functionally divided its target area into subregions according to 'EU status and geographical proximity': EU and EFTA Member States plus Israel; South East Europe and Western Commonwealth of Independent States; and Central Asia, Russia and Caucasus.[27] Thus, formally, little attention seems to be given to Communist legacies, with the first sub-region comprising ten of the new EU member countries (Bulgaria, Czech Republic, Estonia, Hungary, Latvia, Lithuania, Poland, Romania, Slovak Republic, Slovenia) and the latter two sub-regions embracing not only post-Communist or post-Soviet countries. Indeed, in the course of TI's work, some people at the TI-S wondered whether a distinct strategy for the post-Communist region is useful at all:

> Is there a particularly useful analytical framework to talk about post-Communism still? What difference is there, say, to deal with Russia as opposed to Venezuela: you talk about weak institutions, unaccountability, huge state-owned resources ... but is there anything in terms of the uniqueness of post-Communism? (Representative of the TI-S, 2005)

While the TI-S itself has been active since the early 1990s, the TI network has taken root across the Eastern European countries only from the late 1990s and more strongly throughout the 2000s. As Table 3 illustrates, the spread of formally recognised TI Chapters across this region was still under way in the late 2000s.

At the intergovernmental level and usually under the auspices of established international organisations, further membership-based specific anti-corruption networks have been established since the mid-1990s. Most notably, these included the OECD Working Group on Bribery in International Business Transactions (since 1994, with a revised mandate since 1997), the GRECO at the CoE (since 1999) and the ACN as a regional outreach programme of the OECD Working Group for Eastern Europe and Central Asia (since 1998). As mentioned above, these networks have come to play a key role in monitoring the implementation of the OECD and CoE anti-corruption conventions and the Istanbul Action Plan for the post-Soviet countries.[28] In addition, at the UN level, various intergovernmental working groups have been active in relation to the UNCAC. Against this backdrop and given that TI, various donors and, in Eastern Europe, also the EU have actively promoted the CoE and UN conventions, these international treaties present an essential framework for transnational anti-corruption advocacy. For an individual country, subscription to these treaties has entailed the subjection to formalised monitoring procedures, but also eligibility for additional technical assistance.

Four major anti-corruption conventions at a global and European scale – the OECD Anti-Bribery Convention, the CoE Criminal and Civil Law Conventions on Corruption,

Table 3   *The spread of TI National Chapters across Eastern Europe*

Country	Contact Agreement signed	National Chapter Agreement signed
Poland	1996	1998
Slovakia	1997	1998
Latvia	1997	1999
Bulgaria	1998	1999
Czech Republic	1998	1999
Kazakhstan	1998	1999
Georgia	1998	2000
Estonia	1999	2000
Russia	1999	2000
Romania	1999	2001
Azerbaijan	2000	2001
Armenia	2000	2001
Bosnia and Herzegovina	2000	2002
Moldova	1999	2003
Lithuania	2000	2003
Croatia	2000	2003
Serbia	2000	2005
Macedonia	2001	–
Kyrgyz Republic	2004	–
Hungary	2007	–
Slovenia	2008	–

Notes: In chronological order according to the signature of the National Chapter Agreement.

TI Ukraine existed between 1998 and 2007, but was disaccredited. TI Hungary is a new Chapter in Formation; there was another TI Hungary from 1996, which ceased to exist in 2005. TI Macedonia, TI Kyrgyzstan and TI Hungary are currently National Chapters in Formation. TI Slovenia is a National Contact.

Source: Data kindly provided by the TI Secretariat, Europe and Central Asia Department (I am particularly indebted to Miklos Marschall for compiling these data).

and the UNCAC – have been opened for signature and entered into force between 1997 and 2005. A closer look at the processes of signature and ratification again underlines that the process of transnational anti-corruption advocacy is still relatively young, but also increasingly influential (see Table 4). The OECD Anti-Bribery Convention, adopted as the first international anti-corruption instrument in 1997, found relatively little resonance among Eastern European countries, despite the activities of the ACN in this region. This Convention has been ratified only by the Eastern European OECD member countries (Czech Republic, Hungary, Poland, Slovenia) and three ACN countries (Bulgaria, Estonia, Slovakia). In contrast, most Eastern European countries have subscribed to the more recent CoE and UN anti-corruption conventions.

In the case of the CoE conventions, it is further obvious that, in contrast to many Western European countries, Eastern European countries tended to sign and ratify the treaties very soon after their opening or entry into force. Only the post-Soviet countries have ratified these treaties with more delay (Georgia, Moldova, Russia, Belarus, Ukraine) or have not signed at all (Kazakhstan, the Kyrgyz Republic, Tajikistan, Turkmenistan, Uzbekistan). Moreover, illustrating the leverage of the EU in the course of its eastern enlargement, the conventions have been adopted immediately especially by those Eastern European countries who had been preparing for EU accession. The UNCAC further underlines that the leverage of the EU has been limited mainly to the pre-accession negotiations. This convention was only adopted at the eve of the first eastern enlargement round and entered into force after that. Here, the second round EU candidate countries have been more responsive, whereas some new EU member states could afford to sign this convention rather late or not to sign or ratify at all (Czech Republic, Estonia, Latvia). At the same time, the UNCAC seems rather powerful in general, with 135 states around the globe having subscribed within less than five years, including all of the central Asian post-Soviet states. All four conventions, although in principle being open to all countries, have mainly been adopted by member countries of the respective international organisations (Belarus, which is not a CoE member, stands out as an exception).

These patterns suggest that membership of the international organisations may be an important factor. This tendency seems confirmed when looking at the ratification patterns of longer-standing conventions in other areas, such as the OECD Convention on the Organisation of Economic Cooperation and Development, the CoE conventions for the Protection of Human Rights and on the Conservation of European Wildlife and Natural Habitats, or the UN

Table 4 *The international anti-corruption conventions in Eastern Europe*

Country	OECD Anti-Bribery Convention		CoE Criminal Law Convention		CoE Civil Law Convention		UNCAC	
	Signature	Ratification	Signature	Ratification	Signature	Ratification	Signature	Ratification
Armenia	–		2003	2006	2004	2005	2005	2007
Azerbaijan	–		2004	2004	2003	2004	2004	2005
Belarus	–		2001	2007	2004	2006	2004	2005
Bosnia and Herzegovina	–		2000	2002	2000	2002	2005	2006
Bulgaria	1998	1999	1999	2001	1999	2000	2003	2006
Croatia	–		1999	2000	2001	2003	2003	2005
Czech Republic	2000	2000	1999	2000	2000	2003	2005	–
Estonia	2004	2005	2000	2001	2000	2000	–	
Georgia	–		1999	2008	1999	2003	–	2008
Hungary	1998	1999	1999	2000	2003	2003	2003	2005
Kazakhstan	–		–		–		–	2008
Kyrgyz Republic	–		–		–		2003	2005
Latvia	–		1999	2001	2004	2005	2005	2006
Lithuania	–		1999	2002	2002	2003	2003	2006

Macedonia	–		–		–		–	
Moldova	–		1999	2004	1999	2004	2004	2007
Poland	2000	2000	1999	2002	2001	2002	2003	2006
Romania	–		1999	2002	1999	2002	2003	2004
Russia	–		1999	2006	–		2003	2006
Serbia	–		–	2002	2005	2008	2003	2005
Slovakia	1999	1999	1999	2000	2000	2003	2003	2006
Slovenia	2001	2001	1999	2000	2001	2003	–	2008
Tajikistan	–		–		–		–	2006
Turkmenistan	–		–		–		–	2005
Ukraine	–		1999	–	1999	2005	2003	–
Uzbekistan	–		–		–		–	2008

International Convenant on Civil and Political Rights. Also, the two CoE Anti-Corruption Conventions have not been signed by those central Asian post-Soviet countries that are not members in the CoE (Tajikistan, Turkmenistan, Kazakhstan, the Kyrgyz Republic, Uzbekistan), whereas the UNCAC has been signed by these countries as UN member states. However, more precise conclusions about the process of how a particular state has been convinced to adopt these instruments can only be drawn on the basis of more detailed case studies.

Addressing corruption

The multifaceted nature of corruption caused major controversies about how to define or conceptualise the phenomenon. In principle, there is a general consensus among the international actors that corruption, in most general terms, means some kind of 'abuse of power for private gain'. Similar working definitions have been formulated by key international organisations, usually supplemented by typologies or lists of different forms of corruption (EBRD 2006: 4; European Commission 2003: 6; World Bank 1997: 8).[29] TI, in turn, kept revising and refining its concept of corruption throughout the first decade of its work and with a view to the highly contextual experiences of its many Chapters around the world. By the early 2000s, it eventually arrived at a definition of corruption as 'the abuse of entrusted power for private gain'.[30] Only the CoE and the UN seemed reluctant to formulate a framework definition. Rather, underlining its seriousness and global proliferation, corruption has been referred to as 'one of the most widespread and insidious of social evils' (GRECO), 'a prism with many surfaces' (Council of Europe 1996: 15), 'a complex social, political and economic phenomenon that affects all countries' (UNODC), or 'a symptom of something gone wrong in the management of the state' (UNDP 1997: xi).[31] By the early 2000s, the coming into force of the CoE Criminal Law Convention against Corruption and of the UNCAC further entailed a shift in attention towards the variety of possible criminal offences in legalistic terms. While the OECD Convention and the CoE Civil Law Convention focused on defined acts of bribery

(Council of Europe 1999a: Article 2; OECD 1998, Article 1), the CoE Criminal Law Convention contains an elaborate list of offences that shall be established by the state parties as criminal offences (Council of Europe 1999b: Articles 2–15). The UNCAC, in turn, merely contains the following passage (United Nations 2004: Article 61/2):

> States Parties shall consider developing and sharing with each other and through international and regional organizations' statistics, analytical expertise concerning corruption and information with a view to developing, insofar as possible, common definitions, standards and methodologies, as well as information on best practices to prevent and combat corruption.

Thereby, an approach was chosen at the UN level to view corruption 'as an evolving concept' (GC 2004: 5) that should cover various existing forms of corruption while also enabling states to deal with other forms that may emerge in the future. Here, the debate had moved from acknowledging *'the difficulty in finding* universal definitions' (UNODCCP 2001: 7) to recognising that '*[t]here is no* single, comprehensive, universally accepted definition of corruption' (UNODC 2004: 10) and that, in fact, such a definition was *'neither necessary nor feasible'* (GC 2004: 5) (emphases added). Acknowledging that the search for a common definition of corruption encountered legal and criminological, and in many countries also political problems (UNODC 2004: 10), UNODC as the main promoter of this instrument thus upheld the empirical approach of compiling exemplary descriptions of frequently encountered forms of corruption (UNODC 2004; UNODCCP 2001: 14).

In addition the above-mentioned bilateral donor agencies and foundations that have been most active in Eastern Europe have refrained from explicitly formulating working definitions of corruption (with the exception of the GTZ).[32] One would assume that concrete anti-corruption programmes or campaigns have entailed a specification pertaining to a particular target country or region. However, with regard to Eastern Europe it has been more generally recognised that corruption has been particularly high and that there have been new opportunities for and more severe effects of corruption. Assistance programmes seemed to place more emphasis on particular forms of anti-corruption engagement rather than specific forms of corruption (e.g.

awareness-raising, anti-corruption training, anti-corruption agencies and legislation, administrative and judicial reforms, transparency-enhancing measures). As mentioned, anti-corruption programmes have been scattered across other thematic frameworks. This allowed for an increasing number of resonance points when strategically or opportunistically framing corruption, also with regard to the Eastern European transformative countries.[33] Initially, international actors linked corruption mainly to poverty and development. But it was soon also portrayed in connection with democracy, governance, public budgets, administrative reform, investment climate, money-laundering, the development of independent media, civil societies and judiciaries etc. Corruption has also been seen in relation with transnational organised crime, a prevalent issue with regard to Eastern Europe (Athanassopoulou 2005; Rawlinson 2003). In the wake of the events of 11 September 2001, corruption has further been addressed as an international security issue that facilitates terrorism and fosters unpredictability in foreign policy-making. Accordingly, global anti-corruption efforts have been seen as a contribution to counteracting the latter problems, and vice versa.[34]

While such versatile framing has been important in order to keep the issue on the agenda and to initiate a range of actions in many countries, it may not have been unproblematic that corruption has been linked to other phenomena by too many, and at times contradictory, causal arrows. That corruption has been seen as a cause, a symptom, a catalyst, an obstacle, or a consequence of other phenomena may have blurred the design and implementation of anti-corruption strategies. One may thus assume that particular target countries or regions had difficulties in following the state of the international debate about corruption. For example, in search for starting points in post-Soviet countries, a survey of existing instruments led ACN experts to conclude that none of the OECD, CoE or UN conventions would define corruption and that TI's definition was insufficient in focusing on officials in the public sector and excluding the private sector (ACN 2005: 13, 14). As outlined, this was not fully true and TI, by that time, had already opened up its concept towards embracing private-to-private corruption.

Involving civil society

Literally all the international actors introduced above have been underlining their general commitment to involve civil society in their activities and to actively promote civic participation in domestic policy-making. Most international actors have reiterated this commitment through their ambitions to foster civil society development in Eastern Europe and/or to promote civil society participation in anti-corruption efforts. Some have also explicitly promoted civil society involvement in anti-corruption promotion in Eastern Europe.[35] However, while anti-corruption promotion has intensified at an intergovernmental level, donors especially felt a need for a general appraisal of the experiences with actual civil society involvement (see DCD/DAC 2003: 34–6). In the EU context, where considerable funds had been transferred to Eastern European CSOs, concerns about mismanagement and corruption also inside civil society were raised (EUMAP 2003). In this vein, it was noted by the OECD (2003: 7) that

> Civil society plays a key role in fighting corruption. Today, this statement remains unchallenged: it has become a leitmotiv of anti-corruption discourses. But what does it mean in practice? To what extent is it true in all contexts? What is the nature of civil society's involvement?

As outlined in the previous sections, the actual approaches chosen to counteract corruption have been primarily directed at governments. International networks, agreements, and monitoring systems are for the most part intergovernmental arrangements and states, or governments, are the primary addressees. CSOs have been active players at the international level, but mainly in the form of well-established and transnationally active organisations, large foundations, or major business associations. Assistance and information-gathering have included more concrete possibilities of involving domestic civil society, as CSOs have been seen as useful providers of information about a particular country, as important oversight institutions, or as useful channels for providing assistance to the local level. Still, domestic CSOs seemed to play only a marginal role. Only a relatively minor share of anti-corruption assistance went to

CSOs and mainly through bilateral and private donors. Moreover, assistance devoted to 'nongovernmental' activities has often included recipients in the business sector, so that the actual share that went to non-profit advocacy organisations has been smaller than suggested by some activity reports. Also in terms of information-gathering, the trends towards quantitative corruption indices provided through major international outlets and towards formal monitoring regimes in the framework of international conventions seem to reinforce the focus on the nation state as a unit of analysis and on governments and policy-makers as enactors of anti-corruption measures. The UNCAC in particular entails a stronger emphasis on self-assessment by the state parties. GRECO evaluations include consultations of domestic CSOs during field missions. But such interaction seems to be confined to consulting a national TI Chapter and not much is known from official sources about actual practices in this regard.

The global TI network seems to present the most important platform for civil society engagement in this field. At the international level, TI has indeed presented a major civic voice while advocating the international anti-corruption conventions, contributing position papers to many aspects raised in the course of global anti-corruption promotion, and by launching particular campaigns. This role has become widely acknowledged also on the part of the intergovernmental organisations.[36] The TI-S has in many cases also directly approached a country's government, for example through meetings, phone calls, media campaigns, or calling upon other influential governments.[37] TI has further been an essential force for fostering bottom-up advocacy at the domestic level in numerous countries, including most Eastern European countries.

In the anti-corruption field, pressure seemed to be more from above than from below and a core mechanism that could be observed in the case of transnational advocacy in the human rights and other fields – openly pressuring or shaming states from the outside and *in response to* distressed calls from domestic NGOs (Keck and Sikkink 1998: 12; Risse and Sikkink 1999: 11) – has remained a secondary option. Donors have supported mainly non-confrontational and cooperative anti-corruption projects (DCD/DAC 2003; Tisne and Smilov 2004). Among the bilateral donor organisations,

USAID stood out as the only one which explicitly related its anti-corruption policies to US foreign and security interests and which was openly willing to put pressure on governments (Hamm 2006: 14). Even TI remained sceptical of a 'naming and shaming' strategy and made it one of its fundamental policies to be politically non-partisan and non-oppositional (TI 2000: 299).

This chapter has provided a macro-perspective on transnational anti-corruption advocacy in Eastern Europe. It has explicated some more general patterns which underline that this is a very young and highly dynamic field. It has not been uncontroversial, for example with regard to the heavy reliance on corruption indices as main sources of information, to the very concept of corruption, or to the involvement of civil society actors. Anti-corruption advocacy in this region has been particularly strong and could heavily build on pre-existing routines of international collaboration and assistance. While these routines are for the most part played out at an intergovernmental level and under the participation of some highly professional CSOs, one has to ask how civil society actors at the domestic level may have been involved in this process. Much anti-corruption assistance has been provided for domestic CSOs, but mainly through separate programmes offered by bilateral and private donor organisations. More detailed case studies are required in order to understand how these efforts could feed into the transnational promotion of anti-corruption measures in a particular country. To what extent have domestic CSOs actually been able to contribute to the obviously strong external leverage enacted through assistance, information politics, and international legal instruments? This aspect will be studied in more detail in the following chapters with regard to Russia, where the process of anti-corruption advocacy has been more protracted than in many other Eastern European countries.

Notes

1 There had been some earlier efforts to counteract corruption transnationally, but not in a truly global ambition or with little success. See, for example, Moroff (2005) on the attempts to internationalise the US American Foreign Corrupt Practices Act of 1977. The initiation of the

International Anti-Corruption Conference (IACC) as a special forum for anti-corruption law enforcement agencies from various countries by the early 1980s is another case in point.

2 According to the three-phase accreditation procedure, a national organisation is first recognised as a 'National Contact' (usually for two years), then as a 'National Chapter in Formation', and finally as a 'National Chapter'. Accordingly, new and revised contracts have been signed since 2003 also for the previously established National Chapters (interview with a representative of the TI-S, 2004). For an overview of the Chapters and the accreditation process, see also www.transparency.org. On the franchising system, see De Sousa (2009).

3 Interview with one of the founders of TI, 2004.

4 The UN Global Compact, a policy initiative to promote universally accepted principles among businesses, adopted 'anti-corruption' as its 10th principle in 2004 (interview with a representative of the UN, 2005; see also UN Global Compact, at www.unglobalcompact.org). The Stability Pact for South Eastern Europe was launched in 1999 as a comprehensive conflict prevention strategy of the international community, aimed at strengthening the peace-building and democratisation efforts of the countries in this region. In 2000, a particular Stability Pact Anti-Corruption Initiative (SPAI) was adopted within this framework and for this region (see www.stabilitypact.org).

5 For example, explicit efforts to mainstream anti-corruption have been undertaken by the World Bank (DCD/DAC 2003: 17; World Bank 2008), USAID (2004: 2) and the GTZ (2004). USAID (2005b:30–1) identified 22 of its programme types as having an anti-corruption focus or components.

6 Interviews with representatives of the EU, the CoE, the UN, the World Bank and TI (2004–2007). Since the mid-2000s, the major international banks have started efforts to better coordinate their roles and approaches in the anti-corruption field (e.g. ADB et al. 2006; EBRD 2006; World Bank 2006).

7 For example, the CoE Criminal Law Convention against Corruption seeks to further international cooperation in criminal matters. Criminalisation, international cooperation and asset recovery are also cornerstones of the UNCAC. For a summary of international legal instruments against corruption, see UNODC (2005), which refers to 9 different conventions and 12 other documents (resolutions, agreements, decisions, protocols).

8 See World Bank, Governance and Anti-Corruption Diagnostics, at: http://go.worldbank.org/BKSDKT6JC0 (accessed 12/01/2009).

9 See OECD, Anti-Bribery Convention, About, at: http://www.oecd.org /about/0,3347,en_2649_34859_1_1_1_1_1,00.html (accessed 02/02/2009).

10 See, OECD, Regulatory Reform, at: www.oecd.org/about/0,3347 ,en_2649_37421_1_1_1_1_37421,00.html and FATF, NCCT Initiative, at: www.fatf-gafi.org/pages/0,3417,en_32250379_32236992_1_1_1_1_1 ,00.html (accessed 12/05/2009).

11 For the country reports, see the European Commission, Enlargement, at: http://ec.europa.eu/enlargement/index_en.htm (accessed 12/05/2009). For an exemplary analysis of the important role of such reports in terms of anti-corruption promotion, see Ivanov (2010) on Bulgaria and Romania and Börzel et al. (2010) on the new eastern neighbour countries of the EU.

12 For more detail on the evaluation procedures, see GRECO, GRECO Evaluations, at: www.coe.int/t/dghl/monitoring/greco/evaluations/index_en.asp and OECD, Country reports on the implementation of the OECD Anti-Bribery Convention, at www.oecd.org/document/24/0,3343,en_2649_34859_1933144_1_1_1_1,00.html (accessed 02/02/2009).

13 In contrast, it was considered less meaningful to demand Anti-Corruption Strategies of Western countries where usually lower levels of corruption could be observed (interview with a representative of GRECO, 2007).

14 See ACN, Istanbul Action Plan, at: www.oecd.org/document/20/0,3343,en_36595778_36595926_36975252_1_1_1_1,00.html (accessed 02/02/2009).

15 No reports have been made public so far. See UNODC, UNCAC, at: www.unodc.org/unodc/en/treaties/CAC/index.html [accessed 02/02/2009].

16 Since the late 1980s, the Soros Foundations Network had opened offices (which are autonomous institutions) in almost all Eastern European countries (except for Turkmenistan and Belarus) (see www.soros.org). The Washington-based TraCCC had supported local research centres in some post-Soviet countries mainly during the late 1990s/early 2000s (see current website at: http://policy-traccc.gmu.edu/). Tiri is a more recent initiative to support integrity reforms transnationally since 2003 (see www.tiri.org) (accessed 12/05/2009).

17 World Bank, Europe and Central Asia, Anti-corruption, BEEPS Firm Level Data, at: http://go.worldbank.org/Y4YAMUYFS0 (accessed 12/01/2009).

18 See TI, Corruption Measurement, at http://www.transparency.org/tools/measurement (accessed 12/01/2009).

19 See Freedom House, Nations in Transit, at: www.freedomhouse.hu/index.php?option=com_content&task=view&id=196 (accessed 12/01/2009).

20 Only the World Bank team that issued the Worldwide Governance Indicators, while underlining the usefulness of the indicators for cross-country comparison, has refrained from producing 'top-ten' or 'bottom-ten' lists of countries which they consider to be of 'dubious relevance and reliability' (Kaufmann, Kraay and Mastruzzi 2007a: 5).

21 See also The IMF and Good Governance, at: www.imf.org/external/np/exr/facts/gov.htm (accessed 28/10/2008).

22 Interview with a representative of UNODC, 2006. See also UNODC, UNODC and Corruption, at: http://www.unodc.org/unodc/en/corruption/index.html (accessed 03/02/2009).

23 Interview with a representative of the CoE, 2007. See also Council of Europe, Economic Crime/Corruption, at: www.coe.int/t/dghl/cooperation/economiccrime/corruption/default_en.asp (accessed 18/05/2009).

24 See the organisations' websites: USAID at: www.usaid.gov; CIDA at: www.acdi-cida.gc.ca; DFID at: www.dfid.gov.uk; GTZ at: www.gtz.de; and SIDA at: www.sida.se.

25 See TI, About Us, at: www.transparency.org/about_us (accessed 02/02/2009).

26 See TI, global priorities, at: www.transparency.org/global_priorities (accessed 20/09/2008).

27 See TI, regional pages, at: www.transparency.org/regional_pages, and TI National Chapters, at: www.transparency.org/contact_us/ti_nc/europe_central_asia (accessed 20/09/2008).

28 Under the umbrella of the UNDP, another more recent initiative with a particular focus on supporting the establishment of anti-corruption agencies in Eastern European countries, the Anti-Corruption Practitioners Network (ACPN), was established in 2005. Yet in contrast to the formerly mentioned networks, ACPN is based on individual membership, comprising primarily practitioners and experts working in state institutions or international organisations (see UNDP, ACPN, at: http://europeandcis.undp.org/anticorruption (accessed 03/02/2009)).

29 The OECD has been more narrowly focused on bribery in international business transactions. For the IMF, see The IMF and Good Governance, at: www.imf.org/external/np/exr/facts/gov.htm (accessed 23/02/2009).

30 TI, about us, at: www.transparency.org/about_us (accessed 11/10/08) and interview with two representatives of the TI-S, 2004.

31 See GRECO, The Fight against Corruption, at: www.coe.int/t/dghl/monitoring/greco/general/1.%20The%20Fight%20against%20Corruptio n%20–%20A%20Priority%20for%20the%20CoE_en.asp and UNODC, UNODC and Corruption, at: www.unodc.org/unodc/en/corruption/index.html (accessed 23/04/2009).

32 The GTZ defines corruption as 'the misuse of institutional power to obtain unjust advantages' (see GTZ, Good Governance, Corruption, at: www.gtz.de/en/themen/politische-reformen/885.htm, accessed 23/02/2009).

33 On framing as a common strategy of global campaigns and the importance of local resonance points, see for example Keck and Sikkink (1998).

34 It has become a frequently made argument that counteractions against organised crime, terrorism and corruption are interlinked. To mention just a few exemplary references: Council of Europe (2002: 6); TI (2003: 2; 2005c); Gilmore (2004), and UN (2004: 533; 2005).

35 This combined commitment has only very rarely been supported by specific documents (e.g. OECD 2002b; USAID and MSI 2003) or websites (e.g. OECD 2002a). Rather, it has most often been expressed as part of strategies for fighting corruption in the region (e.g. ACN 2003) and for involving civil society in anti-corruption efforts in general (e.g. World Bank 2003).

36 In 2005, the TI-S opened a separate office in Brussels in order to liaise more closely with the EU institutions involved in the fight against corruption. From the very beginning, this initiative has been welcomed among these institutions (interview with a representative of the TI-S, 2005). See also, for example, OECD (2003) and EBRD (2006).

37 Interviews with representatives of the TI-S, 2004 and 2005.

4

External anti-corruption promotion in Russia

The previous chapter has set the stage for the empirical analysis by sketching out international anti-corruption efforts, especially those targeted at Eastern Europe since the mid-1990s. This chapter now portrays in more detail the relevant actors and their various activities in Russia. It casts a stronger focus on the changing agendas and actions during the time of Putin's presidency (2000–8). It will be shown that many international or foreign measures only started during that time. For many international actors, the onset of the Putin era and Putin's declared commitment to the fight against corruption as one of his priorities marked a particular moment. In the course of Putin's presidency, external good governance promoters experienced an increasing reluctance on the part of the Russian government to accept international standards in general. Russia sought to restore its superpower status in international relations. Besides frequent and more self-confident complaints about negative reporting in Western documents and news, this quest entailed a more aggressive foreign policy in its post-Soviet neighbourhood. A representative of the European Commission (2005) thus admitted:

> Before this, I was dealing with the Mediterranean countries ... And there is no country in the Mediterranean that has any similar pretensions as Russia does ... There is a lot of assertiveness.

Some corruption scandals in various international organisations and Western countries during that time, which had been widely publicised in the Russian press as well, also provided a ground for repulsing external emphasis on corruption in Russia and for reminding both the international community in general as well as particular Western countries of corruption problems prevailing in their territories too.[1] In this context, the Russian government did not mind being associated with some controversial acts on the international scene, such as the redemption of Vladimir Kusnetsov, a chairman of the UN Advisory Committee on Administrative and Budgetary Questions (ACABQ) who was charged with corruption, or the appointment of former German chancellor Schröder to a new Russian–German pipeline consortium.[2]

One might thus expect that external anti-corruption promotion was a particularly cumbersome task vis-à-vis an increasingly obstinate Russian government at that time. On the contrary, however, beyond diplomacy and political rhetoric, the Russian government appeared very active and willing to engage in international collaboration against corruption. Most international documents, whilst pointing to persistently high levels of corruption, displayed rather optimistic conclusions about promising anti-corruption efforts under the Putin administration. This position was confirmed by most representatives of international organisations in the interviews:

> So far we didn't have any problems. I think this system [EC Regulation 2584/2000] is a showcase system for the Russians, because it is practically the only system that they have. [...] When we were there in November, the press office of the Ministry of Finance was there because for them this is obviously an aspect worth highlighting. So our experiences have so far been positive actually. (Representative of the European Commission, 2005)

> Still, I was very surprised, I was pleasantly surprised that the [UN] Convention Against Corruption was actually negotiated within a very quick time frame. I was expecting more dissent, there was actually more discussion on the Convention Against Transnational Organised Crime than on this. (Representative of the UN, 2006)

> We've always worked with the Duma ... They are very cooperative. They normally help a lot. They are willing to work. It's been fine so far. (Representative of the CoE, 2007)

International actors thus tended to remain optimistic about Russia's anti-corruption commitment and performance throughout the whole period of study. From 2006, when it became clear that Russia would ratify two major international anti-corruption conventions – the UNCAC and the CoE Criminal Law Convention – interaction was intensified, especially between the UN, the CoE and the Russian government. This strengthened a common focus on assisting Russia in developing a national anti-corruption strategy and specific anti-corruption legislation. However, even when interacting simultaneously with the same beneficiary in the same country, there was little strategic coordination among the various external anti-corruption promoters.[3] It is thus most interesting to analyse more thoroughly the agendas and actions of the latter. The following sections discuss the international engagement in more detail following the main approaches demarcated in the previous chapter: diagnosis and information provision; technical and financial assistance; and international anti-corruption networks and conventions. Two more sections follow on the questions of how corruption had been addressed and how Russian civil society actors had been involved as part of these activities.

Diagnostics and information-gathering

Russia had been included in most of the corruption-related cross-country surveys and indices. According to the survey results of the BEEPS undertaken by the World Bank and EBRD in 1999 and 2002 and published with the first two 'Anticorruption in Transition' reports (Gray, Hellman and Ryterman 2004; World Bank 2000a), Russia performed not that badly among the Eastern European countries: the impact of 'state capture' on firms (one of the buzzwords at that time) proved less problematic than administrative corruption and, importantly, corruption had appeared as a decreasing problem for firms over those years. Also other World Bank projects on related issues such as administrative, judicial or financial sector reform usually contained a budget line for country-specific research and analysis.[4] Although, reportedly, some of this money was subcontracted for surveys about corruption in Russia conducted by domestic research and polling institutes, not much was known about the results of such surveys.[5]

Many other assistance programmes directly oriented at civil society had included support for corruption-related surveys and case studies. To mention just a few: USAID had supported two surveys about the state of corruption in selected Russian regions, realised by members of the region-al Anti-Corruption Coalitions in 2001.[6] The Soros Foundation had supported a major cross-regional survey about corruption conducted by TI-Russia and published as a Russian regional corruption index in 2002 (TI-Russia 2002). The TraCCC, another US initiative with a particu-lar focus on supporting research and policy advice about corruption and crime issues, had maintained several 'over-seas centres' across Russia (including Moscow, St. Petersburg and Irkutsk) whose staff produced a number of case studies about corruption in their regions.[7] However, surprisingly little use had been made of the results of such analyses. Interviewed representatives of international and foreign organisations commonly relied on media reports about the corruption situation in Russia. Even representa-tives of donor organisations whose assistance to Russian groups had led to some kind of publication or report were usually unable to recall the contents of such publications.

At the intergovernmental level, there were other indirectly related assessments that contributed to presenting Russia in a rather favourable light. For example, Russia was reviewed as part of the Non-Cooperative Countries and Territories (NCCT) exercise conducted by the IMF and the Financial Action Task Force (FATF) in 2000. It was identified as an NCCT, which implied that IFIs were urged to give special attention to transactions involving Russia. But in October 2002, FATF removed the country from this blacklist of non-cooperative jurisdictions and withdrew its call for coun-termeasures, given the range of anti-money-laundering and anti-terrorism legislative and institutional measures that the Russian government had undertaken in the meantime (FATF/OECD 2002, 2007). In 2003, Russia became a FATF member, therewith submitting itself to the periodic mutual evaluations which review the member states' compliance with the 40 Recommendations issued by FATF and Nine Special Recommendations on Terrorist Financing.[8] Furthermore,

Russia was the first non-member country of the OECD that was reviewed under the OECD Regulatory Reform Programme. In Russia, this assessment of regulatory policies was conducted in 2004/2005 in order to assist the country's authorities in fostering competition, innovation and economic growth and in meeting social objectives. The final synthesis report presented a major stock-taking of all kinds of reforms relating to these aspects. While outlining several needs for further reforms, the report commented rather positively on the Russian authorities' achievements and reform-mindedness since the year 2000, including the elimination of many opportunities for official corruption (OECD 2005).

As mentioned in Chapter 3, the regular cross-country corruption indices had turned into particularly powerful tools for information politics as part of external anti-corruption advocacy. Yet the Russian case also demonstrates that reporting on this basis drew much attention to quantitative trends rather than to qualitative changes in the corruption situation. According to most of the indices, Russia presented a notoriously problematic case, appearing in the lowest ranks and as a particularly worrying case in comparison with other Eastern European countries. But most indices also indicated a bettering of the situation during the early years of Putin's presidency. Also in the Russian case, the CPI in particular had been widely cited in the international and Russian press each year upon its publication. The CPI was also used as a commonly acknowledged point of reference about the state of Russian corruption in many country reports of international organisations and Western donors.[9] Russia had been listed in the CPI since 1996: it was one of the first Eastern European countries (together with the Czech Republic and Hungary) to be rated in this way. Over the first five years under Putin, and in contrast to the 1990s, Russia's CPI scores (2000–4) had continuously been on the rise (indicating decreasing levels of perceived corruption). Notwithstanding its limited methodological ability to display longitudinal trends, the 'upwards trend' during the early years under Putin was frequently emphasised. In 2005, however, Russia's CPI score suddenly worsened (from 2.8 in 2004 to 2.4). There had been ups and downs in Russia's CPI scoring before, and again afterwards. Still, and again regardless of the accompanying methodological notes acknowledging the CPI's inherent imprecision regarding trends over time (Lambsdorff 2005), the 2005 CPI score caused the most distinct uproar in both Western and Russian news. Many journalists highlighted the fact that Russia fell from place 95 in 2004 to place 128 in 2005, without however mentioning that the number of ranked countries had also increased from 146 to 156.

Most importantly, the 2005 CPI score interrupted what seemed to indicate a steady positive trend since 2000, i.e. since the beginning of the Putin era. TI stressed that Russia's worsening mark was due to a real change in perception rather than statistical error (TI 2005a). Other international assessments seemed to confirm the worrying tendency. For example, in the 2005 GCB, Russia slipped into the category where more than 51 per cent of the respondents thought that corruption affected political life to a large extent (Russia was below the 50 per cent boundary in 2004). According to this survey, the majority of Russian respondents stated that corruption levels had 'increased a lot' over the past three years, and Russian respondents were among the most pessimistic regarding future developments (TI 2005b). Also according to the World Bank's 'Anti-Corruption in Transition 3' report, corruption problems had increased in Russia by 2005, as compared to the 2002 BEEPS (Anderson and Gray 2006), and Russia's Control of Corruption indicator, which had pointed to a bettering of the situation between 2000 and 2004, showed a notably lower score in 2005. But in 2006, critics seemed somewhat appeased as Russia gained a less drastic CPI score (2.5) and also reached better positions in TI's other assessments, the GCB and the BPI. When Russia was first included in the latter ranking of the leading industrial nations in 2002, it took the bottom place (21st out of 21 countries). When the BPI was again issued in 2006, Russia had left China and India behind.[10] Yet also in this case it was hardly mentioned in the press that India for example was a newcomer to the ranking in 2006. Moreover, it was rarely noticed that Russia's score in the World Bank's 'Control of Corruption' assessment continued worsening in 2006. The CPI was clearly the most prominent point of reference. Between autumn 2005 and autumn 2006, obvious peak times of press reporting about corruption in Russia in the context of CPI releases, the Russian government had initiated a range of anti-corruption measures that were well-perceived among international actors and were also noted by many journalists inquiring about recent developments for their articles relating to the newest CPI score.

Financial and technical assistance

Financial and technical assistance presented the more direct avenues of external anti-corruption promotion in a particular country. Russia, which had received the lion's share of Western democratisation assistance during the 1990s (Mendelson and Glenn 2002), was also well supplied with assistance more or less explicitly devoted to anti-corruption measures from the late 1990s.

The World Bank, IMF, EBRD, EIB and other IFIs provided the Russian government with large-scale loans, supplemented by grant-based technical and financial assistance. Altogether, increasing volumes of funds, amounting to $US tens of billions alone during the initial years of Putin's presidency, were provided to support a variety of aspects under the wider headings of administrative and financial sector reforms, legal and juridical reforms, investment policy, social services, environmental protection and capacity building at the local level, as well as analytical work relating to these areas (e.g. EBRD 2002; IBRD/World Bank 2003).[11] In many respects and often implicitly, such assistance programmes also supported measures to prevent or control corruption and fraud in the public and private sectors. Most programmes were directed at authorities and ministries at the federal level, and only a minor share went to particular Russian regions or municipalities.[12]

Also major multilateral and bilateral aid organisations provided technical and financial assistance more or less directly devoted to anti-corruption projects. At the UN level, the UNDP had been active in Russia through its Moscow office and five regional offices since 1997, pursuing a general strategy that combined policy advice and assistance to the federal government and support to regional and municipal administrations as well as civil society organisations. Corruption became an issue during the Putin era, at first more implicitly as part of the human rights, environmental and health components of the 2001–3 grant programme

($US66 million) and then more explicitly as part of a separate 'effective and accountable governance' theme in 2004–7 ($US4 million) (UNDP 2003). Moreover, since the adoption of the UNCAC in 2003, UNODC became a major promoter of this convention. UNODC had been present in Moscow with its 'Russia and Belarus' field office since 1999. But whereas drug-related issues remained in the foreground in Russia, UNODC's anti-corruption engagement was confined to awareness-raising and technical assistance, mainly through supporting professional symposiums or initiating campaigns at the international Anti-corruption Day (9 December), which was also instituted in 2003. From 2004, when an Anti-Corruption Commission was established at the Duma (the lower chamber of the Russian Parliament, see Chapter 5), both the UNDP and UNODC entered closer interaction with this organ. After Russia had signed the UNCAC in 2006, UNODC sought to push the issue of asset recovery, as foreseen by the Convention. However, the Duma Commission considered this as a rather sensitive issue in the Russian context and instead selected integrity in the judiciary as a priority area for the government's collaboration with UNODC. The UN Global Compact started to actively promote corporate social responsibility in Russia from 2005. But again, this initiative started to build its own networks and to search for its own sources of information. [13]

At the level of the EU, Russia presented one of the Eastern European neighbouring countries for which EU membership was not an option. It thus remained outside the leverage to promote anti-corruption measures that the EU could use in the Eastern European candidate countries. Moreover, in contrast to other transitional recipient countries, the EU adopted a rather careful and particularly technical approach to Russia, as it presented the EU's largest European trade partner and a main supplier of oil and gas. Nevertheless, anti-corruption promotion was sought as part of the political dialogue as well as under technical assistance programmes.[14] Cooperation on corruption prevention was one of the objectives declared with the 1997 Partnership and Cooperation Agreement (*Agreement on Partnership and Cooperation* 1997: Article 84). Following 11 September 2001, this was reiterated not only as an economic, but also as a general political and security issue (European Commission 2001b).

Under the programme Technical Assistance to the Commonwealth of Independent States (TACIS, in Russia 1991–2006), about €600 million was allocated to projects in Russia alone between 2000 and 2003 (European Commission 2004). These funds included indirect support to address corruption as part of focuses on the development of the regulatory and legal environment and the requirements for Russia's accession to the World Trade Organisation (WTO). The EU's focus on corruption and fraud affecting EU budgets further triggered the first concrete EU–Russian anti-fraud measure in a specific field relevant to the trade relations with Russia. On the initiative of the European Anti-Fraud Office (OLAF), and mainly arranged between the Directorate-General Agriculture, OLAF, the Russian Department of International Cooperation, and Russian customs investigation units, a Commission Regulation on meat imports to Russia was decreed in 2000.[15] This was an administrative arrangement for transferring information on meat exports from the EU to Russia that aimed to tackle the problem of forged arrival documents from Russia that had emerged during the 1990s. In practice, it meant the establishment of a secure, paperless Anti-Fraud Information System (AFIS) with an electronic database at each end.

Otherwise, in line with the EU's objective to support rather than duplicate existing international anti-corruption strategies, the EU mainly urged Russia to sign the UN and CoE conventions and to cooperate internationally, especially through participation with GRECO. This rather distanced advocacy approach became more pronounced from 2003, on the eve of the EU's first eastern enlargement, when the EU and Russia began to develop a 'strategic partnership' through 'four common spaces', which meant a different approach than the European Neighbourhood Instrument applied to the other neighbouring countries (European Commission 2004).[16] With the roadmap for the Common Space of Freedom, Security, and Justice, agreed upon in May 2005, the EU addressed anti-corruption as one among several other security-related issues. It reiterated its emphasis on Russia's ratification of the UN and CoE anti-corruption conventions and further urged Russia to cooperate with relevant elements of civil society and to incorporate additional anti-corruption elements in national legislation and practices (EU–Russia

Summit 2005). As outlined below and in the following chapter, these promises soon seemed to be fulfilled on the part of Russia.

More indirectly, but to a substantial degree, the EU had financially supported concrete anti-corruption projects implemented through the CoE.[17] As long as Russia was not a member of GRECO, the CoE sought to promote anti-corruption measures through technical assistance programmes. For example, Russia was a participant country of the joint EU/CoE Octopus I+II programmes on the fight against corruption and organised crime in transition countries (1996–2000). In 2000, the Russian delegates who had visited several Western countries as part of these programmes recommended a range of fundamental tasks, including the improvement of the institutional framework (e.g. the establishment of a specialised anti-corruption body); the adoption of an anti-corruption law and an ethics code for public servants; the ratification of the CoE Criminal Law Convention on Corruption; and awareness-raising among experts through training and among the public through the press centre of the Prosecutor General's Office (Council of Europe 2000). As the Octopus programmes ended in 2000, they did not present a substantial push factor during the Putin era.

However, all these recommendations reappeared as the main objectives contained in two subsequent technical assistance projects to Russia – RUCOLA and RUCOLA II – which were equally financed by the European Commission and implemented by the CoE between 2005 and 2007. In addition, the first RUCOLA project had a special focus on corruption prevention in the judiciary and the development of a mechanism for monitoring corruption in the Russian regions (Council of Europe 2006). The second one focused on pilot areas of legislation, namely health, education, and public procurement (Council of Europe 2008). The main Russian partner for these projects was the Duma Anti-Corruption Commission, and the final conference of the second project should have been organised by a Russian civic organisation *Protiv Korruptsii*. However, by the time the conference was eventually held in Moscow in June 2008 (i.e. after the change of government), the term of the Duma Commission had already ended. The conference was then organised in collaboration with the Security Committee at the Duma, the Ministry of Economic Development and Trade (*Ministerstvo ekonomicheskogo razvitiia i torgovli*, MERiT), and a certain Centre for Strategic Development.[18]

In addition, anti-corruption assistance had reached Russia as part of bilateral assistance programmes. From the late 1990s/early 2000s, some technical cooperation programmes to support democratisation and the development of a market economy were opened up towards assisting anti-corruption measures.[19] Most explicitly this was the case with programmes from the USA, Canada and the UK. Although bilateral assistance went primarily to the federal government and regional authorities, CSOs and business associations were also among the recipients.

Western national aid agencies and private foundations presented the main providers of project-related small grants to Russian civil society actors for conducting anti-corruption projects. Specific corruption-related grants were offered from around 1998 by donors who had been active in the country before, first of all: USAID (in Russia since 1992), CIDA (in Russia since 1991), the British government's Global Opportunities Fund (no particular programme for Russia), and US-based private foundations – the Eurasia Foundation, which also used much USAID funding (in Russia since 1993), the Soros Foundation (in Russia since the early 1990s), and the Ford Foundation (in Russia since 1996 and the only donor that was not active in any other Eastern European country). In addition, many small grants went to civic anti-corruption actions indirectly as part of donor programmes to assist democratisation, civil society develop-ment as such, and civic participation in other fields (e.g. environmental protection, municipal reform, research, consultancy, organisation of events, and other service provi-sion to the public and private sectors). Also Western embassies present in the country had occasionally provided local CSOs with small grants for activities in the anti-corruption field. Indirectly, even World Bank and EU money had reached civic anti-corruption activities through various subcontracting arrangements.[20]

Russian NGOs, research institutions, journalistic or other professional associations, but also small and medium-sized enterprises (SMEs) and business associations, could thus apply for small grants, commonly ranging between $US2,000 and $US10,000 per project, under a multitude of programmes and along various channels. The funds were usually distributed on a competitive basis and appropriated for a particular project with an agreed time frame and set of outcomes. Beyond that, grants in this field hardly contained overhead budgets for personnel or equipment. In general, grants to civic groups were offered for projects that would mobilise Russian citizens, contribute to information-gathering or to the provision of training, or advocate anti-corruption reforms vis-à-vis the local administrations. In contrast to governmental programmes, which aimed at building institutions and legal frameworks, the most frequently expected outcome of civic projects was some kind of publication (handbooks, brochures, posters etc.) or forum for information exchange (round tables, public hearings, seminars, multi-stakeholder conferences etc.). The USAID programme supporting regional Anti-Corruption Coalitions also included street action (anti-corruption days or weeks) in several Russian cities (USAID and MSI 2003).

Almost all relevant foreign donors maintained field offices in Russia, more precisely in Moscow (with the exception of the Eurasia Foundation that maintained another regional office in the Far Eastern city of Vladivostok). Yet the programmes themselves mainly supported projects in the Russian regions and were primarily targeted at reform and awareness-raising within these regions. The double focus on civil society and on local vantage points, however, implied that the state (at the federal level) hardly played any role as part of many civic projects. As in other fields of assistance, this strategy may have been partly based on an outdated understanding of decentralisation processes in Russia (e.g. Thomson et al. 2007). In the anti-corruption field, in particular, this was supported by the idea that the local level presented an effective vantage point thanks to greater proximity (e.g. Gole 1999; TI and UN-Habitat 2004). As one Western partner emphasised with regard to Russia:

> A province-by-province approach is the best way to set about tackling the problem [of corruption]. It is unrealistic to expect a quick fix through a policy shift in Moscow that is imposed by the rest of the nation. Russian politics today simply do not work that way (few countries do). Across Russia's vastly diverse political and economic landscape, some areas are more primed for a clean-

hands campaign than others. The battle against corruption must be fought city by city, gang by gang.[21]

The Eurasia Foundation placed particular emphasis on regional diversity. This foundation concluded from an evaluation of its first anti-corruption small grant programme to Russia (1998–2000), that 'success would strongly depend on the consideration of each region's socio-political situation and arrangement of political forces in the project planning'. In a subsequent phase of this programme (2001–2), more emphasis was placed on linking local authorities and civil society.[22] USAID, in contrast, upheld its general practice of expanding successful experiences to other places also in the anti-corruption field. The USAID-financed small grant and technical training programme for assisting the establishment of local Anti-Corruption Coalitions (2001–5) thus aimed at transferring experiences from Russian pilot regions to other regions without much sensitivity to socio-political particularities. This programme was first implemented in three regions in Ukraine (1998–2000) and then extended to other Ukrainian regions and to two pilot regions in Russia in 2001 (Samara and Tomsk oblasts).[23] As the Russian pilot coalitions were viewed as successful (e.g. Spector and Winbourne 2002), these further served as the main model for other Anti-Corruption Coalitions across Siberia and the Russian Far East in 2003 (Irkutsk and Primorskii kray) and 2005 (Khabarovsk kray, Sakhalin oblast, Kamchatka kray) (USAID and MSI 2003; Vol'skaia-Vinborn et al. 2004) (see Chapter 6 for a more detailed case study).

Civil society-oriented anti-corruption assistance through foreign private foundations was rather short-lived in Russia. After the bulk of funding had been distributed during the late 1990s and early 2000s, the foundations began to recognise that these investments had not yielded any major achievements. Some pointed to reasons of a more general nature, such as structural constraints (e.g. the short time intervals of small grant projects, in particular of educational projects) or changing preferences such as counter-terrorism and other issues dominating the international agenda in the aftermath of 11 September 2001 (e.g. conflict resolution and, therewith, a stronger regional focus on central Asia). There was also a re-orientation to fostering civic participation in the provision of basic social services to vulnerable parts of the population (e.g. care for homeless people, orphans, HIV/AIDS prevention etc.). It was recognised that Russian CSOs were more competent and better networked and that their role was better acknowledged by the government in such fields. There were other Russia-specific reasons for private donors to markedly decrease anti-corruption assistance to civil society, such as the passiveness of the population, the inability of local authorities to further develop outcomes of civic projects, or limited information exchange and networking among the various grantees.[24] Regular personnel turnover within the foundations also contributed to changes in programmatic priorities. The Ford Foundation's major programme on good governance and civil society (1996–2001), for example, was discontinued since the new director of the Moscow office decided to focus on different themes for future civil society assistance. This implied not only that the organisation itself was no longer present in the anti-corruption field, but also that much of the knowledge that had been generated with its support was not passed on:

> We make grants in clusters over stretches of time to try to achieve certain objectives. In this case, the entire programme wrapped up, grants had ended, and that was a good five years ago … So we just keep that stuff in the archives in New York and move on. There's not a lot of institutional memory here that stretches back that way. (Representative of the Ford Foundation, 2006)

Importantly, however, foreign donors had experienced increasing suspicion on the part of the Putin administration. Foreign private foundations were more vulnerable to such pressures than governmental or multilateral donors. Among the most important supporters of civic anti-corruption projects, the Eurasia Foundation thus excluded Russia from another special anti-corruption programme which it launched in 2002 to support NGOs in Eastern European and central Asian countries.[25] The Soros Foundation closed down its Moscow office in 2003, following a series of difficulties with the Russian authorities which included the charge that it represented US interests. This incident was not without effect on other donors, as it encouraged them to stick with social-service oriented, non-political programmes.

The Eurasia Foundation chose a totally new operational

approach for Russia. In 2004, the New Eurasia Foundation (*Fond Novaia Evraziia*) was registered as a Russian NGO with an office in Moscow. *Novaia Evraziia* presented a joint project under the auspices of the US-based Eurasia Foundation, the Brussels-based European Madariaga Foundation and Russia's Dynasty Foundation.[26] While even strengthening the Eurasia Foundation's former emphasis on regional development, this new donor also excluded 'anti-corruption' from its official portfolio of social and economic development programmes.[27] Albeit acknowledging the high relevance of various cross-cutting themes for fostering effective regional government and preventing corruption (e.g. higher education, investment, migration, or housing and municipal development), *Novaia Evraziia* would not explicitly label these as 'anti-corruption' projects.[28] USAID, which as a governmental aid agency continued with anti-corruption programmes directly oriented at Russian civil society, thus presented the most important remaining source for CSOs.[29]

International anti-corruption networks and conventions

Russia became involved in various supranational collaborative arrangements against corruption, with most formal commitment starting and intensifying under Putin's presidency.

Immediately in 2000 Russia applied to join the OECD Convention on Combating Bribery of Foreign Public Officials in International Business Transactions (in force since 1999), although it was not an OECD member economy and had not been involved in the adoption of this Convention in 1997. Furthermore, in 2001, it applied to become a full participant in the OECD Working Group on Bribery in International Business Transactions (ACN 2005: 12). However, at that time, Russia could not fulfil the basic requirements for membership of the Working Group and accession to the Convention (national anti-corruption strategy, legal framework for combating bribery, anti-money-laundering legislation, economic factors) (OECD 2004b). Since then, Russia has never seriously resumed the question of signing the OECD Anti-Bribery Convention and has therewith also remained outside the multilateral surveillance system relating to this instrument. Instead, Russia remained a participant in the OECD's regional network ACN (since 1998), which presented the main outreach programme of the OECD Working Group for the post-Soviet region. In the context of ACN, Russia became party to the Istanbul Anti-Corruption Action Plan in 2003 (ACN 2003), another sub-regional strategy endorsed for initially six post-Soviet countries. Before long, Russia stood out as the only ACN country that showed commitment to all major international anti-corruption conventions (see ACN 2005: 12). However, Russia also remained the only participant which never submitted itself to the self-assessment and monitoring process assessing ACN countries' progress in implementing the Istanbul Action Plan. If at all, Russia presented incomplete and outdated self-assessment reports and then still failed to present an official delegation to discuss the assessments and recommendations made on behalf of ACN (ACN/OECD 2005: 2).

Regarding the other major anti-corruption conventions, international cooperation clearly seemed to be on Putin's agenda.[30] On the eve of Putin's presidency, Russia had signed two conventions of the Council of Europe (of which Russia was a member since 1996) – the Criminal Law Convention on Corruption right after its adoption in January 1999 and a few months later the Convention on Laundering, Search, Seizure and Confiscation of Proceeds of Crime (adopted in 1990). Under Putin, Russia further signed the UN Convention on Transnational Organised Crime in 2000 and went on to ratify the CoE Anti-Money Laundering Convention in 2001, to sign the UNCAC right after its adoption in 2003, and to ratify the UN Convention on Transnational Organised Crime in 2004. These steps were well received by the international community. In particular the UN, the CoE and the EU intensified their relationships with the Anti-Corruption Commission at the Russian Duma after the latter was established in 2004 and especially since Russia went on to ratify the UN and CoE anti-corruption conventions in 2006.

In July 2006, the G8 Summit led to the adoption of an international anti-corruption document about fighting high-level corruption (G8 Centre 2006). This document was not specifically related to Russia and the Summit actually focused on different priority issues (global energy security, infectious diseases and education).[31] However, the very occasion of this Summit presented a major push-factor in the given case, since it was chaired by Russia during its first presidency of the Group of Eight (held in St. Petersburg). This Summit was further used as an opportunity by TI for launching a major campaign to lobby for a continuation of anti-corruption commitments made at the previous G8 Summit in Gleneagles, underlining that the overwhelming majority of the eight countries had yet to ratify the UNCAC (Canada, Germany, Italy, Japan, Russia, the United States). TI also stressed the importance of addressing corruption under each of the priority issues.[32] On this occasion Russia could thus present itself as a forerunner state within a club of equals by ratifying the UNCAC during the run-up to the Summit in May 2006. It also demonstrated continuing commitment by ratifying the CoE's Criminal Law Convention on Corruption during the remainder of its G8 presidency in October 2006.

With the ratification of the CoE Convention, Russia also formally agreed on participating in the monitoring procedure of GRECO, even if not being a GRECO member. But very soon, in February 2007, Russia also became a member of GRECO and would thus without any reservations expose itself to this 'process of mutual evaluation and peer pressure'.[33] The external evaluation was conducted in April 2008. During the onsite visit of the Evaluation Team, meetings with representatives of Russian civil society, as proposed by GRECO, had to be arranged by the Russian government. GRECO had chosen leading representatives of specialised anti-corruption organisations with whom the CoE had already been working as part of its previous technical assistance projects (TI-Russia, INDEM, *Protiv Korruptsii*). At first, Russia did not authorise the publication of the resulting report which criticised, amongst many other aspects, the lack of a national anti-corruption strategy and the lack of opportunities for civic participation. The publication of the revised report (GRECO 2008b) only happened under Putin's successor Medvedev in spring 2009. At the UN level, where evaluation was foreseen on a self-assessment basis, Russia more actively participated in the activities of the Conference of the States Parties to the UNCAC from December 2006, a forum aimed at facilitating and reviewing the implementation of the Convention.[34]

TI, of course, presented another major international anti-corruption network which 'included' Russia, albeit in a different way. Understanding itself as 'the global civil society organisation leading the fight against corruption',[35] TI first of all sought to expand its reach by involving CSOs, acting as National Chapters of the global organisation, in as many countries as possible. The Russian TI Chapter, TI-Russia, was set up in 1999/2000, registered as a Russian NGO and located with a small office in Moscow. According to TI's franchising system, TI-Russia was a rather independent initiative of some engaged Russian individuals that received only relatively minor financial support from the TI-S through initial seed money and some project-related allowances. The main assets gained from being a formal member of this global movement were of an organisational and symbolic nature: information exchange, the provision of access points to major international initiatives and to the Russian government, and the possibility of acting under the TI logo.

> We are actually very proud of that structure. We never open an office, or we never hire local people. We don't fund them for instance. So we always wait until there is a local interest [...] And the purpose of this whole strategy is to avoid dependence. Whenever we work within a country, we want the group we work with to be a real genuine civil society, not just an artificial one, funded through international donor agencies [...] Our role at the Secretariat is a role of information sharing. We act like a clearing house of information. So we make the connections between the local activities and global activities. (Representative of the TI-S, 2004)

The TI Secretariat also acted independently as an active anti-corruption promoter at the international level and vis-à-vis certain countries. In the Russian case, the TI campaign in the context of the 2006 G8 Summit also had substantial effects on this country's individual anti-corruption efforts. This campaign had used a major international forum not only to lobby for international collaboration against corruption, as many other TI actions did, but also to push respective developments in a particular country. By 2005, after more than six years of engagement in the Russian case, TI had realised that it was time for another campaign to push for the eventual realisation of much rhetorical anti-corruption commitment on the part of the Russian government. Moreover, following the adoption of a highly controversial and rather restrictive new NGO legislation in December 2005 (see Schmidt 2006b), TI used the G8 Summit for organising a civil society counter-Summit in order to draw international attention to clampdowns on democratic and economic freedoms under President Putin in Russia.[36] Despite the government's efforts to prevent this alternative Summit or, at least, to prevent the participation of Western governmental representatives (Lebedev 2006), it was eventually held as a major two-day conference 'The Other Russia' (*Drugaia Rossiia*) in Moscow just two days before the G8 Summit in St. Petersburg. The organisational committee for this event was composed of leading representatives of the Russian civil society scene, including renowned and opposi-tional human rights advocates as well as the directors of TI-Russia and INDEM, two major Moscow-based anti-corruption organisations.[37]

What kind of corruption?

The essence of the controversial discussions about the defin-ition of corruption, which had been led among and within the main international organisations (see Chapter 3), seems to disappear when looking at particular anti-corruption pro-grammes or projects. Moreover, some of the donors who had occasionally assisted anti-corruption initiatives in Russia did not explicitly mention corruption as part of their agenda and correspondingly did not engage with questions of definition. Rather, within the frameworks of concrete programmes inter-national actors were particularly determined to point to the various consequences of corruption. This strategy was neces-sary in order to justify the relevance of the programmes and the financial resources devoted to them as well as to establish thematic resonance points in the sense of framing. Most strikingly, there had been very little debate about country-specific forms of corruption in the Russian context. On the part of international and foreign actors, internationally rele-vant concerns received overwhelming attention, such as detrimental effects of corruption on the domestic invest-ment climate, on decision-making procedures, or on the unfolding democracy. Rarely discussed on this front were the historically strong roots of some forms of corruption in the particular Russian contexts, such as *blat* (networks of favour), *mzdoimstvo/vziatochnichestvo* (bribe-taking), bureaucratism, or the abuse of administrative resources during elections and other strategic political moves.[38] Similarly, and although respective information was provided even by international surveys such as BEEPS or the GCB, the changing patterns of corruption in certain sectors and within the given political context had rarely received any further attention. As outlined, it was quantitative evidence of decreasing levels of corruption during the Putin era that raised awareness of the fact that things were changing. CoE reports stood out among the international documents by actually using a variety of the existing sources of information and by acknowledging changes in scope *and* kind. For example, the CoE's *Organised Crime Situation Report* in 2005 underlined that economic crime and organised crime in Russia had become qualitatively different in the context of political changes during the 2000s, through a process of consolidation that included a shift from violent to economic crime and a legalisation of illegal business, proceeds of crime, and fraud (Council of Europe 2005: 90–4). However, the official GRECO evaluation report, which had to be negotiated in a plenary meeting, again referred mainly to official sources of information and presented the view that, while there were multiple indications that corruption had grown into a systemic phenomenon in Russia, there was no reliable information on the situation (GRECO 2008b). In general, international programmes and activities seemed to be dominated by a desire to support anti-corruption measures and instruments, rather than to understand the particular corruption patterns in Russia. Moreover, since the question of ratifying the UN and CoE anti-corruption conventions was seriously at the table by the mid-2000s, the anti-corruption discourse experienced a notable legalistic turn. Issues like the criminalisation of concrete corruption offences, the confiscation of proceeds of corrupt offences, or the regulation of investigative and adjudicative competencies under various pieces of legislation moved into the foreground.

Moreover, the Russian case illustrates that spectacular events and scandals contributed to reframing the anti-corruption cause. Since 2002, Russia had entered the radar of international anti-corruption promoters with several hostage takings and terrorist attacks in Moscow and the Northern Caucasus that were made possible through bribes.[39] In the post-11 September climate, this reinforced linkages to international anti-terrorist discourses. The Beslan tragedy, especially, was a key event for TI to remind the international community of the perilous links between corruption and terrorism.[40] Also foreign media and policy briefs used this event for bridging these two major discourses (e.g. *Economist* 2005; JRL RAS 2004; Murphy 2004).[41] By the time the EU and Russia had agreed on the 'roadmaps' for the four common spaces defining their envisioned strategic partnership in May 2005, it was thus hardly surprising that anti-corruption was most explicitly formulated as a security issue (EU-Russia Summit 2005).

Involving civil society?

A commitment to involving civil society was formally made as part of literally all the activities outlined in this chapter. In practice, however, international organisations, programmes and delegations had been primarily interacting with responsible federal authorities. Anti-corruption, from their perspective, presented a political, economic or administrative matter to be dealt with through legal and institutional reforms or through administrative agreements (with regard to given international standards) that were to be instigated at governmental level. For example, notwithstanding a general commitment to civil society involvement uttered by the EU, neither international nor Russian civil society played any part in introducing a first concrete anti-fraud system relating to meat imports through EC Regulation 2584 in 2000. The involvement of Russian civil society in the government's anti-corruption efforts had only been pushed since the mid-2000s in the framework of collaborative projects between the CoE and the Duma Anti-Corruption Commission. On the part of the CoE itself, however, much attention was paid to working with individual civic experts rather than with certain CSOs:

> Basically, we don't work with TI as an organisation. We work with Elena Panfilova who happens to work in TI. (Representative of the CoE, 2007)

Although a formal commitment to assisting civil society in Russia was made by many of the above-mentioned organisations, this was usually realised under separate programmes. In the anti-corruption field, actual involvement of Russian CSOs had remained limited to activities where information-gathering and the provision of financial assistance stood in the foreground. As part of the information-gathering strategies outlined in the first section, some international organisations and foreign delegations directly consulted Russian CSOs, most notably the GRECO evaluation team in 2008. Yet such interaction was most often limited to TI-Russia as the best-known and most easily approachable Russian organisation: based in Moscow, with English-speaking staff, and well-networked at the international level. Not least, this role of TI-Russia as a main lynchpin for civic expertise in corruption-related matters was explicitly fostered by the TI Secretariat.[42] A number of Western donor organisations, in turn, devoted financial assistance to civic anti-corruption projects in many regions across the country. The provision of small grants to Russian CSOs presented another most substantial form of involvement. However, interaction between international partners and domestic beneficiaries was limited to the implementation of certain projects and thus framed by formal terms and conditions. There was not much continuance beyond the limited time frames of overall programmes or individual projects. In particular US foundations tended to transfer project reports to their head offices in Washington, DC or New York after only a few years.[43] A rather frequent turnover of personnel within international organisations further contributed to disrupting opportunities for further collaboration or, at least, exchange of information. At the same time, representatives of key anti-corruption promoting international organisations regretted that hardly any Russian CSOs were active in this field, as perhaps best illustrated by the following statement:

> There are not that many civil society organisations [in Russia] working on corruption. And this is an unfortunate side. Of course you have journalists that provide a lot of useful information [. . .] And in terms of civil society, NGOs in themselves are

of course the usual suspects for the UN – [you have] TI-Russia. But, really, the network is not well established yet in this country, unfortunately. (Representative of the UN, 2006)

Financial assistance to CSOs primarily aimed at fostering the role of the latter as providers of information and expertise. The fruits of such efforts, however, were not reflected in official country reports of other international organisations, which were commonly based on CPI data about the level of corruption in Russia, on official data about anti-corruption measures, including reports of the Supreme Court and the Prosecutor General's Office (PGO) (about the number of prosecutions, the downsizing of civil service staff, adjustment of salaries etc.) and newly adopted legislation, as well as statements of Russian government officials, judges and (mostly legal) scholarly experts. With only a few exceptions (EBRD 2004; GRECO 2008b), there was hardly any mention of information about corruption in Russia provided by Russian CSOs. Also, with the exception of TI, the inter-national *anti-corruption* community seemed to pay little attention to the generally degrading operational conditions of Russian CSOs under the Putin administration (see also Chapter 5).

Civil society involvement through the government, in contrast, was identified as a remaining and even increasing deficit in Russia's anti-corruption performance. In particular, UN agencies and the CoE criticised top-down public participation mechanisms and urged for better civil society participation in future reforms (GRECO 2008b; UNDP 2007). The possibility that NGOs were co-opted or manipulated was taken into account:

> But we have to be very careful because corruption obviously also is intertwined with the political process. And this is why I, especially in corruption, am hesitant to take information that is received from civil society organisations at face value, unless I know what the real driving force behind that NGO is. That it is not manipulated politically, that it is not seeking other ends. So, again, it's a very delicate area to go in, and I've seen NGOs appear doing key political election processes and then disappear. (Representative of the UN, 2006)

However, this stood in contrast to a rather uncritical interaction with dubious and obviously government-supported organisations such as *Protiv Korruptsii* (see Chapter 6 for more detail). Moreover, external support of civil society involvement had sometimes remained rather vague. For example, the UNDP Country Programme for Russia 2008–10 (a $US76.3 million programme adopted in July 2007) contained an overall target that 'sustainable mechanisms of civil society involvement in administrative reform, budgeting process and actions against corruption' should be developed in at least 10 of the Russian regions (formulated under the 'democratic governance' component, for which resources of $US5.8 million were scheduled – presenting the smallest amount per component). However, while the partners for this component were clearly identified at the governmental level (particular federal ministries, the Federal Accounts Chamber, the Duma Anti-Corruption Commission, and regional authorities in 10 pilot regions to be selected), only vague reference was made to 'civil society; business associations and corporate sector'. The concrete output envisioned for this component and target was even more broadly formulated as 'Networks of decision-makers and experts' (besides training officials and introducing performance-based budgeting tools) (UNDP 2007, Annex).

Finally, the TI network clearly presented the most strategic approach to involve Russian civil society in global anti-corruption advocacy through a National Chapter. As such, however, the whole TI network presented a civil society actor itself. It still had to search for access points to the activities in the intergovernmental sphere. Moreover, in the Russian context, the TI strategy was confined to supporting and interacting with one single Russian organisation – TI-Russia. In contrast to the emphasis placed by foreign donor organisations on channelling support for anti-corruption projects through local organisations across a number of regions, the TI-S left it to its Moscow-based Chapter to develop networks with other CSOs across Russia. The representatives of the TI-S believed that TI-Russia was indeed well networked across the Russian regions.[44]

This chapter has outlined the various international approaches to promoting anti-corruption efforts in Russia. It has identified a variety of actors and programmes that sought to foster the development of a range of anti-corruption measures during the Putin era. These have been similar and closely linked to the overall anti-corruption advocacy directed at Eastern Europe. While external assistance included the generation of information about country-specific patterns of corruption, quantitative evidence about (rising) corruption levels provided by cross-country indices presented a main point of reference. Moreover, the international activities were for the most part targeted at the Russian government. In practice, the CoE and UN agencies, which emerged as key anti-corruption promoters in Russia from the mid-2000s, had entered closer interaction with the Commission for Counteraction against Corruption in the Russian Duma, which had been established in 2004 (see Chapter 5). Despite a general commitment to involving civil society in anti-corruption advocacy, actual participation remained rather limited in practice. While several financial assistance programmes had been devoted to supporting civic anti-corruption projects in particular, these were largely fostered by different external actors and under separate programmes. Moreover, foreign private foundations, especially, tended to cease anti-corruption assistance around 2002–4. During the remainder of the Putin era, such assistance was continued basically only by USAID and some Western embassies.

In terms of process, this chapter has further shown that anti-corruption promotion markedly intensified from the mid-2000s and especially in the context of the G8 Summit held in Russia in 2006. Although this acceleration included a pooling of different international efforts that sought to push Russia's ratification and implementation of international anti-corruption conventions, direct coordination in planning and implementing the various programmes in Russia remained limited. Moreover, although the stronger focus on the UN and CoE conventions generally implied a strengthening of intergovernmental collaboration, especially on legalistic matters, the increasing presence of CoE also fostered the inclusion of *some* core Russian CSOs into the implementation of international projects and measures such as the GRECO evaluation. In order to establish a better understanding of these changing patterns of interaction, further analysis is needed of domestic anti-corruption initiatives as undertaken by the Russian government (Chapter 4) and various Russian civil society actors (Chapter 5).

Notes

1 For example, interview with a UK consular service official based in Russia, 2005.

2 In the context of the controversy on the UN Oil-for-Food Programme and as part of UN accountability and ethical conduct reforms, Secretary-General Kofi Annan waived the diplomatic immunity of Vladimir Kusnetsov, who was arrested by US officials in connection with the investigation of Alexander Yakovlev, the former UN procurement officer, both suspected of corruption (UNA-USA 2005). In November 2005, the Russian government delivered $US500,000 bail money for Kusnetsovs' release (RFE/RL 2005a). Also in 2005, as extensively criticised in the German and other Western media, following Schröder's election defeat, Putin offered him a leading position in the consortium that would coordinate the pipeline deal between Russia's (state-owned) Gazprom and Germany's companies E.On and BASF. The TI-S launched a campaign on this issue directed at the governments of Germany, the UK and others, criticising this 'mixing of political and business activities', especially by using a company that was not up to international corporate standards (interview with a representative of the TI-S, 2006).

3 Some international organisations invited each other's representatives to attend their various events in Russia. Also Russian and foreign experts were recommended across international programmes. However, the organisations tended to not coordinate the designing and implementation of their various anti-corruption programmes (interviews with representatives of the EU, 2005; the UN, 2006; and the CoE, 2007).

4 The $US50 million Judicial Reform Programme for Russia (implemented through MERiT since 2007), which had a strong focus on transparency in the judiciary, is just one more recent example. See for an overview of World Bank projects: The World Bank, Projects and Operations, Country Reports, Russia, at: www.worldbank.org.

5 Several Russian interviewees mentioned that World Bank money had been used (by other than their own organisations) for research about corruption in Russia.

6 See, for example, MSI (2002a, 2002b, 2004) for Samara, Tomsk and Irkutsk.

7 See TraCCC, 'Russia Centers and Projects' at: www.american.edu/traccc /projects/russia.html (accessed 06/04/2006), also old version 'Overseas Centers' at: www.american.edu/traccc/centers.htm (accessed 23/05/2003).

8 See FATF, the 40 Recommendations, at: www.fatf-gafi.org/document /28/0,3343,en_32250379_32236930_33658140_1_1_1_1,00.html (accessed 12/05/2009).

9 The CPI or, more precisely, recent news based on the CPI, was also referred to in most interviews with representatives of international organisations, usually before I asked a question related to this or other indices.

10 The Bribe Payers' Index has been issued irregularly: in 1999, 2002, 2006, 2008.

11 Amongst others, the increase in assistance was due to the resumption of IMF disbursements to Russia, following an interruption between 1999 and 2002 due to disagreements with the Russian government over a

common strategy in the aftermath of the 1998 Russian financial crisis, and the onset of the EIB lending mandate in 2001, which was extended across sectors and regions in 2003 (after it was initially confined to environmental projects in north-west Russia, in the context of the EU's Northern Dimension) (e.g. EBRD 2002).

12 See, for example, The World Bank, Projects and Operations, Country Reports, Russia, at: www.worldbank.org or EBRD (2004). The EBRD directly financed €5.5 billion and mobilised several billions of euros through co-financing up to 2003, representing the largest volume among its countries of operation.

13 Interviews with two representatives of the UN, 2005 and 2006.

14 Interviews with three representatives of the EU, 2005 and 2006.

15 European Commission (2000) and interview with a representative of OLAF, 2005.

16 See Arbatova (2007), Borko (2004) and Johnson and Robinson (2008) for more details about the development of EU–Russia relations in general. On the ENPI and anti-corruption promotion, see Börzel et al. (2010).

17 These project-related grants had been subcontracted through tenders. Reportedly, in the Russian case, no other organisation but the CoE had won these tenders (interview with two representatives of the CoE, 2007).

18 The conference was entitled: 'Practices and prospects of development of the legislation regulating anti-corruption expertise of legal acts and draft laws in Russia and other countries of Eastern Europe and Asia' (GRECO 2008a: 3).

19 Between 2000 and 2002 alone Russia received several $US billions of assistance from Germany, Japan and the USA and several hundred million $US from Canada, Finland, Sweden and the UK in support of democratisation, economic reform and environmental protection (EBRD 2002: 59–60).

20 Precise channels were difficult to trace in official documents. In several interviews, Russian groups mentioned that they had benefited from EU funds. The RUCOLA projects, which were financed by the European Commission, presented but one concrete example where Russian civic groups had been involved as experts or for the organisation of conferences as part of projects primarily led in cooperation with governmental authorities (interview with a representative of the CoE, 2007).

21 United Research Centers for Organized Crime in Eurasia, Washington, quoted in Rutland and Kogan (2001: 146).

22 See *Fond Evraziia*, 'Otsenka Programmy po Preduprezhdeniiu Korruptsii', at www.eurasia.msk.ru/programs/corruption/evaluation .html (accessed 06/06/2006).

23 Under the same programme, national coalitions were set up in Albania, Bulgaria and Macedonia around 2000 (Tisne and Smilov 2004). Also interview with two representatives of MSI, the organisation implementing this programme in Ukraine and Russia, 2007.

24 See *Fond Evraziia*, 'Otsenka Programmy po Preduprezhdeniiu Korruptsii', at: www.eurasia.msk.ru/programs/corruption/evaluation.html (accessed 06/06/2006), also interviews with representatives of the Eurasia Foundation, Ford Foundation, New Eurasia Foundation, 2004 and 2006.

25 See Eurasia Foundation, Anti-Corruption, at: www.eurasia.org/programs /anticorruption.aspx (accessed 25/01/2009).

26 Following this, between 2005 and 2007, the Eurasia Foundation revised its whole organisational strategy by creating autonomous locally registered foundations also for the other regions where it was engaged – Central Asia, South Caucasus, and Eastern Europe. Together with the Eurasia Foundation as their American counterpart, these organisations were intended to 'represent a new type of institution for the region, combining local knowledge and leadership with international best practices of program management and financial stewardship, all carried out under the governance of international boards of trustees' (see Eurasia Foundation, About, at: www.eurasia.org/about/ (accessed 25/01/2009).

27 See *Fond Novaia Evraziia*, at: www.neweurasia.ru (accessed 25/01/2009).

28 Interview with three representatives of *Novaia Evraziia*, 2006.

29 In general, civil society-oriented programmes presented the second-largest budget line among USAID anti-corruption programmes (see USAID, Fighting Corruption, at: www.usaid.gov/our_work/democracy_and _governance/technical_areas/anti-corruption/ (accessed 25/01/2009)).

30 With the exception of the Civil Law Convention on Corruption of the Council of Europe (adopted in 1999), which had hardly been part of the discussions in Russia and remained unsigned.

31 See G8 Summit 2006, Agenda, at: http://en.g8russia.ru/agenda/ (accessed 12/04/2009).

32 See documentation of the whole TI campaign at TI, G8 Russia, at: www.transparency.org/news_room/in_focus/2006/g8_russia   (accessed 12/04/2009).

33 CoE, 'What's the GRECO?', at: www.greco.coe.int (accessed 28/09/06).

34 See protocols of the Conference of State Parties at UNODC, United Nations Convention against Corruption, at: www.unodc.org/unodc/en /treaties/CAC/index.html (accessed 15/04/2009).

35 See TI, About us, at: www.transparency.org/about_us (accessed 20/05/2009).

36 Interview with a representative of the TI-S, 2005.

37 See *Drugaia Rossiia*, at: www.theotherrussia.ru (accessed 20/04/2009).

38 See, for example, Ledeneva (1998) on the persistence of *blat* in post-Soviet times, Bondarenko (2002) on various forms of corruption and their historical roots, or Kliamkin and Timofeev (2000) on corruption and the shadow economy in Russia.

39 The hostage-takings in the Moscow theatre Dubrovka in October 2002 and in a school in Beslan in September 2004 were widely covered in the international and Russian news.

40 In Beslan, a southern Russian city, Chechen rebels seized a primary school on 1 September 2004 (traditionally school enrolment day). They took hostage more than 1,000 people, including hundreds of pupils and their parents. Three days later, a firefight between Russian security forces and hostage-takers left over 325 people dead, almost half of them children.

41 Also interviews with representatives of the TI-S and TI-Russia, both 2004.

42 Interview with a representative of the TI-S, 2004.

43 In an effort to receive project reports and documents about past projects, I had sent several emails to US-based head offices of the relevant donor organisations. However, all of them remained without reply.

44 Interviews with two representatives of the TI-S, 2004 and 2005.

5

Governmental initiatives against corruption

The previous two chapters have introduced the main actors engaged in anti-corruption promotion at the international level and have outlined their changing agendas and actions relating to Eastern Europe and to Russia. The following two chapters will now direct the focus towards Russia's domestic level. This chapter starts with governmental anti-corruption initiatives throughout the Putin era. Here too, the course of the governmental engagement was traced with due attention to the precise timing of the actions and events.

President Putin had been reiterating his anti-corruption ambitions throughout his two terms in office. Russia's corruption problems and the need to tackle them were core issues in each of the President's Annual Addresses to the Federal Assembly of the Russian Federation (henceforth Annual Address) and in other public speeches or interviews with key domestic and foreign audiences. Indeed, during his eight and a half years in office, tens of thousands of officials and numerous high-profile politicians and entrepreneurs were convicted, and an unprecedented anti-corruption system was brought underway which included institutional and legal measures, Russia's integration into the most significant international anti-corruption regimes, and outreach to the domestic citizenry. At first glance, the record of governmental anti-corruption action seems to present a steady commitment. However, a more attentive tracing of the actions reveals several twists and turns. While prosecutorial measures continued throughout the time frame studied, two main phases can be distinguished. As outlined in the following section, the first phase (2000–5) set in with Putin's explicit anti-corruption promises and some spectacular arrests. But it also saw a widening of the official anti-corruption agenda and actions in scope and kind while the government opened itself up to the international anti-corruption discourse and established anti-corruption institutions. The next section then traces the new anti-corruption drive since 2006, when the government turned to more determined commitment to international collaboration as well as to integrating civic expertise and popular opinion at home. Finally, the two remaining sections summarise what forms of corruption were addressed and how civil society was involved during these two phases.

Prelude (2000–5): anti-corruption promises, showcases and institutions

Almost immediately after Putin's inauguration, the presidential administration and the PGO started to implement the anti-corruption promise by charging various Russian oligarchs, who were extensively involved in politics, with grand fraud and misappropriation. According to the rhetoric of the new President, Russia was plagued with transition-related corruption caused by the introduction of market mechanisms and a simultaneously unregulated legal sphere. Following Putin's first State of the Nation Address in July 2000, where he reiterated his intention to clamp down on the oligarchs and rebellious regional governors (Putin 2000), the oil giant Lukoil, car manufacturer Avtovaz, and the Media-Most broadcasting conglomerate were at the focus of investigations into tax fraud. Vladimir Potanin, former deputy prime minister and chairman of the financial conglomerate Interros was ordered to reimburse the government $US140 million which he had allegedly underpaid for the purchase of the Norilsk Nickel company, and the Parliament launched investigations into the sales of shares in 'Unified Energy Systems' (*Edinaia Energeticheskaia Sistema*) – an electric monopoly chaired by former finance minister Anatoly Chubais – and of a company established by atomic energy minister Yevgeny Adamov, allegedly profiting from US government contracts to improve Russian nuclear plant safety. Also the corrupt management of the state-owned gas monopoly Gazprom was reformed (The Center for Public

Integrity 2004). In 2001, media tycoons Vladimir Gusinsky and Boris Berezovsky were forced to leave the country, and full governmental control was reinstalled over their national TV networks ORT and NTV, Media-Most, and two major daily newspapers (Oates 2006; Rutland 2006). Countering criticism that these moves were politically motivated and that the free media were harassed, Putin repeatedly underlined the need for order and law enforcement. He also noted that the mass media in particular would need to be economically independent in order to be free. In 2002, Railway Minister Nikolai Aksyonenko was fired when the Duma Audit Chamber reported that his ministry fixed freight rates to benefit companies owned by members of his family. In 2003, several high-profile cases were filed for gross extortions and abuse of office, including the arrests of Georgy Oleinik, former chief financial officer of the Ministry of Defence, of seven senior law enforcement officers, and of three border guards from Moscow Sheremetevo airport (Coalson 2003; The Center for Public Integrity 2004).

In October 2003, Yukos founder Mikhail Khodorkovsky was charged by the PGO with, amongst other things, tax evasion, forgery, fraud and illegal party financing. The government took further actions against Yukos in 2004, and in May 2005 Khodorkovsky was sentenced to nine years in prison. In addition, his philanthropic foundation *Otkrytaia Rossiia* (Open Russia) was closely audited by tax inspectors in November 2003, April 2004 and February 2005. In October 2005, the foundation's offices were searched by the PGO and some of its former recipients, mainly Russian CSOs, were probed. In 2006, the foundation was eventually put out of action.[1] The Khodorkovsky affair was intensely followed up by the international media. While it was not uncontroversial, it was largely seen as a politically motivated act, not least responding to Khodorkovsky's public announcement in 2003 that he might run for president during the upcoming elections. Many observers understood the arrest as an assault against democracy and the rule of law. Russian NGOs contended in an open protest letter in October 2003 that it happened precisely because Khodorkovsky started to promote a more transparent and socially responsible entrepreneurship and to support democratic parties and organisations.[2] Several other petitions were posted online during the following months, and a number of sympathetic Russian and Western websites and blogs emerged that continued to pool day-to-day updates about this case and background information about Khodorkovsky and his family over the coming years.[3]

In addition, Putin's initial anti-corruption campaign was directed against the bureaucratic corruption that was not only at the focus of many international anti-corruption programmes but also the main concern of business actors and common people in Russia. Putin frequently blamed Russian 'public officials' and 'bureaucrats' (*chinovniki*) in general for abusing existing regulations and using their leverage for personal enrichment. During his first term, the President arranged that thousands of officials were charged with economic crimes. In 2000, about 18,000 officials were charged, including more than 1,000 officials at the Ministry of the Interior (*Ministerstvo Vnutrennykh Del*, MVD), 120 customs officials, more than 20 tax police officials, 30 judges and 10 prosecutors.[4] In 2001, more than 25,000 officials were investigated for crimes involving corruption, including the former Railway Minister, Nikolay Aksyonenko, among the more prominent ones.[5] In 2002, about 21,000 police officers were censured for criminal or other offences and 17,000 officials were dismissed by the action of the MVD, most of them engaged in petty corruption (Kupchinsky, Chirkova and Savintseva 2004: 249).

Besides prosecution of corrupt individuals, Putin's campaign also envisaged systemic reforms. He repeatedly noted that the way in which the Russian administrative and bureaucratic system was organised would naturally foster corruption (Putin 2000, 2002). However, the first steps in this direction were rather muted and did not show any major progress.

In March 2000, an anti-corruption commission was established within the State Duma, headed by the former Prime Minister and newly elected deputy Sergei Stepashin (Yabloko). However, not least due to its restricted advisory mandate, it did not play a major role during the coming years. The Putin administration did not remain completely inactive in terms of legal reforms, which was one of the foremost objectives of international anti-corruption campaigns. In 2002, a Code of Conduct for Civil Servants in the Russian Federation, after passing the first Duma reading almost unanimously, was eventually turned down by the presidential administration and the government. The Code was based on recommendations of the Committee of Ministers of the CoE and was intended to help Russia to achieve European anti-corruption standards. Yet it came under severe criticism among Russian experts, journalists and civil servants, not least for using a terminology not found in Russian law and making provisions that contradicted Russian traditions (Vasiliev 2002).

Moreover, particular anti-corruption legislation had been repeatedly recommended on the part of the international community. This recommendation was echoed by Russian officials who had participated in the Octopus programmes of the CoE/EU (see Chapter 4). Also some groups of Russian reform-minded deputies as well as nongovernmental experts proposed drafts of a national anti-corruption strategy or legislation to the new government almost on a yearly basis. From 2004, the call for an anti-corruption policy and legal framework was intensely pushed by the new Duma Anti-Corruption Commission (see below). These calls were not taken up by the President or the Duma. Nevertheless, the government initially reported to the international community that the respective documents were underway (e.g. Council of Europe 2000; European Commission 2001b: 9). It should be noted, up front, that concrete anti-corruption legislation remained a pending issue throughout the Putin era (this matter would only be settled by Putin's successor Dmitry Medvedev who eventually signed a comprehensive National Anti-corruption Plan in July 2008 and a package of anti-corruption laws in December 2008).[6] Still, the Putin administration could refer to numerous other legal reforms that covered crucial facets of a comprehensive legislative basis addressing corruption and that were largely welcomed by the IFIs and international organisations, including: a list of laws and regulations as part of a 'Conception of Public Service Reform in the Russian Federation' (2001); a new Criminal Procedural Code (2001); a new Customs Code in line with WTO norms (2003); laws on political parties and electoral procedures (since 2001); a law on the securities markets (2002); and several amendments to these regulations further on. In addition, several measures against money-laundering (since 2001), against the financing of terrorism (since 2002) and against trafficking (since 2003) had been undertaken. As mentioned earlier, the anti-money-laundering efforts (including the establishment of a Financial Monitoring Committee in November 2001)[7] convinced the FATF and IMF, by 2002, to remove Russia from their 'blacklist' of non-cooperative territories.

In accordance with Putin's call for institutional reforms in his second Annual Address in 2001 (Putin 2001), new governmental commissions and central organs were established that were charged with the development of policies in various areas – all of which were also on the agenda of international actors (e.g. federal securities markets, government across administrative levels, intergovernmental fiscal relations, human rights, anti-terrorism, anti-organised crime, anti-corruption). Yet soon after, most of these were again abolished and their powers transferred to respective Federal Services operating directly under the jurisdiction of the federal government. Most notably after Putin's re-election in March 2004, administrative reforms aimed at strengthening the structure and performance of the federal agencies and their control over regional governments. The comprehensive reforms were justified with regard to Russia's economic development as well as security concerns. Reducing corruption or patronage was an often an implicitly formulated goal.

New anti-corruption institutions were established by the end of Putin's first term in November 2003 with a Presidential Council and Commission for Combating Corruption and a Commission for the Resolution of Conflicts of Interest.[8] The official purpose of the latter institutions was to cover both prevention and monitoring by improving the state policy against corruption in the federal, regional and local organs, addressing conditions generating corruption, reducing the abuse of official positions, and guaranteeing the observance of official ethics standards by civil servants. The establishment of these presidential anti-corruption organs was welcomed by IFIs and international organisations. However, while this fell into the context of Russian parliamentary and presidential elections which attracted overwhelming international attention (in late 2003/early 2004), it was subsequently rarely noticed that these anti-corruption bodies remained relatively inactive in practice.

In April 2004, another Commission was created within the newly elected Duma which indeed became a central coordinating office in anti-corruption matters during Putin's second term. The 'Commission for Counteraction against Corruption' (henceforth: Duma Anti-Corruption Commission) was formed by some Duma deputies. A rather young deputy, Mikhail Grishankov (United Russia), who was formerly active in anti-narcotics and anti-terrorist initiatives, was elected as chairman by an overwhelming majority within the Duma.[9] This Commission sought to address a number of issues, including the consolidation of the various anti-corruption efforts of the state, media and public associations, pushing the preparations for the ratification of the UN and CoE anti-corruption conventions, the development of a legislative reform programme, and analysing proposed bills and other materials coming from regional authorities or from citizens in order to develop positions and to identify corruption-fostering tendencies (*korruptsiogennost'*) contained in such proposals. To realise this, three subcommittees within the Commission were responsible for specific analytical tasks (the study of incoming documents, of legal projects presented to the Duma, and of federal and regional legislation). Grishankov further initiated the formation of an expert council within the Commission, whose 24 members (half of them holding a doctorate in law or economics) were recommended by Duma deputies, the Supreme Court, the PGO, the Audit Chamber, the MVD, the FSB, the federal customs service, the Financial Monitoring Committee, and leading research institutes of the Russian Academy of Sciences. Also the leaders of the 'specialised CSOs' TI-Russia and INDEM were allowed into the council (Gosudarstvennaia Duma 2005).

The Duma Anti-Corruption Commission made several recommendations to the President, the Duma, the Supreme Court, the PGO, political parties, and regional authorities. Recommendations to the President included the ratification of the UN and CoE conventions, the adoption of a governmental anti-corruption policy (through the still existing Presidential Anti-Corruption Council and Commission) and the strengthening of the PGO as a core actor in the fight against corruption. In accordance with its high attention to analysing legal documents, the Duma Anti-Corruption Commission came to propose amendments to the Criminal

Code and a number of legal acts (ranging from regulations about advertising, competition and tourism, to state control on gambling, privatisation of state and municipal property, to public procurement). In accordance with its emphasis on the need to ratify the UN and CoE conventions, the Commission further paid attention to legal provisions for the criminalisation of corruption and the recovery of assets (from abroad). In 2004, the Duma Commission initiated a joint project with the CoE (financed by the European Commission) in order to reconcile the Russian legislation, in particular provisions for punitive and reactive measures, with international tandards.[10] Following the consultations with regional authorities, it further called upon these authorities to develop anti-corruption policies in accordance with their specific regional conditions (Gosudarstvennaia Duma 2005, 2006).

As outlined in the previous chapter, in particular the institutional and legal (however indirect) anti-corruption measures were noticed and largely welcomed in official international documents and evaluations. Within the country, however, experts and the general public remained somewhat sceptical about Putin's anti-corruption campaign.[11] Even some of those personally involved in governmental anti-corruption institutions remained doubtful about the viability and effectiveness of the new anti-corruption efforts under the Putin administration. For example, Boris Reznik, member of an earlier Duma anti-corruption commission, stated: 'I do not know how corruption is fought in other states, but as for Russia, we actually only simulate the campaign, while in fact we do nothing – that's the truth' (Reznik 2001). Also Prosecutor General Vladimir Ustinov admitted that a large-scale operation similar to Italy's 'Clean Hands' campaign in the 1980s was unfeasible, given that over 80 per cent of Italy's politicians either resigned or were brought to jail (Vernidoub 2002).

This has to be seen in a historical context where both politicians themselves and citizens had lost belief in any official anti-corruption campaigns. Especially during the first post-Soviet decade these campaigns had commonly occurred around elections, on the eve of strategic political changes, or following major crises. They used to be means to attack political rivals, to legitimise a new team in power by denouncing predecessors, and to justify policy changes. Moreover, the assumedly more independent Russian media, which were increasingly dominated by political and economic interest groups, had a major stake in condemning almost any government policy as dictated by cronyism and corruption. With endless denunciation campaigns, culminating in a veritable 'kompromat war' in 1999, the overall impression was left that 'everyone had given and received so much that practically speaking, only the morally crippled and dead remained on the political stage' (Szilágyi 2002: 224).[12] By the eve of Putin's presidency, the 'chasm between discourse and reality was so great that everyone who denounced corruption was now perceived as corrupt himself' (Coulloudon 2002: 203).

Putin's initial campaign seemed to be no exception from Russia's anti-corruption legacy, given the many spectacular cases targeting grand corruption and fraud, especially among oligarchs and high-ranking politicians who had appeared as bothersome political figures, if not outright political opponents (as in the case of Khodorkovsky). Moreover, the Russian media remained full of contradictory reports relating to corruption during the Putin era. In many regions, journalists who had reported on cases of corruption in the higher ranks of the federal and regional administrations, were arrested, dismissed, otherwise harassed or even murdered. While information about the background of such cases and about those ordering sanctions on the journalists usually remained hazy, and most cases of murder remained unsolved, these developments certainly contributed to impeaching the credibility of any official anti-corruption efforts and of Putin's proclaimed policy of zero tolerance for corruption. Among the international anti-corruption community these developments went largely unnoticed.[13] It was a different community of international organisations promoting human rights, democracy and free media that sought to draw attention to some of the dubious cases involving journalists.[14] Since the early 2000s, some international actors also started to publicly honour selected individuals for their personal commitment to raising awareness about or to investigating cases of corruption.[15]

Breakthrough (2006–8): anchoring anti-corruption efforts internationally and domestically

From late 2005/early 2006, governmental anti-corruption initiatives clearly gained new momentum. The new governmental anti-corruption drive started mainly in response to the 2005 CPI, in which Russia suddenly received a lowered score, interrupting a previously steady upwards trend that could be observed since the beginning of the Putin era. This CPI, published by TI in October, was backed by a major domestic survey undertaken by the Russian NGO INDEM, the results of which had been made public since July 2005. The INDEM survey supplemented the CPI score with more detailed data about corruption in various sectors and across the country. Compared with the results of a similar survey that INDEM had undertaken in 2001, it confirmed that despite all anti-corruption initiatives corruption had drastically increased under Putin (INDEM 2005). As such, this kind of evidence was nothing new at that time. A number of Russian surveys had previously recorded erratic levels of corruption in Russia, including those presented by institutions close to the government, such as the All-Russian Public Opinion Research Centre (VCIOM, since the late 1980s) or the Public Opinion Foundation (since 1992), and by the internationally visible ROMIR holding (since 1989), as much as by independent organisations, including INDEM (since 2001) and the Levada-Center (since 2003).[16] The latter independently led surveys, however, presented a new feature during the Putin era, and the INDEM team had actively made its survey results public. Although it had equally done so in the case of its earlier corruption survey in 2001, the official reaction was much less rigorous then. The finding that business bribery had a volume of over $US30 billion in Russia was simply waved off by Putin with a remark that, according to him, it would be half this volume (Argumenty i fakty 2005). As outlined in the previous chapters, the CPI and other international anti-corruption assessments had meanwhile turned into major points of reference for practitioners, analysts and the media at both international and domestic levels. The sudden drop of Russia's CPI score in 2005 was also explicitly commented upon by TI (TI 2005a), and other international evidence at that time seemed to confirm the fact that corruption in Russia was on the rise. Most importantly, in 2005, it was not only evidence of a *high* level of corruption in Russia, but also of *growing* corruption that could not possibly be ignored by the Russian government, all the more since the latter found itself unable to provide alternative data: the efforts of the Duma Anti-Corruption Commission to gather more information had only just started and had focused more on legislative texts than on information about corruption itself. Moreover, by that time the Russian government was generally very concerned about the restoration of Russia's image, more precisely the image of the Russian 'state', both internationally and domestically.[17] In this particular context, the 2005 CPI was the final straw.

The year 2006 was announced as a critical year in the Duma's struggle against corruption.[18] More determined governmental action should have demonstrated to both the international community and the Russian citizens that it resumed full responsibility for taking care of anti-corruption efforts in this country. A special section on 'opposition to corruption' was included in the plan for administrative reforms and for the whole planning period from the first quarter of 2006 to the fourth quarter of 2008 (Gosudarstvennaia Duma 2006). Since autumn 2005, reporting in the Russian press on corruption and more importantly on various official anti-corruption efforts had markedly increased. In his 2006 Annual Address (which was, for the first time, officially translated into English) Putin (2006) admitted that:

> despite all the efforts we have made, we have still not yet managed to remove one of the greatest obstacles facing our development, that of corruption.

Indeed, various governmental bodies came to launch a new flurry of anti-corruption activities in 2006. As earlier, the government openly accused various culprits, including the customs services and unspecified businessmen and civil servants. Ardently supported by Prosecutor General Vladimir Ustinov, Putin inspired a series of corruption probes that hit senior security, legal and customs officials and regional leaders. Within one month after Putin's 2006 Annual Address, 14 federal-level officials were dismissed, 6 high functionaries were put on trial, and dozens of regional offi-cials were investigated (Holm 2006; RIAN 2006a).

Most surprisingly, after the PGO had dismissed three high-ranking customs officials, Ustinov himself was sudden-ly removed from his post as Prosecutor General, which he had held for two consecutive terms since 1999. The PGO had frequently been accused of failing to properly investigate corruption cases. But, as with earlier dismissals in the upper hierarchies of the state apparatus, Ustinov's dismissal too was interpreted as a personal power struggle. Amongst others, Ustinov's relations to his protector Igor Sechin (deputy head of the presidential administration, head of the supervisory board at the state oil company Rosneft, and a most influential player among the *siloviki*) were strengthened with a marriage between Ustinov's son and Sechin's daugh-ter (Holm 2006; RIAN 2006b).[19] Putin again nominated Ustinov's predecessor, former Justice Minister Jury Chaika, as Prosecutor General.[20] Chaika's long service record in the justice system and his moderate support of judicial reform as well as the upcoming implementation of the UNCAC implied a new emphasis on this so far neglected area of anti-corruption reform. When Chaika took over in June 2006, he immediately started a major re-organisation of the PGO. While praising the office's ability to fight corruption in terms of its political will and functions, he stressed the need for further 'careful and deliberate' reforms (RIAN 2006b). One week later, Chaika removed several prosecutors because of incompetence or corruption, including the chief military prosecutor Alexander Savenkov. The latter case, however, caused much consternation among Russian soldiers' rights activists, since Savenkov had been reputed to be independ-ent, qualified and fair.[21] A Department on Anti-corruption Legislation Oversight was also established within the PGO.

The Duma Anti-Corruption Commission was concerned that new manifestations of corruption in the PGO, and in the judicial and law enforcement systems, had a negative effect on the ongoing anti-corruption efforts. It proposed the estab-lishment of a legal advice centre for citizens in order to restore public trust in courts and in the judiciary. Again, it criticised the lack of coordination between the centre and the regions in anti-corruption matters. By the end of 2006, it noted that it had received an unprecedented amount of requests from citizens relating to corruption and anti-corruption efforts in Russia.[22] By the end of its mandate in December 2007, the Duma Commission again underlined the rapidly growing variety of tasks it had solved and the constantly increasing volume of work it had undertaken. It strongly recommended the creation of an analogous commission with the newly elected Parliament in 2008 (Gosudarstvennaia Duma 2007b).

Others had joined the official anti-corruption discourse in 2006, also by instrumentalising it for their own causes. For example, Vladimir Zhirinovsky, leader of the (nationalist) Liberal Democratic Party of Russia (LDPR), Vice-Chairman of the Duma and known proponent of a police-state, called for more radical control systems and accused 'Russia's southern areas' of being a major breeding ground for corruption, contending that there was no corruption in the Russian Empire and Soviet Union (Itar-Tass 2006; Shkolnikov 2006). In June 2006, the Supreme Arbitration Court proposed amendments to the federal law on judges, concerning regulations for reporting income, cars, apartments and property. According to the court's chairman, European standards should be applied to the Russian judiciary in an effort to combat corruption (Medetsky 2006). Also MERiT, which had so far mainly focused on corporate governance and business ethics, resumed comprehensive reform measures in 2006 that were intended to target the constantly blamed bureaucrats.[23] In July 2006, MERiT further announced a $US44.5 million pilot programme to apply 'customer charters' in 19 federal agencies and their counterparts in 29 regions, in order to reduce the demand for bribes – thereby tackling petty corruption as the main concern among the general public (agencies issuing driving licenses and passports), among local communities (agencies approving state subsidies for utilities costs and welfare payments), and among entrepreneurs (agencies registering firms, real estate and cars) (Yablokova 2006).

The entry into force of the UNCAC in December 2005 and the 2006 G8 summit, which was held in Russia (St. Petersburg) that year and which contained a particular focus on international anti-corruption collaboration at the G8 level, presented welcome opportunities to demonstrate political will and international commitment. The latter event also guaranteed much visibility in the West and at the international level. Russia thus ratified the UNCAC in February 2006. On this occasion Putin blamed his justice staff for a lack of perseverance to ratify anti-corruption agreements and ordered a bill from the Ministry of Justice 'within two weeks' concerning Russia's ratification of the CoE Criminal Law Convention on Corruption (signed in 1999) (AFP 2006). The CoE Criminal Law Convention was eventually ratified in October 2006.

As mentioned in the previous chapter, all international anti-corruption promoting organisations intensified their work with the Russian government in 2006. In order to ensure effective implementation of the standards of the two conventions, the CoE had designed a second project to support the Duma Anti-Corruption Commission in elaborating a wider range of preventive, pro-active measures (July 2006–November 2007). According to previous experience of the CoE, this focused on opportunities for corruption created by the legislation in particular spheres (education, health and public procurement). In addition, again, this project was intended to push the elaboration of proposals for a national anti-corruption strategy.[24] For its collaboration with UNODC, the Duma Anti-Corruption Commission chose corruption in the judiciary as a priority area.[25] In October 2006, UNODC and the Duma Commission organised a seminar on ethical principles and responsibility in the judicial system. The Commission further established an interparliamentary working group for the development of bills (Gosudarstvennaia Duma 2007a).

On the part of the international community, differences between the existing presidential and the Duma anti-corruption organs were hardly noticed. Even from the perspective of foreign Moscow-based representatives, who might have had better insight into these details, the facts that there was 'somebody' to work with at all and that highly motivated individuals emerged in this field seemed to outweigh the importance of institutional design:[26]

[We] work closely with the Duma committee against corruption, headed by Mikhail Grizhankov, and I think that this was a good investment, definitely [...] It has been successful. Again, the human factor is very important. Because, if you have a dynamic person that you can work with, then also some of the international principles, which may be difficult to grasp here, will then more easily be introduced in a context where not always international best practice is seen as applicable. (Representative of the UN, 2006)

Following the ratifications, Russia itself became more actively involved in the international activities around the implementation of the UNCAC and the CoE Convention. Regarding the former, the Russian government was represented with one of the largest delegations (along with China and the host countries) at the first and second session of the Conference of the States Parties to the UNCAC (Jordan, December 2006/Indonesia, January 2008). The Russian delegation included representatives of various ministries, a Department of new challenges and threats (Ministry of Foreign Affairs/MID), the Duma Anti-Corruption Commission, and the FSB. Since the very beginning of intergovernmental coordination through the Conference of State Parties, Russia was among the countries which actively participated in the reporting process (including development of the self-assessment checklist and the submission of a self-assessment report). At the same time, while reporting that article 5 of the UNCAC (preventive anti-corruption policies) was only partially implemented in Russia, the government refrained from requesting technical assistance to achieve full implementation.[27] Regarding the CoE Convention, Russia joined GRECO in 2007 and thus submitted itself to the joint evaluation procedure. The GRECO Evaluation Team visited Russia in April 2008 and met not only with government officials but also with representatives of TI-Russia, INDEM and the inter-regional movement *Protiv Korruptsii* (GRECO 2008b). The Russian government did not authorise the publication of the resulting report (this only happened with much delay under Putin's successor Medvedev in spring 2009). Nevertheless, the Russian government demonstrated its commitment by organising an international roundtable on anti-corruption legislation and expertise in Russia and Eastern Europe in cooperation with the CoE (held in Moscow, also later than expected, in June 2008).[28]

Besides demonstrating stronger commitment to the international community, the government also sought to better integrate popular opinion and nongovernmental professional expertise at home. With this new campaign, the government started to utilise a variety of media channels, including TV and radio as the most important traditional information sources for Russian citizens and the Internet as a main medium for the younger generation and professionals with a particular interest in the issue. Common people and experts were invited to participate through various interactive components.

For example, in February 2006, state-owned *Radio Rossiia* launched a talk show about corruption on Saturdays where citizens could call in with questions and let these be answered by key anti-corruption experts.[29] On March 2006, the head of the Duma Anti-Corruption Commission, Mikhail Grishankov, was invited into the studio. On this occasion he stressed that the Commission's priorities were to immediately reconcile the Russian legislation with international standards and to establish public control, supplemented by better coordinated anti-corruption efforts at the regional level. Furthermore, the government made use of the print media for a major stock-taking of actors, opinions and data in the anti-corruption field. In April 2006, the Ministry of Justice's journal *Chelovek i Zakon* (Man and Law) announced an annual Russia-wide competition 'Against Corruption' among journalists and media outlets who had published on corruption in Russia in 2005–6. This competition would, amongst other things, help to expose myths about the invincibility of corruption; create a climate of opposition against corruption among the readers; support the professional activity of journalists and encourage the journalistic community to further objective investigation into cases of corruption and the fight against it; and analyse 'the *true state* of the corruption market in Russia' (thereby using the term 'corruption market' as coined by the much-cited INDEM study) in order to adapt anti-corruption means and methods. The nominees were to be selected by an expert council, comprising several 'best-known and competent authorities concerning the problem of corruption' (Chelovek i Zakon 2006). The Internet too was harnessed as a media for governmental anti-corruption campaigns. From early 2006, the Duma Anti-Corruption Commission and Mikhail Grizhankov presented themselves on their own websites. By providing unprecedented documentation about the Commission's activities (including transcripts of lengthy parliamentary hearings about the ratification of the international conventions, often lasting more than ten hours), these sites also alleviated the sense of secretiveness traditionally characterising governmental action in this field.[30] As a more interactive tool, the websites of some governmental bodies also started to provide sections where people could submit corruption-related complaints or participate in mini online polls (posting only one question at a time for several days or weeks).[31]

Despite an impressive range of activities, including various efforts to bring official anti-corruption campaigns closer to the citizenry, the Russian population tended to remain doubtful about the motives and effectiveness of these measures (e.g. Levada Analitycal Center 2008: Tables 7.2.7, 7.2.8, 10.27), not least because this new campaign too had included some ambivalent cases of sanctioning politically bothersome officials. There was also not an end to the tendency that journalists reporting on corruption were removed.[32] At the same time, there was a persistently high share of the population that believed that, in general, it is impossible to eradicate corruption in Russia and that the law enforcement organs and the President were primarily responsible for the fight against corruption in Russia.[33]

What kind of corruption?

The official anti-corruption campaigns addressed a diversity of forms of corruption, albeit in different ways. Reactive countermeasures, mainly led by the President and the PGO, were directed at grand corruption, fraud and financial crime, through some spectacular cases of prosecuting oligarchs or high-ranking politicians. In most cases, in particular during the first years of Putin's presidency, it was obvious that the anti-corruption discourse was instrumentalised as a means to remove bothersome individuals from their post or completely from the business-political scene. In this regard, public as much as private sector corruption were addressed. In fact, it would have been difficult to properly distinguish between these two forms in Russia at that time. Furthermore, petty bribery in the state's administrative apparatus was tackled through charges against and dismissals of spectacular numbers of lower-ranking public officials. Petty corruption in the private sector, however, did not seem to be an issue at all. There had never been a debate about how to define corruption. It was obvious that the anti-corruption discourse implicitly built on a common understanding of corruption as 'abuse of public position'. Instead, it seemed of utmost importance to clarify the causes of the rampant corruption in Russia and the measures envisaged to counteract this problem. Putin himself thus repeatedly underlined that corruption had sprung from the transition period. As with many other problems that beset Russia at that time, corruption should be tackled through his proclaimed 'dictatorship of the law'.

From 2004, the work of the Duma Anti-Corruption Commission added somewhat more specificity to the anti-corruption discourse within the government. The Commission directed the focus towards corruption in certain sectors and called for the development of specific anti-corruption programmes. These included initially a range of sectors and areas of greatest political relevance to the government, such as law-enforcement, the judiciary and customs controls, privatisation of state and municipal property, the financial spheres (banking and taxation), and the private energy sector (Gosudarstvennaia Duma 2005). In 2005, interaction with international actors (the CoE) and domestic nongovernmental experts (INDEM) had inspired attention towards two more socio-political areas: corruption related to public health (where the Council of Europe had just accomplished a European pilot programme) and in the education system (on which INDEM provided materials). Beyond that however, and despite the Duma Commission's heavily analytical mandate and initial efforts to push the gathering of statistical data about the situation of corruption in various sectors, its activities did not contribute to a more specific debate about corruption itself. Rather, the prime focus of the Commission was on identifying viable anti-corruption measures, including an overall anti-corruption policy as much as departmental, sectoral and regional anti-corruption programmes. Moreover, its attention to the ratification of international conventions, to legal texts (corruption-fostering tendencies in a range of regulations and anti-corruption legislation), and to two collaborative projects with the CoE had prompted the Duma Commission to focus on the criminalisation of corruption and legal issues such as the seizure of property and recovery of assets achieved through criminal means (Gosudarstvennaia Duma 2006).

Only with the new anti-corruption campaign in 2006, was the quest for data and more detailed information about corruption in Russia raised again, and this time more forcefully. This should be hardly surprising since a major impetus for this very campaign was the evidence of rising corruption levels provided by international and independent domestic organisations. The new governmental anti-corruption discourse thus mainly called for better insight into the *actual* corruption situation in Russia. New collaborative projects with international actors, in turn, added a new emphasis also on preventive measures.

Involving civil society?

Although intense official discourses relating to both anti-corruption and Russian civil society had unfolded during the Putin era, these were pursued in parallel and remained largely unrelated.

Regarding anti-corruption efforts, practically no role was seen for civil society actors until the Duma Anti-corruption Commission had been established. The Commission allowed representatives of two core Moscow-based specialised organisations (TI-Russia and INDEM) into its expert council. It further recommended to the President consultation not only with state research institutes but also with CSOs and independent experts while developing a governmental anti-corruption policy. With the new official anti-corruption drive since 2006, however, the need for a stock-taking of non-governmental actors and discourses in the anti-corruption field had been acknowledged (most notably realised through a Russia-wide competition for journalists). Moreover, following the ratification of the CoE Anti-Corruption Convention and the accession to GRECO, the onsite visit of the GRECO evaluation team also included meetings with TI-Russia, INDEM, another movement *Protiv Korruptsii*, the Chamber of Commerce, and the media.

Parallel to the specific anti-corruption debates and activities, the operational conditions of civil society in general changed substantially throughout the Putin era. The Putin administration had repeatedly questioned the presence of foreign donors and their assistance to civil society in the country, starting with several instances where particular Western foundations (e.g. German, US or British organisations) were accused of 'supporting dubious institutions' in Russia since 2001, accompanied by criticism against Russian NGOs in general for pursuing the interests of foreign donors.[34] Also since 2001, efforts had been launched to formalise the interface between Russian CSOs and the Kremlin through the Civil Forum (see Fein 2002). A number of Russian organisations, individual activists and journalists interfering with political matters while advocating democracy, human rights, or environmental protection experienced direct repressive actions, ranging from personal harassments and office raids to arrests and even murder. Among the foreign donor community and other international actors, however, the state's gradual encroachment upon the foreign-funded civic sphere was fully realised only with much delay. This was then perceived as a rather sudden move with regard to some key events following Putin's controversial re-election, including the establishment of quasi-nongovernmental, Kremlin-supportive social movements (especially the youth movement *Nashi* in 2005) and of a Civic Chamber as an official representative body of Russian civil society in 2005/2006.[35] Although Western and international organisations criticised these actions as indications of an authoritarian turn, they still regarded them as domestic affairs.

Only in reaction to a new NGO law, introduced by Putin in December 2005, which also fortified administrative barriers against and control over foreign funding, did international and Western organisations fully realise the state's intention to supplant foreign influence from the civic sphere. At this stage, the European Commission and the CoE became involved and accomplished some amendments to the originally highly restrictive version of the law.[36] However, in this regard, these institutions were represented by departments and persons that were different from those concerned about anti-corruption. A major impetus for more restrictive actions was given with the series of so-called colour or flower revolutions across the post-Soviet region at that time

(Georgia in 2003, Ukraine in 2004, the Kyrgyz Republic in 2005), which in the eyes of the Russian government demonstrated the potentially destructive implications of foreign assistance in the post-Soviet world, given the involvement of USAID-assisted organisations and the celebration of these events in the Western press as bottom-up movements for democracy and against corruption. The Putin administration responded rather resolutely to the practice of foreign civil society assistance, not least because Russian civil society in general (in its NGO-based version that emerged during the 1990s, see Schmidt-Pfister 2008) was severely over-dependent on foreign funding, and as such overly prone to supporting foreign agendas.

This chapter has added the governmental dimension to the overall picture of transnational anti-corruption advocacy. Tracing the process of anti-corruption engagement at this level also reveals that international and domestic campaigns were indeed closely interrelated. Many steps were taken by the Russian government that in fact responded to the proposals, demands and assistance coming from the international level, as outlined in the previous two chapters. Overall, despite recurring complaints about persistently alarming corruption levels in Russia and resistance from the Russian government against external anti-corruption promotion, the international organisations expressed satisfaction with the anti-corruption efforts undertaken by the Russian government during the Putin era. In 2000, in the context of intense global anti-corruption promotion, a first phase had started with eager anti-corruption rhetoric on the part of the new President, prosecutions and dismissals of large numbers of corrupt entrepreneurs and officials, and the building of some anti-corruption institutions. A second phase was established by 2006 that has seen renewed enthusiasm and further substantial measures on the parts of both the government and the international community. Domestically, the Russian government sought to restore its image as a leading anti-corruption promoter through better outreach to the citizenry and the presentation of more official information about corruption in Russia. This implied a noticeable re-centralisation and strengthening of the leverage of governmental anti-corruption discourses and bodies. Only one core measure, although repeatedly called for by both international and domestic actors, was fully blocked throughout the Putin era: the development of a particular anti-corruption policy and legislation.

The second major anti-corruption drive clearly came as a response to the simultaneous presentation of data through the CPI and the domestic INDEM survey in 2005, which both attested a rising level of corruption in Russia. Increased commitment to international collaboration was further pushed by other factors including the new anti-corruption enthusiasm at the international level following the ratification of the UNCAC and the G8 Summit held in Russia in 2006, but also Russia's growing concern about its international leadership role. The Russian government did not want its country to be treated as one among many problematic transitional countries. The G8 Summit was thus used as a major occasion to demonstrate that it was on par with, and even ahead of, countries such as the USA, Japan, or Germany in terms of anti-corruption efforts. Looking only at these two levels of action, at first sight, one might assume that Russia presents a case of successful international norm promotion corresponding to conventional models about transnational advocacy (see especially Keck and Sikkink 1998; Risse and Sikkink 1999). However, one crucial element contained in these models seems missing from the analysis so far: an active domestic opposition that would have mobilised external advocacy in the first place, thus effecting 'pressure from above and below' towards the government.

Except for the cumulative effect of the INDEM study and the CPI in 2005 and the consultation of CSOs during the GRECO onsite visit in 2008, interaction between Russian civil society and international actors remains largely invisible as a driving force behind the increasing governmental anti-corruption commitment. In general, the analysis presented in this chapter seems to suggest that civil society did not play a major role in pushing the anti-corruption efforts of the Russian government. Still, recalling Chapter 4, much international assistance also went towards anti-corruption projects conducted by Russian CSOs. The question thus remains whether there had been any of the powerful synergies between international actors and domestic civil society that brought about the most essential driving forces according to conventional assumptions about transnational norm promotion. The next chapter will therefore turn to an analysis of civic anti-corruption initiatives at the local level in three different Russian cities: Moscow, St. Petersburg and Irkutsk.

Notes

1   On 17 March 2006, the bank accounts of the Open Russia foundation were frozen by a Moscow district court (see e.g. RFE/RL 2005b, 2005c). In July 2006, the foundation's website (www.openrussia.info) was also closed.

2   The official letter of protest was posted by the Western branch of the international human rights organisation 'Memorial' (active in Russia, Ukraine, Belarus, Kazakhstan, Latvia, Poland and Germany), see Memorial, at: www.memorial.de/nachr.php?nid=53 (German translation, accessed 29/10/2003).

3   For example, the US-American NGO 'Jurist' has been tracing all news related to the trial (see http://jurist.law.pitt.edu/currentawareness /khodorkovsky.php). A Russian-Ukrainian group 'Sovest' (www .sovest.org), the anonymous 'Mikhail Khodorkovsky Society' (http://mikhail_khodorkovsky_society.blogspot.com/), the Observatoire de l'Affaire Yukos et du procès Khodorkovsky (http://affaire-yukos .blogspot.com/) and many others have been archiving personal and trial-related information, photographs and protest letters (all accessed 02/02/2009).

4   According to PGO data (see Ledeneva 2001: 41; 2003: 92; Timtschenko 2003: 74–7).

5   According to PGO data (see Vernidoub 2002).

6   See Medvedev's first State of the Nation Address and meetings with Prosecutor General, Juri Chaika, in 2008 (transcripts at www.kremlin.ru), and the list of anti-corruption laws at www.transparency.org.ru (accessed 23/02/2009).

7   The Financial Monitoring Committee was chaired by Viktor Zubkov – one of the *Pitertsy* ('those from St. Petersburg') that Putin had introduced into his administration – who was appointed First Deputy Finance Minister at the same time.

8   The Commission for the Resolution of Conflicts of Interest was part of the Anti-Corruption Council. The Presidential Council and Commissions were formed by Presidential Decree No. 1384 'On the Council with the President of the Russian Federation on the Fight against Corruption' in November 2003 which defined their respective functions (see *Rossiskaia Gazeta*, at: www.rg.ru/2003/11/26/sovet-doc.html (accessed 12/09/2006)).

9   384 Duma deputies voted for Grishankov (without a dissenting vote and only 3 abstentions), see minutes at: www.duma.gov.ru/ (accessed 20/05/2008).

10   The project 'Harmonisation of Russian anti-corruption legislation with international standards', lasting January–December 2005 was financed under the European Union Policy Advice Programme; see also European Commission and Council of Europe (2006a).

11 In 2004 and 2005, the fight against corruption and bribery was considered as one of the largest failures of President Putin (together with 'solving the Chechen problem') (Levada-Center 2006: Table 7.2.3). Also interviews with representatives of Russian civic anti-corruption organisations, 2006.

12 *kompromat* (russ.: short for *kompromatiruyushchii material*, compromising material) stands for a ruthless smear campaign practice that seeks to morally and politically discredit an opponent rather than exposing the truth. Earlier a KGB method, it was adopted by Russian oligarchs in the late 1990s who collected and deployed material against competitors and senior officials (Holm 2006; Szilágyi 2002).

13 Only one of the foreign interviewees acknowledged: 'And that culture [of reporting] is not being facilitated by the fact that this is the country which has the highest number of reporters who are killed because they are investigating corruption cases. Very few people know that.' Interview with a representative of the UN, 2006.

14 The international network Reporters Without Borders (www.rsf.fr) and the broadcaster Radio Free Europe/Radio Liberty (www.rferl.org), which both considered Russia under Putin as a country where a free press remained absent, covered some of the cases where Russian journalists experienced serious difficulties in retaliation for reporting on official corruption and embezzlement, including the killings of Natalia Skryl (2002), Alexei Sidorov (2003) and Paul Klebnikov (2004), and the arrests of many others. Obviously, however, there had been many similar cases across Russia that never came to the attention of these outlets (interviews with Russian journalists, Irkutsk, 2005 and Moscow, 2006; see also Fish 2005: 68).

15 For example, TI had launched particular 'Integrity Awards' in 2000 (See TI, Integrity Awards, at: www.transparency.org/news_room/award /integrity_awards. Also the 'EVawards Europeans of the Year', awarded by European Voice since 2001, has had a category 'Journalist of the Year' since 2002 (See European Voice, EVawards, at: www.europeanvoice .com/microsite/evawards/29.aspx (accessed 10/12/2008)).

16 After the All-Russian Public Opinion Research Center, VCIOM, had been re-organised as a joint-stock company under full state ownership in 2003, all staff members quit their jobs in order to continue the research programmes they had conducted during the 1990s under renowned Russian scholars such as Tatiana Zaslavskaya and Yury Levada. The team went on to work as VCIOM-a and since March 2004 as *Levada-Center* (see www.levada.ru/ (accessed 08/08/2006)).

17 In 2004, for example, Putin spoke to about 130 Russian ambassadors who had been summoned to Moscow for a meeting at the Foreign Ministry, urging them to more actively promote a less biased and more favourable image of Russian foreign and domestic policy abroad. He further stated: 'The way people view Russia in the countries where you are based it often far from reality. *Planned campaigns to discredit the country* – and their harm to the state and Russian business is obvious – are not rare' (Yablokova 2004). See also Sakwa (2008: 371).

18 E.g. Mikhail Grishankov (Radio Maiak 2006) and vice-chairman of the State Duma, Vladimir Zhirinovsky (Itar-Tass 2006).

19 The term *siloviki* (from russ.: *sila*, force) is commonly used for former and current chief officials from the security-intelligence services and so-called power ministries (Ministry of Defence, MID, MVD).

20 Chaika was Deputy Prosecutor General in 1995–99 and served as acting Prosecutor General in 1999 under the then President Boris Yeltsin (RIAN 2006b).

21 Savenkov had been concerned about investigating army crimes and had repeatedly publicly criticised Defence Minister Sergei Ivanov for failing to prevent hazing, a serious problem in the Russian army (Yablokova and Abdullaev 2006).

22 About 560 requests from citizens reached the Commission in 2006, presenting more than the total number of requests during the first two years of the Commission's existence (Gosudarstvennaia Duma 2007a).

23 MERiT was headed by liberal-minded minister German Gref, who had become known for his promotion of investment, openness and accusation of mid-level bureaucrats during the 2000s. Gref had developed an economic reform strategy already in 2000 on Putin's order, which included a public administration reform component, but was delayed not least because it seemed too liberal.

24 The project was again funded by the European Commission (under the European Union Policy Advice Programme) with a budget of €209,988 (European Commission and Council of Europe 2006b).

25 Also interview with a representative of the UN, 2006.

26 Also interviews with a representative of the EU, 2005 and of the CoE, 2007.

27 See UNODC, Conference of the States Parties to the United Nations Convention against Corruption – (CAC/COSP), at: www.unodc.org /unodc/en/treaties/CAC/CAC-COSP.html (accessed 18/01/2009).

28 'Practices and prospects of development of the legislation regulating anti-corruption expertise of legal acts and draft laws in Russia and other countries of Eastern Europe and Asia', organised by the Security Committee of the State Duma, the Ministry of Economic Development and Trade, and the Centre for Strategic Development, in cooperation with the CoE, see GRECO (2008a).

29 See Radio Rossiia, *Ochnaia stavka s Olegom Vakulovskim*, at: www.anticorr.ru/news/news134.html (accessed 22/07/2008).

30 See *Komissiia Gosudarstvennoi Dumy Federal'nogo Sobraniia Rossiiskoi Federatsii Po Protivodeistviiu Korruptsii*, at: www.duma.gov .ru/anticorcom/index.html and *Deputat Gosudarstvennyi Dumy M.I. Grishankov*, at: www.grishankov.ru/KORR_PAGE.htm (accessed 15/12/2008).

31 The Federal Registration Agency provided an 'Anti-Corruption' (*Antikorruptsiia*) page for citizens' inquiries about registration-related corruption (www.rosregistr.ru/index.php?menu=1560000000 (accessed 17/02/2009)). The MVD site hosted a hotline for more general inquiries (www.mvdrf.ru/priem/ (accessed 17/02/2009)) and a forum that posted daily, mostly police-related, questions and comments (www.mvdrf .ru/forum/, launched in 2006, but soon inactive).

32 Reporters Without Frontiers concluded that the working conditions of Russian journalists had worsened alarmingly in 2005/2006. Several journalists had been arrested and at least one more journalist (Yevgeny Gerasimenko) murdered for looking into corruption (See Reporters Without Frontiers, Russia – Annual Reports 2006 and 2007, at: www.rsf.org/). The most distinctive uproar in the Western media, however, was caused by the murder of Anna Politkovskaya, who had

been known in Russia for her investigative reports on human rights abuses committed by the Russian military in Chechnya (see, for example, the international Committee to Protect Journalists, *anna-politkovskaya*, at: http://cpj.org/tags/anna-politkovskaya). In 2008, Russian investigative journalist Roman Shleynov received the TI Integrity Award (together with UK journalist David Leigh). TI under-lined their 'untiring determination to expose corrupt dealings in the face of formidable odds [which] serves as inspiration to the anti-corruption movement'. See TI, Integrity Awards, at: www.transparency.org/news_room/award/integrity_awards (accessed 28/03/2009).

33 For example, Levada Analytical Center (2008: 7.4.23); VCIOM, Press-vypusk No. 481, 29/06/2006, at: http://wciom.ru/arkhiv/tematicheskii-arkhiv/item/single/2826.html; FOM, *Korruptsia v Rossiiu*, December 2005 and November 2006, at: http://bd.fom.ru/map/ (accessed 28/03/2009).

34 Critical remarks against foreign-funded NGOs appeared most frequent-ly in public speeches given by President Putin and foreign minister Sergei Lavrov.

35 The Civic Chamber (sometimes translated as Public Chamber) was a formal civic organ with partly appointed, partly selected representatives that could issue recommendations to the government; see also Evans (2006: 151).

36 For more detail on the international and domestic debates around the new Russian NGO law, see Schmidt (2006b).

6

Civil society actors against corruption in Russia

This chapter will now add a thorough analysis of the remaining key dimension pertaining to transnational advocacy 'on the ground': civic anti-corruption efforts in Russia during the Putin era. It will reveal that much anti-corruption engagement occurred in the civic sphere in Russia throughout that time, indeed much of it with international and Western support. However, a more precise tracing of the processes of civic anti-corruption engagement in three Russian cities – Moscow, St. Petersburg, and Irkutsk – shows a more complex picture. Local actors are simultaneously linked to, and indeed embedded into, the developments at international, domestic, and local levels. Yet the nature and implications of the linkages may differ in different places even within a single country. The chapter presents the empirical findings for each city following the same process-tracing logic as in the previous chapters: while introducing local anti-corruption efforts actor by actor, much attention is paid to the timing of the actions and events in each case.

Moscow

As already indicated in the previous two chapters, Moscow as Russia's capital city is the linchpin of the country's interaction with the international sphere. It hosts all representations of international organisations and foreign governments. Domestically, under Putin's presidency, it has again become the single centre of federal decision- and policy-making. Administratively, Moscow is one of Russia's two Federal Cities, alongside St. Petersburg, which also count as regions separate from the surrounding oblasts (Moscow and Leningrad) and whose regional governors simultaneously officiate as local mayors. Moscow and St. Petersburg together are sometimes referred to as 'the capital region' and in both of them federal activities are much more entangled with local politics. Also in both cities during the 1990s, the mayors, Yury Luzhkov and Vladimir Yakovlev, had a reputation as 'the two "criminal managers"' or 'the two "monsters"' (Szilágyi 2002: 227). The Moscow city government group became known as a particularly tough political interest group (Coulloudon 2002: 194) and the capital's *chinovniki* were in disrepute for their particular brusqueness and belligerence. Corruption became most pronounced in the construction sector and during the City Duma elections. Both the local elections in December 2001 and parliamentary elections in December 2003 had demonstrated good relations between the Kremlin and the city administration. But the local elections in December 2005 were unprecedented in terms of deploying administrative resources. Yet similar to the rhetoric at the national level, the local leadership tended to redirect the blame for corruption and criminal behaviour towards unspecified masses of local public officials or citizens. The series of terrorist attacks as well as increasing immigration flows from southern Russia during the early 2000s provided another ground for heightening security measures and police control. During the mid-2000s, the Moscow city administration was among the first to signal growing intolerance towards irregularities and crime in the civil service and public life, for example with institutional and educational measures such as a community watch system or behavioural lectures.[1]

Although the Moscow city administration had maintained a reputation for non-democratic governance, a comprehensive, diverse and vigorous civil society scene had been unfolding there. Yet this scene was heavily fragmented and NGOs, too, had an ambivalent image in the eyes of the population (Forum Donorov 2005). With an estimated 12 million inhabitants, the metropolis had become troubled by a range of socio-economic problems, including unemployment, poverty, homelessness, alcoholism and HIV/AIDS, all of which had been tackled by a variety of local CSOs and under many international or foreign assistance programmes.[2] For transnational advocacy, corruption was thus only one among many concerns. At the same time, the Moscow context had been conducive to a variety of civic anti-corruption activities, including specialised anti-corruption advocacy organisations. More than elsewhere, these groups were working in close proximity with federal politics, law enforcement agencies and international networks.

Actors, approaches and interrelations

In Moscow, there had been numerous nongovernmental anti-corruption activities during the late 1990s/early 2000s. With the arrival of foreign grants for corruption-related issues, several CSOs, educational institutions and professional associations had been conducting projects in areas ranging from housing and municipal development, to exchange programmes for investigative journalists and to monitoring electoral processes or providing specific anti-corruption training.[3] Such programmes were mainly oriented towards the municipal level. Moreover, conducted by organisations whose main missions were related to other fields, these initiatives were usually confined to the duration of a given project.

In the business sphere, leading Russian associations such as the all-Russian association for small and medium enterprises (*Obshcherossiiskaia obshchestvennaia organizatsiia malogo i srednogo predprinimatel'stva*, OPORA) or the Russian Union of Industrialists and Entrepreneurs (*Rossiiskii Soiuz Promyshlennikov i Predprinimatelei*, RSPP) had taken up the issue. OPORA maintained many regional branches working closely with local administrations. From 2004, its Moscow office became closely involved in the activities of the Duma Anti-Corruption Commission, including its collaborative projects with the CoE. Anti-corruption initiatives pushed by the RSPP were essentially driven by concerns about international reputation and foreign investment. These concerns also entailed criticism against international corruption rankings based on foreign perceptions, notably the CPI. In 2002, the Union thus provided a considerable budget to support international PR measures (including the establishment of an English-language Internet portal), established a Charter of Business Ethics, and promoted the idea of integrity pacts between companies, NGOs and authorities

(Savintseva and Stykow 2005: 201). In 2003, after RSPP leaders were explicitly asked by Putin to 'destroy the breeding ground for corruption' (Murray and Panfilova 2003) it established a working group for developing reform proposals.

Later in 2003, RSPP was brought into disrepute when Mikhail Khodorkovsky, then head of RSPP's working group for foreign relations, openly criticised the pervasiveness of corruption within the executive and presented administrative reform proposals to the Kremlin through RSPP (Mulin 2006; Savintseva and Stykow 2005: 200). While Khodorkovsky himself was arrested, amongst others, for charges of fraud and tax evasion, in the same year RSPP continued to be an active promoter of corporate responsibility, increasingly in cooperation with international and foreign networks (at UN level and in the USA more than in Europe).[4] Foreign business associations, in turn, kept underlining the immense investment potential of the capital and the long-standing investor-friendly policy of the city administration under Luzhkov.[5] Most importantly, these various anti-corruption activities remained isolated from each other as well as from the civic anti-corruption advocacy outlined below.

In 2000, TI-Russia had been established as a National Chapter of the global TI network. By design, this organisation had been most intrinsically linked to the international level. Within this network, financial assistance was secondary. TI-Russia had only received a start-up grant ($US10,000) and minor project-related funding from the TI Secretariat (TI-S), and like any other Russian NGO had to secure funding from a variety of other, mainly foreign sources (until 2004 mainly from the Soros Foundation and recurring support from the British government's Global Opportunities Fund). Within the TI network, TI-Russia could benefit from various forms of organisational support, including access to international conferences and organisations, to other national TI chapters, and to its own government. In terms of access to information, the relationship was more reciprocal as the TI-S not only assisted the Russian Chapter in obtaining information about developments outside Russia, but was also most interested in supporting the Chapter as a source of information on corruption in the Russian situation. TI-

Russia itself and furthermore its director Elena Panfilova, who came from an OECD background, thus became quite well known and well networked within a short period of time.

> And if I get a request on Russia, of course, I always turn to the [Russian] chapter to provide me with information, if it is about some important detail [...] So whenever we are asked by an international donor or media about specifics, we are one of the few international NGOs that can relatively quickly mobilise local knowledge. (Representative of the TI-S, 2004)

The anti-corruption engagement of TI-Russia was strongly directed at federal-level politics. In this regard, TI-Russia had in a sense emancipated itself from its international Secretariat. Initially, the Russian Chapter was more intensely devoted to the strategies pursued and promoted by the TI-S, including advocacy for access to public information, setting up a resource centre, or networking with TI Chapters in other post-Communist countries. With the development of a corruption index for the Russian regions in 2002, TI-Russia undertook a first attempt to develop more context-specific approaches. By demonstrating the variance across the regions this index was intended to correct some sweeping conclusions about corruption in Russia as based on TI's CPI and 'enable the public and [regional] authorities to monitor changes in the levels and structure of corruption' (TI-Russia 2002). Many of the initial objectives turned out to be illusory after a few years. For example, legislation on information access could only be accomplished in one pilot region (Kaliningrad, the only region where the EU had a particular stake);[6] the local resource centre was abandoned (instead prioritising the website as an archive for corruption-related documents and news);[7] and plans to establish a cross-country Anti-Corruption Coalition or to expand the regional indices across all Russian regions and to conduct such surveys on a regular basis were not realised. Partly it was acknowledged that these approaches proved inappropriate within the Russian context (especially the resource centre, the only project financially supported by TI-S); partly this was related to the vanishing of the main funding sources for these activities with the departure of the Soros Foundation from Russia in 2003 and the fading of support from other donors.

TI-Russia developed a particular interest in political corruption, more precisely in furthering research into the abuse of administrative resources during elections (i.e. the means used to influence the voters and the electoral process in general). Following the Russian regional index, subsequent Soros funding (then received via OSI Budapest) was used for monitoring a number of newspapers and periodicals during the federal Duma elections in 2003 and the local Moscow elections in 2005.[8] During that time, TI-Russia and the Secretariat were often in disagreement about the most appropriate position vis-à-vis the Putin administration. As outlined in Chapter 4, TI-S allowed the Russian Chapter great latitude in deciding on situational strategies. But TI-Russia's rather critical position against the new government essentially contradicted the overall TI philosophy of 'working with everybody'. Only by late 2005, in the context of the generally intensifying international critique of Putin's authoritarian turn, and most notably at the sight of the new NGO draft law, did TI-S come to acknowledge the need for a more critical stance. At the same time, TI-Russia never understood itself as an oppositional organisation and always sought to maintain a neutral working relationship with the authorities.

> Many of us were quite supportive of Putin. He deserves credit for restabilising the country, making sure that taxes were paid, and salaries were paid to teachers. You know, Russia was on the brink of a total collapse before he took over [...] Now this is a pretty closed regime with a full control on everything, from the economy to the media. This is something everyone is a little bit surprised at [...] So I think this is a very sad development and now it opened up the eyes of many, including myself. (Representative of the TI-S, 2005)

> We never had warm relationships with the authorities. We try not to bother each other. Sometimes they ask something from us, sometimes we ask for something [...] We are not a political organisation. (Representative of TI-Russia, 2004)

During 2005/2006, the time when foreign assistance to Russian CSOs had become a highly sensitive issue and when the government started its major anti-corruption campaign (see Chapter 5), TI-Russia itself remained rather cautious regarding its activities and publicity (e.g. it had not used any foreign grants in 2005 and most of 2006 and had desisted from contributing country-specific case studies to the TI Global Corruption Reports since 2006).[9] It was certainly a bonus that TI-Russia had been able to insist that it never used funding from USAID (which was a major catalyst for the controversy about foreign funding to Russian NGOs) and that it had indeed remained critical against the latter. In autumn 2006, furthermore, TI-Russia started an educational project to increase the understanding of the then ratified UNCAC, in particular among officials, entrepreneurs, journalists and the younger generation (with UK funding). By that time, the domestic situation also seemed to allow the resumption of research into the abuse of administrative resources as well as the acceptance of a major USAID grant for doing so with regard to the campaigns for the federal and regional elections in 2007. Although conducted under the evocative heading 'Fighting Against Political Corruption' and bolstered by an exceptionally voluminous grant ($US400,000 for two years – almost equal to the total that TI-Russia had received in grants during the previous seven years), this project's design and timing were well chosen in order not to affront the government. Most importantly, by that time the government had already taken the lead in the anti-corruption field. Also the project itself was designed in a very analytical manner and almost free from normative or political advocacy. Conducted in cooperation with a professor at the State University, legal experts and other analysts, it entailed the development of highly abstract mathematical models and typologies, and, rather than confronting the official discourse with 'alternative' information or voices, it built on interviews with officials, deputies and those involved in election campaigns (in addition to analysing the media and relevant legislation in 14 Russian regions).[10]

Since early 2008, TI-Russia in collaboration with the Youth Human Rights Movement has established an Anti-Corruption Advice Centre (*Antikorruptsionnyi setevoi kabinet i priemnaia*, ASKP) (with CIDA funding).[11] This was primarily oriented towards the general public and SMEs, who suffered most from the multiple pressures of petty and administrative corruption, through a combination of awareness-raising, legal advice in concrete cases of corruption, and the development of regional anti-corruption strategies. The advice centre entailed the launch of 'the first anti-corruption website in Russia' on 9 December (Inter-national Anti-Corruption Day) 2008.[12] With these latter projects, TI-Russia again undertook a subtle balancing act between realising priority tasks envisaged by the TI-S (UNCAC, corruption in politics, Advocacy and Legal Advice Centres/ALACs) and insisting on the need to adapt global ideas to the particular Russian context.[13] At home, these projects could claim to be constructive rather than oppositional as they built on preceding governmental anti-corruption efforts and discourses (implementing the UNCAC; emphasising the special nature of 'Russian corruption' and of the country's political-administrative system; tackling petty corruption and bringing anti-corruption efforts closer to the citizens; expanding a federal strategy across the regions).

TI-Russia had been closely cooperating with some other Moscow organisations, including the Information Science for Democracy Foundation (INDEM) and the *National'nyi antikorruptsionnyi komitet* (National Anti-corruption Committee, NAK). INDEM was already established in 1990 as an independent organisation devoted to the analysis of and projects on democratic governance. Its leaders and its team included some former Kremlin officials, most notably Georgy Satarov (INDEM President, one of the organisation's founders and an assistant to President Yeltsin during the mid-1990s), mathematicians and social scientists. Since 1996, INDEM had conducted research on corruption and sought to develop anti-corruption methods. In autumn 1999, on the eve of Yeltsin's resignation, NAK was established on the initiative of the INDEM Foundation as a specialised group to push the development and implementation of measures that might eliminate contextual conditions that fostered corruption in post-Soviet Russia. NAK was composed of almost 50 politicians, high-ranking (mostly retired) law enforcement officials, journalists and entrepreneurs. Different from an ideal grass-roots NGO concept, both INDEM and NAK were thus highly elitist and professional groups.

The INDEM team cultivated its Yeltsin-affiliated legacy and also pursued a broader range of topics during the Putin era. Although their publications were highly critical of the enormous corruption problems, especially within the political context during the Putin era, they also contained constructive proposals for viable anti-corruption measures. Moreover, the texts were based on sociological analytical methods, including quantitative and comparative assessments of Russia's situation (internally and internationally) and sought to further develop the methodology of corruption studies. NAK, in contrast, sought to cooperate closely with new governmental agencies and 'individual honest politicians' and focused on advocating anti-corruption reform at the federal level.[14] Also NAK had always refrained from using any foreign assistance and had been working without much publicity (e.g. without its own website and without any public campaigning). Yet through its close collaboration with TI-Russia, NAK was also, however indirectly and whilst remaining less visible to international actors, hooked up to international networks. Both TI-Russia and NAK were located within the same office building and their leaders often referred to by other Moscow interviewees in one breath. INDEM did use foreign funding for their projects, including grants from a Western national aid agency for its first major corruption survey in 2001, and actively sought to present this study to an international audience (e.g. through its website in English, via American colleagues, or at the occasion of the visit of US President George Bush to Moscow in 2002). It caused some controversy that this major study on domestic corruption was accomplished on the basis of Western funding. For the second round of this survey in 2005, INDEM thus avoided foreign assistance. This study too was widely reported in the Russian media as well as among Western analysts. In fact, and regardless of the many corruption-related studies and articles that the INDEM team had produced since the late 1990s, it was mainly with this study that INDEM became known beyond Russia as a professional think tank in the anti-corruption field.[15]

Less visible to outside observers, the activities of TI-Russia, NAK and INDEM were closely linked. In 2001, when INDEM released its first major 'diagnostics of corruption' survey, NAK brought in a comprehensive blueprint, 'Basic directions of anti-corruption policy in Russia' (NAK 2001). The latter advocated the need to establish an anti-corruption strategy as a separate, permanent element in the national policy. It contained proposals for mechanisms to address corruption in the short term, recommended reform of almost all parts of the Russian governance system, ranging from the civil service to the legislature and the executive organs, and called for possibilities of public participation and international cooperation. In 2002, TI-Russia published its regional corruption indices, which presented empirical survey data and recommended their use for regional policy-making (without providing concrete policy advice). As outlined in Chapter 5, the government was far from receptive to such advocacy at that time. In 2004, a team under the INDEM President Satarov published a higher education textbook on 'Anti-corruption policy' (Satarov 2004) that they hoped would be used among the many independent research institutes across Russia – admitting that they were in no position to propose changes to the curricula in state universities.[16] In the same year, NAK issued another paper expressing serious concerns that corruption had increased during the Putin era, that corruption problems had reached a critical level for the Russian citizens and the Russian economy, and that it might even turn into a national threat and lead to a new systemic crisis (NAK 2004). The paper harshly criticised further the fact that proposed systemic reform strategies were not implemented 'as they contradict the interests of the bureaucracy' and that, behind the rhetoric of strengthening the state and anti-oligarchic policy, the activities of many officials were shielded against public attention and criticism, political opposition and mass media were eliminated, and political competition replaced by intrigues. Corruption, in turn, had grown as a side-effect of the vertical executive power, pre-reformist privileges of the bureaucracy had been revived, and the bureaucracy had tripled in size and become increasingly ineffective. While this critique was presented in an impersonal style it contained a note that Putin had allowed this to happen and that he should be more assertive in this field:

> The President must personally head the struggle against corruption [. . .] V. Putin, after designating importance to the struggle against corruption, stood aside from these problems until recently, allowing exceptionally bureaucratic structures to be renewed. It is today obvious that this fight is only an imitation. (NAK 2004, original in Russian)

What may read like an anti-Putin campaign on paper was in turn mediated by TI-Russia to an international audience in a much softer tone and perhaps with different connotations, when presenting NAK in TI's Global Corruption Report as an organisation which 'believes that Putin is the only person able to rid the system of corruption [and] recommends that Putin use his broad popular support as a resource in anti-corruption battles' (Savintseva and Stykow 2005: 201). In February 2004, INDEM, NAK, TI-Russia, and OPORA had also created a nongovernmental Anti-Corruption Council. This institutional measure may have inspired the first noticeable reaction on the part of the government, namely the establishment of the Duma Anti-Corruption Commission in April 2004. Not least, the latter clearly adopted one of the NGO Council's core objectives, to further anti-corruption legal projects, as its own priority. Yet only in late 2005, after INDEM published their second 'diagnostics of corruption' study *and* Russia's CPI score suddenly worsened, did the government feel impelled to more forcefully react to the activities of these Moscow groups, in particular to their generation and dissemination of information about corruption in Russia (see Chapter 5 and below).

Despite their different organisational make-up and strategies, TI-Russia, INDEM and NAK shared the view that corruption in Russia was something particular, historically rooted in the complex Russian administrative and political system. This included emphasis on the considerable variation across the Russian regions. In the latter perspective, Moscow had to be singled out as a particularly exceptional case, 'a country within the country' (Elena Panfilova, in Chudodeev 2006), being the locus of the top level of power, of the largest number of officials, and of the highest turnover of money. Moreover, despite a critical stance against the Putin administration, they agreed that the government needed to play a leading role in realising anti-corruption efforts.

In summer 2005, a new player appeared in Moscow: the Russian movement *Protiv Korruptsii* (Against Corruption) which, as the name implies, focused explicitly on anti-corruption advocacy. It was officially registered as a Russia-wide (inter-regional) movement, which was a common organisational form in many fields where public participation was encouraged via local administrations and communities rather than NGOs. Up to 2008, it had indeed considerably expanded its outreach activities towards other regions all across the territory of the Russian Federation. Also its website and electronic newsletters became tools for providing corruption-related information about each of the more than 80 Russian 'federal subjects'.[17] This movement, too, distanced itself from foreign financial support. Yet unlike NAK, it appeared to rely on governmental support instead. While concrete links remained invisible, there were indications such as its leading members working closely with the government (the executive secretary, Leonid Troshin, was a former MVD official, general of the tax police and leading PGO representative under President Putin), Duma deputies sitting in the experts' council (including Mikhail Grizhankov, head of the Duma Anti-Corruption Commission, see Chapter 5), or the movement's access to state-owned media and to regional governors. Although *Protiv Korruptsii* was in search of its constituency among nongovernmental experts, nobody of the existing Moscow groups had been considered for inclusion. The combination of actively used foreign funding and the production of internationally well-received analytical work was a major thorn in the eyes of the government, all the more since it had no alternative data to present. *Protiv Korruptsii* gave expression to these concerns:

> They [INDEM] have the monopoly on Russia's corruption assessments. They have the wrong figures, but there are no figures with which to compare. (Representative of *Protiv Korruptsii, 2005*)

The scholars at INDEM became a particular target of open accusation by *Protiv Korruptssi* for providing wrong evidence to international actors. INDEM's 2005 study on the rising corruption problems was thus commentated as a 'fruit either of nonprofessionalism or political order'. The data, it was claimed, were 'deliberately impossible' and without doubt fed into the 'momentous but foolish international ratings'. Such exaggerated data presented a threat to Russia's position, not least in the global energy market (*Protiv Korruptsii* 2006). The plethora of daily information about corruption in Russia provided by this movement was thus meant to counteract rather than to supplement existing information. This was not least illustrated by its well-maintained website, which used a very similar URL to that of INDEM's corruption-related site (www.anticorr.ru instead of www.anti-corr.ru).

In terms of its own anti-corruption strategy, *Protiv Korruptsii* presented a well-devised hybrid. It actively promoted the inclusion of the Russian public in the anti-corruption discourse; it brought together a diversity of relevant actors who were situated within different nongovernmental and governmental networks; it promoted international collaboration. Essentially, it thus took over all features that were declared, however imperfectly realised, by earlier transnational efforts. But unlike its forerunners and remaining counterparts, *Protiv Korruptsii* was very much working in line with the state rhetoric of that time and was organised closer to the Kremlin. Regarding transnational networking, it openly questioned the use of foreign funding and the provision of information to foreign partners as viable means to support anti-corruption efforts in Russia. The movement's own international orientation started from the level of high politics where the government was equally involved. It was, for example, involved in organising the final conference in 2008 for the RUCOLA-II project that the Duma Anti-Corruption Commission had led in cooperation with the CoE.[18] Regarding its domestic coalitions, it chose partners who could guarantee essential links to federal-level agencies, to local authorities, and activists in the Russian regions. Regarding outreach, it refrained from organising street action or issuing grey literature and instead used the mass media and actively involved journalists. For example, one of its members initiated the Saturday radio broadcasts mentioned in Chapter 5. Still, all this was less strategically designed from above than it may seem. The movement had initially changed its membership and organisational strategies several times and had been playing around with ways to adapt to the historical context in a sufficiently flexible manner.[19]

The capital: a nucleus of civic action

The anti-corruption scene in Moscow was divided into several spheres which were not necessarily overlapping. A number of CSOs and projects had been addressing corruption problems in daily life as one of several problems these organisations were primarily devoted to (e.g. housing, environmental protection, bureaucratic procedures, electoral processes). While many of these activities had been support-ed, in fact often inspired by, various foreign grant programmes, they were also confined to the duration of the various projects. More enduring and, in fact, increasingly influential anti-corruption advocacy had been undertaken by TI-Russia, in close collaboration with NAK and INDEM. This circle of organisations, which had become active since 1999/2000, presented a fortunate constellation: TI-Russia and NAK pursued anti-corruption advocacy as their main mission, while INDEM presented the professional head behind the methodology used for TI-Russia's analytical pro-jects. Moreover, in terms of their organisational forms, INDEM and NAK were well connected to Moscow (especial-ly federal-level) political circles, while TI-Russia could use the leverage of an increasingly powerful international network. The analyses and rhetoric of these anti-corruption advocates heavily built on evidence of growing corruption in Russia. While they were critical of the Putin administration, their argument that the immense corruption problems presented a threat to the nation itself was not in contradic-tion with the official rhetoric. In 2005, the contemporaneous publication of the second major INDEM study and Russia's worst CPI since Putin's inauguration eventually contributed to a more determined governmental reaction. Besides a new governmental anti-corruption campaign, this included the introduction of the Kremlin-close anti-corruption move-ment *Protiv Korruptsii* as a new player within the civic anti-corruption scene. The latter started with a campaign against the established circle and the rephrasing of their main argument by claiming that the (exaggerated) data about corruption presented a national threat. Since 2006, both camps had pursued their anti-corruption efforts. Both under-lined the need to comply with international (European) standards, to involve civil society, and to generate viable information. Not least, the context of intense governmental anti-corruption engagement also paved the way for new and indeed most comprehensive projects under the roof of TI-Russia. In terms of anti-corruption strategies, this entailed a reorientation from analysing corruption towards providing legal advice and focusing on concrete cases.

St. Petersburg

St. Petersburg, Vladimir Putin's home town, was able to revive its historical legacy as the 'northern capital' or rival capital (rooted in the eighteenth-century ambitions of Peter the Great) during the 2000s. Putin inserted a dominant faction of *pitertsy* ('those from St. Petersburg') into his administration, recruited mainly from reformist circles of economists, lawyers and *siloviki*.[20] This had not only affected federal policy-making and reform, but also the other way round: local governance in St. Petersburg became more firmly tied into domestic politics. This city region seemed to enjoy 'privileged access to Putin's ear and favourable treatment by the federal government' (Duka and Rutland 2004: 56), not least as persons close to Putin were appointed as regional leaders, including the North-West Presidential Envoy Viktor Cherkesov and Governor/Mayor Valentina Matienko. After a first unsuccessful attempt to replace Governor (since 1996) Vladimir Yakovlev with the Kremlin-supported Valentina Matienko in 2000, this take-over was accomplished in an unprecedented Kremlin-backed campaign in 2003.[21] Given Yakovlev's reputation for corruption, this may be interpreted as an anti-corruption success. Yet the personal feud behind his removal was too obvious in this case.[22] The 2003 elections raised major concerns that the local media were finally brought under control. But a number of small independent media outlets were able to survive, perhaps more than in Moscow.[23]

Yet also, St. Petersburg's historical reputation as Russia's 'window to the west' could be restored. It was often referred to as the most Westernised city in the country and it became a 'standard stop' (Duka and Rutland 2004: 56) for foreign heads of state visiting Russia. Presidential Envoy Cherkesov strengthened the 'gateway role' of the region as part of his economic but also security policies (*Ibid.*: 55). The surrounding Leningrad oblast shared a border with EU member state Finland, across which bilateral economic, cultural and research exchange had flourished. Both the oblast and St. Petersburg city benefited from assistance under the EU's Northern Dimension framework and from collaborative US–Scandinavian grant and technical assistance programmes. Through its port, St. Petersburg maintained intense trade relations with the Baltic Sea countries and was thus closely involved in the implementation of the EC Regulation 2584, the first concrete collaborative anti-fraud measure between the EU and Russia in 2000 (see Chapter 4). Foreign investment, after a slump between 1999 and 2004 (from 5.2% to 1.8%), had significantly increased under Governor Matvienko. Foreign businesses even came to consider St. Petersburg as a city with maximum potential and minimum risk for investment (e.g. VDW 2004: 27).

The city of St. Petersburg further attracted extraordinary international attention during its 300th anniversary in 2003 and during the G8 Summit, together with Russia's 10th International Business Forum, held here in 2006. At both events, the issue of corruption was addressed, in 2003 with a focus on the city administration's mismanagement and in 2006 with regard to Russia's growing corruption problems in international comparison. Yet both events also fostered scepticism among local CSOs and experts against prodigal use of local and federal budgets for 'potemkin village'-style PR campaigns towards the international community at the expense of local circumstances. Official preparations for these events came with highly questionable measures: in 2003, a wall was erected to fence off the airport highway – and international visitors' views – from the hinterland, and local citizens' vegetable gardens close to the highway were burned. Long before the G8 Summit in 2006, notorious activists and trouble-makers had been advised to leave the city, homeless animals were removed from the streets (by slaughter), and the annual university entrance exams that would have coincided with the summit were postponed in order to avoid crowds of students coming in from the regions.[24] In the context of the G8 Summit in particular, the authorities were 'trying to make sure that the city of St. Petersburg functions with as little inconvenience as possible' (Russia Profile 2006: 30), amongst other ways by officially accrediting some selected NGOs to work in the summit's press centre. Still, local news showed rather sarcastic responses to Russia's G8 membership and protest actions were initiated in particular by young activists.

In St. Petersburg, a lively civil society scene in general has developed since the early 1990s, where civic rights activists (*pravozashchitniki*), environmental activists, journalists and research groups have played a central role. Some branches of bigger Moscow organisations and some umbrella organisations devoted to civil society development in general were located there. Yet this scene was highly clustered and interaction across various subnetworks remained low.[25] This context made it particularly difficult for 'newcomers' to get access to the existing civic sphere. Also new ideas had to be introduced and implemented via in-group members, unless foreign funding allowed a sufficient degree of independence to follow up on a certain idea.[26] In terms of anti-corruption engagement, St. Petersburg presents a case where much had been done since the early 1990s even without any specialised anti-corruption organisations (as in Moscow) or a specific Anti-Corruption Coalition (as in Irkutsk). Instead, the issue of corruption was taken up by a number of organisations working on a range of issues. But even those groups would claim that hardly any anti-corruption activities could be found in their city.[27]

Actors, approaches and interrelations

The organisations the Leontief Centre, Strategia, *Grazhdanskii Kontrol'* and the Regional Press Institute (RPI) presented a circle of local people who had been actively engaged in promoting local reforms since the early 1990s. All of them had been addressing corruption-related issues, albeit to a different extent and with different underlying motives.

The Leontief Centre, a think tank type of organisation, was founded in 1991 on the initiative of the then mayor Anatoly Sobchak and Nobel prize laureate Wassily Leontief who, despite having lived in exile for most of his life and being affiliated with Harvard and New York universities after the Second World War, was considered as a St. Petersburg native. The centre was closely affiliated with the local administration and business representatives and, according to Leontief's expertise in economics, primarily devoted to advising on market reforms in St. Petersburg. With this focus on economic policy, the Leontief Centre was touching upon anti-corruption advocacy indirectly through concerns about transparent laws and procedures. During the 2000s, times changed for this organisation not only with regard to the domestic context, but also because Leontief himself had died in 1999. It remained one of the largest organisations among those discussed here, relying on over 60 (part-time) staff members and more than 150 consultants.[28] It continued to provide economic expertise to the city administration, but its potential to actually influence economic reform policies was increasingly limited while their recommendations, if accepted, underwent fundamental adjustment (CISR 2004: 10).

A more active player in the anti-corruption field was the Centre of Humanitarian and Political Studies (Strategia), located with its offices and staff in the same building as the Leontief Centre and actively cooperating with the latter. Strategia had been working as a Russian NGO since 1993, when it was founded by a group of deputies from the city council, activists from early democratic parties, journalists and entrepreneurs. It had been addressing anti-corruption reform at the regional level since 1998, when the first foreign grants for anti-corruption projects arrived in Russia. Strategia's anti-corruption work was thus almost exclusively financed from abroad (mainly through US-based private foundations, such as the Eurasia Foundation, Ford Foundation, National Endowment for Democracy, and Soros Foundation, but also through the CoE). The Strategia team regarded Western support as useful not only in financial terms but also with regard to experiences and theories. TI and World Bank publications were actively used references as they dealt with many concrete problems and viable analytical concepts, such as 'conflict of interest'. They adopted a focus on 'public policy', which included concerns about non-transparent budgeting and abuse of resources during elections.[29] In this regard, they were closely cooperating with TI-Russia and INDEM in Moscow. Starting with a grant under the Eurasia Foundation's programme 'Preventing corruption by virtue of civil society', it also became one of the declared goals of Strategia to foster civil society involvement in anti-corruption activities. Only the idea of 'whistleblowers' seemed to be totally unacceptable to Strategia leaders:

> We are not such watchdog organisations, we are not such dogs. (Representative of Strategia, 2005)

Rather than actively seeking to influence local policy-making in St. Petersburg, which they admitted became almost impossible after the appointment of Matvienko as new mayor in 2004 (see also CISR 2004), Strategia adopted an analytical approach and a focus on anti-corruption reforms at the regional level across Russia. Strategia saw the main role for CSOs in conducting analyses about their various local situations, including local legislative acts, in developing reform proposals, and in raising awareness about the actual problem of corruption. They sought to foster this role through supporting research and conference activities and through providing seminars in various thematic areas, including prevention of corruption through civil society, transparent budget, public participation and public policy.[30] In various conversations and interviews with other Russian groups, Strategia conferences were mentioned as worthwhile experiences by those who participated. However, while these events certainly brought together various anti-corruption activists from European, Siberian, and Far Eastern parts of Russia and from abroad, they were less integrative than it may seem. This was not only a failure of the rather informal and interpersonal recruitment practices used by the organisers themselves; but also, among potential participants, some Russian group leaders who knew about future conferences were neither willing to participate nor interested in the outcomes only because they had not been personally invited. Strategia itself had been in a rather privileged position and was able to gain insight into ongoing and planned initiatives across the country thanks to its involvement in the realisation and evaluation of the Eurasia Foundation's anti-corruption grant programmes in Russia.

The various projects and conferences resulted in a respectable series of publications, for the most part edited volumes. Both authorship and readership of these publications were mainly confined to the circle of project partners and participants. In terms of content, the publications comprised practically all facets of civic anti-corruption initiatives, ranging from analysis of corruption, to election campaigns, transparent budgeting, access to information and mass media, to monitoring the legislature and civic participation (e.g. Gornyi 2002; Strategia 2003). International experience was included in a rather arbitrary way, presented through some papers that had appeared at some of these events (e.g. in Strategia 2003; Sungurov 2002). In addition, translations from press releases on TI's CPI and BPI, on TI-Russia's Russian regional indices, as well as excerpts of some international documents, entered some of the volumes, mainly through TI-Russia and INDEM.[31] Some representatives of other Russian groups underlined the usefulness of Strategia books, but they were primarily referring to the importance of learning about experiences and opinions of other Russian organisations while expressing little interest in international agreements and documents.

Grazhdanskii Kontrol' (Citizens' Watch), the Regional Press Institute (RPI), and the the Centre for Independent Social Research (CISR) presented other examples of longer-standing organisations in St. Petersburg that understood concerns about corruption as an integral part of their ongoing work. However, due to their different main missions as much as due to an overreliance on long-established personal relations, they were hardly interacting with each other or with the organisations introduced above in terms of anti-corruption advocacy.

Grazhdanskii Kontrol' was established in 1992 by a group of human rights activists, lawyers, journalists, and deputies of the Duma and St. Petersburg city council. The organisation had always maintained close ties to Moscow-based 'colleagues'. It had also been using foreign assistance for work related to democratisation and human rights. Also during the 2000s, *Grazhdanskii Kontrol'* acted upon its goal 'to assist in establishing parliamentary and civic control over police, security service and armed forces, in order to help prevent violations of constitutional rights by these governmental agencies'.[32] By the mid-2000s, the organisation's leaders considered Russia to be far from a normal market economy and democracy. In addition to the wild capitalism that had fostered much corruption, the previous few years had entailed a liquidation of fair elections, free press, and independent political parties. The organisation thus saw many of its activities being closely related to anti-corruption advocacy, including their lobbying for free access to information, transparent judicial proceedings, and access to justice, or their assistance to police reform and the modernisation of the police education system. *Grazhdanskii Kontrol'* had organised international and national conferences on the quality of the Russian legislation, in order to develop amendments in accordance with international human rights standards that could be proposed to the government.[33] It had also translated documents of the CoE and other international organisations into Russian. Some of its publications met high demands as they put forward practical advice on concrete issues to particular audiences, such as guide books for police officers on first contact with victims of crimes and for crime victims on their legal rights.[34] An envisioned English/Russian publication specifically on 'fighting corruption' could not be realised since it has not sparked much interest among its traditional audience.

The Regional Press Institute (RPI), established in 1993, presented an initiative of journalists who were concerned about the development of free media and objective, neutral reporting. This concern was very much rooted in the experience of business-owned, manipulated mass media during the early 1990s. Originally, the RPI was a branch of a Moscow-based network, but decided to register as an independent organisation by the mid-1990s, following an affair of misappropriated US funds and accusations of corruption against the centre in Moscow. The network eventually fell apart during the early 2000s when all regional branches cancelled their affiliations with Moscow. The RPI itself continued to closely cooperate with American partners and donors. Besides the badly needed financial assistance, its director also considered the exchange of ideas as a main asset. For example, among the seminars offered by the RPI, those that were held by one Western and one Russian expert were perceived as most successful. Financially, after the closure of the Soros office in Russia in 2003 (see Chapter 4), USAID remained the only stable source. Similar to Strategia, the RPI had been cooperating with 'colleagues' and offering its seminars to journalists in regions across Russia rather than in St. Petersburg. Following its separation from the founding umbrella network, the institute further refrained from offering seminars in Moscow, acknowledging that 'they have their own experts', although maintaining close contacts with journalists in the capital. The RPI maintained a critical stance against Putin, not least since the institute's director, Anna Sharogradskaya, knew him from his earlier St. Petersburg times. But their Western colleagues tended to not believe their warnings about prospective challenges for the Russian media sector for a long time while regarding Putin as 'resolute, effective and fluent in foreign languages'.[35]

The RPI understood anti-corruption advocacy as a key element of its ongoing activities, given its prime concerns about 'closedness' as a main cause for corruption and about the massive bribing of print media during elections and other political key events. The daily work of RPI staff consisted in intensely monitoring the press and other publications. Foreign grants were mainly used for providing seminars for journalists, editors and entrepreneurs. One seminar on 'lobbying and media', for example, sought to show that lobbying did not only mean to be bribed by businesses (as in the Russian sense of the term), but could also mean to actively fight against corruption. The authorities obviously disliked the RPI's work, although they remained careful not to take sides. Only within the restructured local governance context under the new mayor, did the RPI feel an increasing need for juridical consultation. However, it lacked the financial means to realise this kind of support.

A small team of local researchers at the Centre for Independent Social Research (CISR) may also be worth mentioning. Under the leadership of renowned St. Petersburg sociologists Viktor Voronkov and Elena Zdravomyslova, since 1991 mainly sociologists and anthropologists had been working at the CISR, on a variety of issues ranging from environmental sociology to border studies or gender studies.[36] Only two of the staff members during the early 2000s had adopted a research focus on corruption issues, mainly with regard to the informal post-Soviet economies in a wider sense (Olimpieva and Pachenkov 2003), but also regarding possibilities to counteract business-related corruption in St. Petersburg from below (Olimpieva, Pachenkov and Nikiforova 2004). They developed this direction independently from the rest of the centre, but in close collaboration with research teams abroad (especially in the USA and Hungary) and in other Russian cities (especially in Irkutsk, where the CISR maintained a branch, see below). Such collaboration was considered beneficial for all partners, as the Western partners commonly brought in the needed financial resources, including grants from various donors, and the Russian and other Eastern European teams made use of their local embeddedness by realising empirical case studies in their home towns. From the view of the St. Petersburg team, these research projects thus sprung from a partly path-dependent and partly random process of continuously developing research partnerships and seeking financial support for their daily work.

Regarding the recentralising governance context from the mid-2000s, CISR staff in general quite self-confidently continued their various research projects, which was facilitated by the fact that these focused on social rather than political aspects and that they sought to generate objective knowledge. Besides the directors and some project leaders, most team members were relatively young, many of them enrolled in a masters or PhD programme at the European University in St. Petersburg, one of the most independent Russian universities (founded in 1994 with the support of Anatoly Sobchak).[37] Yet those who were personally critical of Putin and of the political developments in Russia and St. Petersburg at that time, were so in their private lives rather than in their professional work context. Some staff members were also invited to give lectures or presentations at official agencies and mostly readily accepted the opportunity to present their findings in such contexts:[38]

> As an anthropologist, I am free to ask what I want. I want to find out how people live, what they experience. So I ask them. There is nothing political about that, there is nothing to be afraid of. (Researcher at the CISR, St. Petersburg, 2004)

In addition to these corruption-related activities in the framework of longer-standing organisations, a number of activities were undertaken by more recent local organisations that were founded by a younger generation of professionals (rather than activists) in the fields of business and legal consulting.

Business ethics programmes were well received in St. Petersburg. Various local NGOs and business associations had been collaborating with international business organisations to organise symposia or to provide consultative and educational services to investors, enterprises and authorities. During the late 1990s/early 2000s, some foreign foundations supported NGOs in organising events where SMEs and financial institutions could get together, hoping that these would open up a market for consulting services as well as alternative funding sources for the NGOs (e.g. Golishnikova 2002). Some of these events also addressed corruption-related issues and fostered some exchange between various parties interested in anti-corruption promotion from a business perspective. However, conferences in this sphere were usually supported by bigger budgets and took place at rather prestigious locations. They were thus part of a totally different milieu that never attracted any of the above-mentioned activists, even if they knew about them. They felt that this was very different from their concerns about fundamental citizens' rights or research. Moreover, even within the business community, it was obvious that, when it came to corruption, foreign businesses and multinational companies referred to security, street crime, corporate social responsibility and codes of conduct, whereas local and smaller businesses were more concerned about the experience that the numerous inspections and bureaucratic hurdles could only be overcome by using *blat* and bribes.[39] The former discourse received more attention from the mid-2000s, in the context of increasing efforts to attract more foreign investment to Russia and to St. Petersburg on the part of the federal and local administrations. Not least, this came in response to an OECD assessment which called for more foreign direct investment in Russia (OECD 2004a). In the following years, several large-scale conferences were organised that would attract foreign investors, Russian regional companies and authorities in order to trigger grand investment projects. At the occasion of some large-scale events, which were held in St. Petersburg in 2005/2006, the need for more business integrity and public–private interaction in the fight against corruption was underlined.[40] At the opening of the 10th International Business Forum, held by MERiT during the run-up to the G8 Summit in St. Petersburg (see Chapters 4 and 5), President Putin himself underlined the importance of anti-corruption initiatives.[41] At this level, however, and within the context of the summit in particular, independent CSOs felt completely out of place.

Juristic activity presented another field where professional expertise rather than activism indirectly fed into anti-corruption efforts. The Institute for Information Freedom Development, a local NGO established only in 2004, was but one example of small offices around Russia that sought to further work on the legal aspects of information freedom and state secrets at the federal level. Following a law pushed through in 2003, not least resulting from TI-Russia's advocacy, each federal ministry and governmental executive agency was obliged to maintain a website providing certain information on its activities (legal acts, events, statistics, vacancies). The St. Petersburg institute sought to push the relevant agencies to comply with this duty, if necessary through initiating court cases. Within a short period of time, this work achieved considerable success. By 2004, 53 out of 83 relevant agencies did not have their own website. Following a series of letters and correspondence, this number was reduced to 12 by 2005. Yet these remaining agencies were mainly 'power ministries', which were hard to influence even through court cases. Nevertheless, such cases proved conducive to the institute's overall goal to attract more public attention to these obligations and to the fact that the rule of law was not totally absent in Russia. Since 2005, the institute has followed up on its initial quantitative success by regularly monitoring the quality of the existing websites. Indirectly, and in fact unconsciously, this initiative thus contributed to the continuation and implementation of civic anti-corruption efforts pursued earlier in Moscow. Still, it came from a different direction, namely the former personal engagement of its founding director, Ivan Pavlov, who had been devoted to defending activists who were put on trial as 'spies' after making public information on resource mismanagement. Although Pavlov had been among the defence lawyers of Nikitin and Pas'ko, who both continued to be active in the field of environmental rights (with their own organisations in Moscow and St. Petersburg), no further synergies were sought. Instead, the institute pursued its own professional role in the field of freedom of information which offered a whole range of different possibilities to network and to acquire funding (from both Russian and foreign sources).[42]

The weight of local traditions and politics

St. Petersburg presented a pattern of civic anti-corruption advocacy that was rather different from Moscow. There were no specific anti-corruption organisations. Rather, various CSOs had been addressing corruption-related issues as a side issue in addition to their ongoing work. Most of these groups did not perceive themselves as being anti-corruption advocates and did not look out for collaboration in this particular field. While some seemed to be sharing common concerns, such as access to information or fraud during elections, they pursued different organisational missions (e.g. economic policy, citizens' rights, free media, business ethics, or awareness-raising, professional training, policy advice, research, or judicial work on certain issues) and were thus oriented towards different wider discourses and networks. Moreover, while it was important for all of them to maintain contacts with peers and potential donors in Moscow and abroad, they were usually not concerned about influencing federal policy-making (with the exception of the team of jurists working on access to governmental information). Although foreign funding had been used for most corruption-related activities, it had come from a variety of sources and programmes rather than through specific grants for anti-corruption projects. Strategia was the only exception, since it had been working under the specific anti-corruption assistance programme of the Eurasia Foundation. This organisation had become connected to other anti-corruption activities all across Russia (rather than in St. Petersburg) and had established close collaboration with TI-Russia in Moscow.

Furthermore, the St. Petersburg scene was clustered into relatively strong sub-networks which proved quite effective within their respective area. In addition to professional self-perception and the thematic interests of the various groups, personal cleavages were reinforcing these divisions. Although most members of St. Petersburg CSOs knew each other, they tended to interact 'behind the scenes' through personal contacts rather than publicly at formal meetings and events. Similarly to Moscow, one cluster of organisations that had actively taken up on corruption-related issues was built on longer-standing and rather elitist circles of senior *pravoza-shshitniki* who had been involved in (local) politics and science during Soviet and perestroika times. But those who were concerned with local reforms had in particular faced more obstacles since 2004 because the appointment of a more Kremlin-loyal governor and mayor had meant that they had lost crucial personal contacts in the city administration. Another cluster was composed of younger organisations founded by younger professionals in fields such as business consultancy or juridical work. Although a governmental anti-corruption discourse related to business and investment policy was being fed by 2005 and 2006, when much international attention was directed at St. Petersburg, consultants in the field of business ethics understood their work as apolitical and oriented towards individual companies. Juridical work related to governmental information provision, in turn, contained some political engagement but no synergies were sought with specific anti-corruption networks – although this meant a continuation of earlier efforts undertaken by TI-Russia.

Irkutsk

Although not a metropolis like Moscow or St. Petersburg, Irkutsk city is the capital of a region that has always played a key role within Russia. Together with the Republic of Buryatia, Irkutsk oblast flanks the shores of Lake Baikal, the world's largest freshwater reservoir and a unique ecosystem.[43] Moreover, possessing valuable natural resources (oil, gas, metals, timber, fish etc.), it was Siberia's commercial and administrative centre in the mid-eighteenth century, the centre of gold mining in the mid-nineteenth century, and a priority region of Soviet industrial development during the twentieth century, with enormous investments devoted to grand hydro-energy and industrial projects. By the 2000s, Irkutsk still counted as one of the relatively well off, resource-exporting, and urbanised regions in Russia. Although the number of inhabitants markedly decreased in Irkutsk city (from 620,000 in 1989 to 580,000 in 2004), the oblast remained one of the most populated Russian regions with low out-migration.[44] Nevertheless, it was among the lowest-rated regions in terms of investment. The re-orientation from processing to exporting raw materials from the mid-1990s implied that little local-level employment was generated and not much profit was redistributed within the region. Between 1997 and 2003, growing injections from the federal budget should have countered significant decreases in the gross regional product and real incomes. Yet the effectiveness of budget subsidies seemed questionable, not least since above-average salaries were found in the regional administrations.[45] There were persisting conflicts between the regional governor, Boris Govorin, formerly Irkutsk city mayor who had won the post in 1997 through the use of administrative resources, and the respective city mayors. In August 2005, Putin appointed Alexander Tishanin as the new regional governor. In contrast to his predecessor, Tishanin was Kremlin-loyal and without ties to the regional political and business elites. From that point, *siloviki* grew more influential in the region. Similarly to St. Petersburg, this could be interpreted as an anti-corruption measure. In the local context, however, this measure fell into a temporal climate when Govorin had been favoured over the then mayor Vladimir Yakubovsky (United Russia), and it was therefore hardly welcomed by the local population.

Irkutsk had been the locus of intense transnational advocacy during the 1990s when protracted struggles for nominating Lake Baikal as a UNESCO World Natural Heritage Site were under way (which happened in 1996, followed by a controversy about endowing the lake with the status 'World Heritage in Danger').[46] While international attention to these issues had already faded by the mid-2000s, the local environmental scenes in Irkutsk and Buryatia had remained lively and influential. In general, the life of the people there had always been intrinsically linked to Lake Baikal. Yet the closure of previously state-owned industries and a persisting lack of investment in sustainable and social development had contributed to a range of severe problems, including shadow economic and criminal activities in the timber and oil sectors, serious environmental pollution and contamination in the industrial agglomeration around Irkutsk, increasing levels of poverty and unemployment, and accompanying socio-economic problems.[47] For many households, a secondary economy became the main source of survival. Civic anti-corruption activities could in this context build on a rather active civil society scene concerned with environmental protection, indigenous rights, social and educational projects, and corruption problems in connection with large-scale illegal logging, oil exploitation or pipeline constructions. Also business actors of various kinds played an active role. In contrast to Moscow and St. Petersburg, no offices of international organisations or foreign donors were located in Irkutsk.

Actors, approaches and interrelations

In Irkutsk too, various activists, journalists, and entrepreneurs had become engaged against corruption since the early 1990s. Still, except for two, none of the interviewees there knew anything about the international activities outlined in Chapters 3 and 4. Most interviewees were not even aware of TI-Russia or TI in general. None of the Irkutsk organisations was familiar with the TI Source Book, which presented a frequently used reference on the shelves of various Moscow and St. Petersburg groups. Among the international anti-corruption activities, only some of the anti-corruption assistance programmes directed at civil society had reached Irkutsk during the 2000s.

Local activists in Irkutsk were embedded within a rather strong tradition of civic engagement relating to environmental protection and local governance. In the 1960s, plans to build a pulp and paper mill directly on Lake Baikal gave rise to the Soviet Union's first public protests where scientists played a leading mobilising role. From then on, a comprehensive environmental movement grew around Lake Baikal, which still includes many scientists but also journalists, educators, entrepreneurs and other activists and professionals. This movement cannot be introduced here in detail. But it is worth mentioning that it presents a highly successful example of locally rooted activism that had grown very influential in local and federal politics. Regardless of ongoing quarrels between political and economic elites in Irkutsk oblast and the Republic of Buryatia,[48] common concerns about the protection of the lake had inspired active collaboration among nongovernmental activists in both regions. Intense struggles relating to the nomination of Lake Baikal as a UNESCO World Natural Heritage site during the 1990s had further fostered close interaction with environmental networks and legal experts in Moscow and abroad.

Also throughout the 2000s, this wider movement was exceptionally successful in warding off several pipeline construction projects that were planned in protected drainage areas or nearby National Parks, including a Yukos gas pipeline to China in 2003 (Bel'skaia 2003) and a Transneft oil pipeline to the Pacific coast in 2006. In the latter case, resolute protests against the Kremlin-backed construction had even resulted in Putin's personal order to reroute the line further away from the lake.[49] With the help of Moscow-based experts complaints and court cases against fraudulent environmental assessments could be initiated and more powerful actors at international and national levels could be involved (e.g. Greenpeace, WWF, UNESCO, or the Russian social-democratic political party Yabloko). At the local level, international assistance was furthermore important in the form of knowledge provision (e.g. about global energy markets, environmental conditions, citizens and indigenous rights). The local groups themselves had engaged in on-site investigation, organised public hearings, initiated information campaigns, and mobilised mass protests in the streets. Although presenting environmentally motivated protests and while the 'boomerang effect' against Transneft was not quite as strong as proclaimed in the local press, this presented a major assertion against political power in a domestic context of largely silenced opposition.[50] These activities contained successful mobilisation against political corruption and fraud. Clientelism and patronage behind the pipeline project was obvious.[51] Moreover, the protesters appealed against false 'civic ecological impact assessments' that were provided by GONGOs, permitting construction within ecologically sensitive areas.[52] In this context, another interesting aspect was that the Yukos oil company, together with Khodorkovsky's foundation *Otkrytaia Rossiia*, were perceived as opponents who sought to build pipelines at the cost of local communities and ecosystems, rather than as supportive donors:

> When they tried to get the Yukos pipeline through, that involved only Irkutsk and Buryatya and Chita, and Yukos was able to buy all the politicians along the route and to buy the media along the route [...] I think we have good ground for being sceptical. Because the way the company was working here within the Baikal region, trying to get this pipeline through, breaking the law, there was corruption, it was rife with corruption, and buying the media – I mean is this 'Open Russia'? (Representative of a local environmental organisation, 2005)

This was rather different from Moscow and St. Petersburg, or Samara as a pilot region of the Anti-Corruption Coalition project outlined below, where *Otkrytaia Rossiia* was appreciated as a main Russian donor among journalist and activist communities.[53] When the government put *Otkrytaia Rossiia* out of action in 2006, an act that was elsewhere perceived as a strike against the beginnings of corporate social responsibility and domestic civil society assistance (see Chapter 5), this was for some Irkutsk groups only another illustration of clan fights.

One Irkutsk-based environmental group deserves further comment as it was also included in the local Anti-Corruption Coalition introduced below. *Baikal'skaia Ekologicheskaia Volna* (Baikal Environmental Wave, locally known as 'the Wave') was from 1990 devoted to fostering citizens' control over environmental protection and became actively involved in influencing decision-making about resource exploitation and industrial construction projects in the region. Its many activities included environmental education for youth and the general public, monitoring and protests, and, if needed, law suits against illegal projects.[54] Corruption as a main facilitator of such projects dealt out between regional and federal authorities and businesses had always been a major concern for the Wave. Corruption related to illegal logging and resource exploitation was also on the agenda of international anti-corruption promoters such as TI and EITI.[55] Yet synergies with the global discourse and action were not utilised in this case. Russia had never become part of the EITI initiative. On the part of TI, as outlined in Chapter 4, support was concentrated on TI-Russia in Moscow and the establishment of cross-country collaboration was entirely left to the latter. TI-Russia, in turn, had itself never worked on resource exploitation. Moreover, TI's non-confrontational approach stood in contrast to the Wave's commitment to conducting investigations into particular cases of corruption and to rallying opposition.

Local entrepreneurs and journalists had also been addressing corruption in Irkutsk. Some of the key anti-corruption advocates among the entrepreneurs had entered the local business sector after they had vainly tried to further reforms as deputies during the 1990s. Having realised through experience that much genuine political engagement was forestalled by entrenched corruption and administrative rigidity, they shared a common interest in fostering research and information exchange. They disliked the tendency that Russian citizens 'sit and wait', under Putin even more so than during the perestroika time.[56] Yet their efforts to counteract corruption and mismanagement were rather different.

One of the entrepreneurs had, in addition to his own company, launched his own journal as well as a regional Association of Entrepreneurs. He actively used both forums to mobilise the owners of small-scale businesses in Irkutsk and surrounding towns to stand up for their rights, including the rights not to pay bribes and to have a say in reforms related to the business sector (e.g. tax reforms).[57] Another one became vice-president of the East Siberian Chamber of Commerce and Industry. In an individual move, he added anti-corruption advocacy to his professional duties, focusing on access to information, administrative barriers, and legislation. These two business representatives later participated in the Anti-Corruption Coalition. Yet not everybody was willing to unite forces with local civic groups. Some admitted outright that they would never listen to NGOs. Another entrepreneur, who had established a local corporate fund, *Baikal, Tret'e Tysiacheletie* (Baikal, Third Millennium), did not enter the Coalition and remained sceptical about this approach, mainly because the grantees could not develop their strategies independently from the donors. Instead, he himself initiated an anti-corruption campaign in 2004 that included support to local research groups and a grant competition for journalists through the Third Millennium fund. This anti-corruption initiative was essentially a response to a recent blackmailing attack against him. The strategy he used was inspired by successful experiences with a business-sponsored anti-corruption initiative in Yekaterinburg (in Central Russia). He wanted to use the competition to mobilise financial assistance for anti-corruption initiatives from the local entrepreneur community and, in a context of a self-interested local press, to assist the formation of a journalist community as a forum to express civic positions. While the former objective could be realised, the competition was perceived with mixed feelings by local journalists, precisely within this context of low trust and probably reinforced by the comparatively generous grants offered (the three winners of the competition would have received 100,000 / 50,000 / 30,000 roubles).[58] According to participants in the accompanying press conference, the expensive location (a central hotel hall) and the presence of only one TV camera further fostered distrust amongst the journalists.[59]

Among the local journalists themselves some had, since the 1990s, been engaged in publishing on corruption in the region. This was not easy in a climate where the Governor was well respected and connected to local elites and media outlets. Some themes were simply taboo, such as illegal property, the Mafia, and anything critical about the Governor. Especially around election time, some journalists were playing on the conflict between the Governor and the Mayor. But this was a difficult venture when Yakubovsky (United Russia) was mayor during the mid-2000s, as there was much official intervention from Moscow in support of this mayor. There was thus much self-censorship among journalists. The journalistic scene was also highly factioned. Besides many personal cleavages, tensions had emerged between well-established investigative journalists and students from the Faculty of Philology and Journalism at Irkutsk State University (IGU). The latter had been educating professional journalists since 1961. Since the late 1990s, and partly via an NGO founded by one of the lecturers, a group of people there had sought to improve the ethical reporting culture of young journalists and to motivate them to take up on corruption. They used NGO newsletters and some private local newspapers to regularly publish articles written by student journalists. Yet after some uncomfortable experiences with stories that led to court cases because somebody felt offended, these outlets tended to reject articles with a high potential for conflict. Senior investigative journalists, in contrast, preferred to publish articles about actual criminal incidences. They were frequently indicted or harassed themselves but then usually supported through their editorial departments.[60] The team at IGU had also conducted some awareness-raising projects related to corruption with the assistance of foreign grants (from, e.g., the Ford Foundation or the Soros Foundation). Yet some investigative journalists who tended to survive financially only through their affiliation with various newspapers considered the young generation that was attracted by foreign and local grant competitions as 'unprofessional and shady'. Moreover, while the latter claimed that primarily governmental authorities (*vlasti*) and the procuracy should fight corruption, the former strongly believed in the power of organised civil society. The IGU-based group thus also joined the Anti-Corruption Coalition in 2004.[61]

Specific foreign funding for civil-society-led anti-corruption projects had reached further to Irkutsk in 2000, when two local organisations received small grants under the second round of the Eurasia Foundation programme 'Preventing corruption by virtue of civil society'.[62] One grant went to the Irkutsk Economic State Academy for conducting a sociological study on corruption in the higher education system. However, neither the outcomes of this project nor any ongoing research on corruption within the Academy were known among other local groups. In contrast, the other recipient, the Eastern Siberian department of the Russian Union of Cameramen (henceforth cinematographers) literally made the most of this grant. Headed by two senior, very agile ladies, this group produced a series of short documentary films about various civic anti-corruption projects, including many of those that had been conducted under the Eurasia Foundation programme since 1999. The producers were highly engaged in tracing these projects and actively sought out interested audiences all over Russia. Similarly to the above-mentioned entrepreneurs, they searched for active people 'who really want to do something instead of sitting around and waiting, passively, indifferently'. The film series provided perhaps the first overview of how civic projects in Russia could address corruption in various spheres of life, ranging from child care and housing to corruption in local administrations and courts. The cinematographers too were later included in the Anti-Corruption Coalition where they continued this work by producing another series about anti-corruption projects and by distributing their video tapes across Russia.[63]

In 2003/2004, the USAID programme for supporting Anti-Corruption Coalitions, which was implemented by the American contract organisation Management Systems International (MSI), arrived in Irkutsk.[64] In contrast to the earlier anti-corruption grants from the Eurasia Foundation, which were part of a Russia-wide programme (distributing small grants of about $US10,000 to 15 civic projects all across the country),[65] Irkutsk oblast was one of the few designated target regions under the USAID programme. The programme envisaged a pooling of anti-corruption initiatives in this particular region and therefore provided seven small grants alone to Irkutsk groups ($US6,500 for each 9-month project). Following the Ukrainian experience, such regional coalitions had first been set up in two pilot Russian oblasts – Samara and Tomsk – in 2001. The extremely successful experiences with these two coalitions would next be transferred to Irkutsk oblast and Primorskii kray (Vladivostok) in 2003, and to Khabarovsk kray, Sakhalin oblast and Kamchatka kray in 2005 (USAID and MSI 2003). While the first impetus came from the local administration who had heard about and applied for participation in this USAID programme, and while the programme in general aimed at supporting 'public–private partnerships against corruption',[66] the then established Coalition for Counteracting Corruption in Irkutsk Oblast (henceforth Coalition) was primarily a civil society initiative. It was composed of 23 local individuals, including leaders of various NGOs (in the fields of journalism, education, research and environment) and of business associations (including the Irkutsk branch of OPORA and the Eastern Siberian Chamber of Commerce and Industry).[67] Following the termination of the first round of grants in 2005, negotiations about possible continuation of these activities had been dragging on for many months. But eventually, the programme was suspended. Shortly after, the website of the Coalition was abandoned and the various participating organisations went back to their main work; some disappeared from the local civic scene. In the meantime what had happened to make the Irkutsk Coalition such a failure in comparison with its forerunners? The launch of this coalition involved an impressive dedication and range of rather comprehensive projects undertaken by local groups. The Coalition had received wide coverage in the local press and relatively positive reactions on the part of the regional and local authorities. For example, the 'anti-corruption week', one of the start-up measures organised by all Russian regional coalitions, proved rather promising also in Irkutsk. As in the pilot regions, this awareness-raising event included an 'anti-corruption bus' staffed with legal advisers, and other street action involving activists and local students. It thus attracted people from the local administrative and political circles, including MVD officials with whom the local organisations had not been in contact before. The authorities could hardly respond negatively to such a public offensive and collectively organised event.

> They [MVD officials] came to us and confessed their helplessness in these matters and offered their cooperation.
>
> When students were going around, asking whether they could put up a sign 'zdes' korruptsii net' [no corruption here] at their office doors, the officials simply had no choice. They could not send the students away. Many also knew them personally. (Coalition members, Irkutsk, 2005)

Also formally, the Irkutsk Coalition was designed exactly the same way as in the pilot regions: it had a Charter, a Secretary (appointed by MSI), and a local Coordinator (chosen in agreement between MSI and local participants). The Coalition members held regular councils. Seven among the participants had received small grants on a competitive basis in the very beginning for realising individual anti-corruption projects. Also according to the pilot experiences, some of the grant-based projects produced information booklets on corruption-related issues such as 'What is corruption?', 'Free access to medical service', 'Corruption in higher education', a 'Model code of ethics' etc.[68] At a closer look, however, a variety of factors put sand in the wheels of the Irkutsk Coalition, some related to the particular local context (pre-existing patterns of civic engagement, including anti-corruption activities), some to the particular timing (key events in the domestic and international contexts in 2004/2005), and some to the design of the programme itself (foreign assistance and Russian model regions).

First, the pre-existing patterns of civic engagement, outlined above, provided the main ground for the envisioned coalition. As much of this engagement included anti-corruption efforts, in principle, valuable resonance points in terms of previous experience and continuing enthusiasm would have been in place. However, the various groups had entered the Coalition with different expectations, understanding it as another means to further their individual efforts and agendas.

The MSI programme, in contrast, was very much focused on the coalition as an end in itself and the grants were offered under preconceived thematic headings. Although most of the Irkutsk participants had applied for a grant, many were rather reluctant to give up on their previous efforts in exchange for some fashionable ideas and methods or for 'reinventing the wheel'. Eventually, among the seven recipient organisations only three felt that they realised a project according to their previous experience: *Molodyie Zhurnalisty protiv korruptsii* (Young Journalists Against Corruption), *Grazhdanskaia Advokatura* (Citizens' Legal Advice Office), and *Pravovoe Pole* (Legal Field). The latter project presented the above-mentioned documentary series produced by the cinematographers. These grantees admitted that they had learned much about corruption and anti-corruption engagement in various parts of Russia through their work under this and the previous Eurasia grant and that they wanted to share this knowledge. Still, they considered themselves as professional producers of educational films and therewith as mediators between the subjects of these films and educating institutions (thus not as anti-corruption advocates). They also insisted that they produced 'videomaterials' rather than 'movies'. This does not mean that they were not disappointed about the fact that almost nobody within the Coalition showed an interest in these documentary series about civic anti-corruption projects. Their production may also have seemed rather old-fashioned to the American donors who were seeking cutting-edge projects. But knowing that they had indeed received some good feedback from other Russian experts across the country, they went on to pursue their mission outside the Coalition. When the MSI programme was discontinued in 2005, they had already gained a follow-up grant from the US Embassy which they went on to use for visiting about 12 of the 30 districts (*rayony*) within Irkutsk oblast in search of anti-corruption and other projects that would be worth recording. Similarly, the environmental organisation the Wave, who had not won a grant, seemed not unhappy about it. This organisation realised that its own goal of investigating concrete cases of corruption could not to be met through this USAID grant programme, and vice versa. In 2006, the Wave secured a USAID grant through a Programme for Third Sector Development led by an inter-regional Siberian umbrella organisation for a project on the development of a legal culture of public hearings at the municipal level in Irkutsk.[69]

> We just understood that we haven't got time to deal with campaigns, theoretically fighting corruption, because in our understanding, the fight against corruption is through the law. We have to deal with concrete cases [...] Our grant application

together with our participation in the seminars indicated [to the donors] that we were dealing very closely, too closely with corruption to be able to trust us, not to unearth some corrupt practices. (Representative of the Wave, 2005)

Second, in Irkutsk more than in the pilot regions, the founding phase of the Coalition in early 2004 was affected by crucial developments at the domestic and international levels. Domestically, it fell into the time when Putin was just re-elected and a massive restructuring of the Russian governance system was under way, including the reinstallation of federal control over the regions. On a more positive site, the Irkutsk Coalition coincided with the initiation of the Duma Anti-corruption Commission at the federal level. Irkutsk authorities thus felt obliged to follow Moscow's action plans. Amongst others, anti-corruption commitment emerged as a new demand if they wanted to attract investment and federal subsidies. At least formally, they were thus rather accessible to requests of the Coalition. In summer 2005, when the decision about the continuation of the USAID programme in Irkutsk was pending, the regional governor was replaced by a person who was Kremlin-loyal. The Coalition programme was ended under the latter and not least with regard to the controversial image of USAID following its involvement in the recent Orange Revolution in Ukraine (where the USAID regional Anti-Corruption Coalition programme had originally started as well).

Third, the design and organisation of the coalition-building programme itself contained elements that contributed to the failure of the Irkutsk Coalition, some of which were reinforced under these particular local and temporal contextual conditions. A factor that was irrelevant in the pilot regions was the discrepancy between the donors' objectives to support locally grounded initiatives, on the one hand, and to transfer best practices across Russian regions on the other. In many respects, Irkutsk participants felt uneasy about how this transfer was realised. Following a pre-screening visit to Irkutsk, MSI initiated a seminar about the Coalition project in September 2003. The participants from Irkutsk, Samara and Tomsk were selected by MSI. MSI held a two-hour presentation and three separate meetings with representatives from the business, NGO and media circles. Two months later, an international conference was held in

Irkutsk. Among the 60 participants, roughly, were included American experts, Russian coalition members, and officials from the local administration, procuracy and MVD. After the Irkutsk grantees were selected, two training days followed, where members from the Coalitions in Samara and Tomsk presented their experiences with the MSI grant programme. That the anti-corruption activities had already been 'tried and tested' in Samara and Tomsk and that these pilot coalitions should serve as prime models presented an asset from the perspective of the donors (Vol'skaia-Vinborn et al. 2004: 115).[70] Also the selection of the grantees, based on a voting system that granted equal weight to the votes of experts from MSI, Samara and Tomsk, and Irkutsk (one-third each), should have weakened the component of importing foreign ideas into Russian target regions. From the perspective of Irkutsk participants, however, this was perceived as a share of two-thirds actually being 'imported' projects. In general, Irkutsk Coalition members felt confronted with a double burden of rather concrete expectations coming from both their foreign donors and their Russian counterparts. In this regard, it was also noticed that the pilot projects were build on longer and more context-specific planning periods.

> The lecture-type trainings provided little opportunity for open discussions, questions and answers. And local experts had little say in selecting the grantees.

> Just remember the trainings. Everything went so fast, especially when the people from [one of the pilot coalitions] presented. (Members of the local Anti-Corruption Coalition, Irkutsk, 2005)

At the same time, Irkutsk actors in their narratives were strongly oriented towards MSI or 'their US donors'. Most of the grantees had previous experiences with foreign foundations which they used as a point of reference. When the problem emerged in Irkutsk that the finalisation of several grant projects was delayed, this came as a surprise also to the local organisations themselves. The grantees complained about unrealistically high expectations, tight schedules, low remuneration, and the neglect of local contextual conditions which had entailed complicated experiences during the realisation of some projects. At a more personal level, tensions with the appointed secretary were frequently mentioned. It also seemed odd to the Irkutsk participants that several organisations had encountered similar problems during the realisation of their projects but that a discussion of these problems was not taken up by MSI.

> We were afraid about the life of the people who did our data collection.

> We have experiences with conducting big projects. But in these cases we received 16,000 dollars and not 6,000. (Members of the local Anti-Corruption Coalition, Irkutsk, 2005)

When it was debated whether the Irkutsk Coalition should continue its work under another round of MSI grants, the members seemed less concerned about the venture of the Coalition itself. For most of them, ongoing work in their individual organisations clearly was in the foreground. For some, this included concerns about their future funding prospects (some feared that they were now on this donor's 'black list'). Based on the experience with the first round of grants, others feared a continuation of the prescriptive organisational modus as well as colossal workloads that would exceed their resources and competencies. All the participants underlined their additional duties (as one member put it: 'We don't have only this one coalition'). In addition, most felt ill-prepared for the three new thematic priorities proposed by MSI for the second round of grants (transparent budgeting, access to information, tender procedures). Although these were not alien concerns to them, only one participant actually had previous experiences with tender procedures. Some thus underlined that a reorientation towards these areas might overstretch the problem-solving capacity of the local civic community and eventually damage its image. Moreover, some members were unhappy about two future steps that had been agreed in April 2005: the consolidation of a Russian network among the coalitions in Samara, Tomsk, Primorskii Kray and Irkutsk (*Rossiiskoe Antikorruptsionnoe Partnerstvo* / Russian Anti-Corruption Partnership, RAP) and its further expansion towards the Far Eastern regions Khabarovsk, Sakhalin and Kamchatka.[71] Finally, the coordinator of the Irkutsk Coalition, although obviously much appreciated in this role by the other participants, refused to carry on with this task in the future and nobody else seemed keen to replace her. Overall, it was thus also in the interest of the participants themselves that the venture should be discontinued.

> If grant proposals come to us, it doesn't mean that we have to accept them.

> We first need our own clear position. We need to consolidate as a coalition, not as another partnership. (Members of the local Anti-Corruption Coalition, Irkutsk, 2005)

In the end, the failure of the Anti-Corruption Coalition was not particular to Irkutsk. Except for the coalition in Samara, which was still active by the end of the study period, all the other coalitions and the trans-regional partnership became inactive by 2006 or slightly later. However, in the Irkutsk case, the failure was not without consequences for further collaboration in the anti-corruption field and beyond this region. For example, some of the participating organisations had been eager to get access to European networks and TI. According to TI-Russia, however, successful coalitions were located in Samara, Tomsk, Khabarovsk and Vladivostok, whereas this type of activity seemed to be premature for Irkutsk oblast.[72] Vladivostok was the peer target region to Irkutsk, with Samara and Tomsk as model regions for establishing Anti-Corruption Coalitions. The coalition in Vladivostok, which had been established in parallel with the Irkutsk coalition, had become known to TI-Russia through its work on a proposal for a federal anti-corruption law.[73] Yet access to the networks around TI-Russia was also barred because the former coordinator of the Irkutsk Coalition had joined the expert council of the *Protiv Korruptsii* movement in 2005.

The weight of local traditions and politics

In Irkutsk, the civic activism related to protecting the environment around Lake Baikal had been strong and influential since Soviet times. During the 1990s, journalists and entrepreneurs too became engaged in advocating various reforms. Preventing corruption was a common concern to all of them. Similarly to St. Petersburg, anti-corruption advocacy was taken up by various groups and individual activists concerned about local politics, but all of them had been addressing corruption-related questions in addition to their prime missions. Moreover, distrust and conflicting mutual perceptions among entrepreneurs, journalists and environmental activists hindered collective action. In this regard, ambivalent perceptions about the role of foreign assistance played a crucial role in this remote Siberian city.

During the early 2000s, some CSOs had conducted specific anti-corruption projects with the assistance of foreign grants. In 2004/2005, under a USAID programme, efforts were undertaken to pool the various local anti-corruption efforts by establishing an Anti-Corruption Coalition. This had inspired a more concerted anti-corruption discourse and a range of anti-corruption projects. However, a number of factors related to the particular context and timing contributed to the failure of this coalition: first, the various local groups had entered the coalition with rather different expectations. Most participants found it difficult to devote sufficient time and resources to the coalition as an end in itself. They welcomed it as a means for furthering their individual efforts, but did not understand themselves as anti-corruption advocates. Second, the coalition project fell into Putin's second term when domestic governance underwent a drastic recentralisation. After a rather promising start at a time when local administrations were eager to promote anti-corruption efforts (the Duma Anti-Corruption Coalition had just been established), several coincidences thus hampered the continuation of the coalition project, including controversies about the involvement of USAID funding in the Ukraine's Orange Revolution and, more decisively, the appointment of a Kremlin-loyal regional governor. Third, the design of the programme itself was perceived as bringing about a double burden of having to assume projects that not only had to meet the expectations of the US donors but were also judged against the successes of previous pilot coalitions in two other Russian regions. That the transfer of experiences even from one Russian city to another may always be difficult was also demonstrated by the competition held by the Third Millenium Fund in 2004. Yet the failure of the Irkutsk Coalition also determined further collaboration with Moscow-based anti-corruption networks for some local groups, as it impeded access to the network around TI-Russia while opening up links to the Kremlin-close movement *Protiv Korruptsii*. At a supra-regional level, this may have led to a further strengthening of cleavages between competing networks and inhibited strategically linked anti-corruption mobilisation.

This chapter has presented three rather different pictures of civic anti-corruption advocacy 'on the ground'. In Moscow, specific anti-corruption groups had emerged which had become increasingly influential throughout the Putin era. In St. Petersburg and Irkutsk, in contrast, a variety of CSOs had adopted corruption-related work as part of or in addition to their main missions and activities, which were very much focused on local politics. Yet collective action in this field had been hampered by the fact that most of these actors would not identify themselves as anti-corruption advocates. This was perhaps best illustrated by the efforts to establish an Anti-Corruption Coalition with the assistance of foreign funding in Irkutsk. Timing and contextual conditions played a crucial role in all cases. Moreover, in the latter two cities in particular, it seems that most of the developments outlined in Chapters 3, 4 and 5 disappear when zooming in to the local level. The following chapter will therefore return to a macro perspective and, by contrasting and summarising the analyses so far presented in the four empirical chapters, will elaborate on the nature and implications of the various link-ages between the actors and processes at the international and domestic levels and in different locations. On this basis, further conclusions regarding civil society involvement into transnational advocacy can be drawn.

Notes

1 Primarily as an anti-terrorism measure, Luzhkov started a community watch programme according to the Soviet system of 'house seniors', a network of informants with recruits in each apartment block who report suspicious persons and incidences to the police (Sandul 2004). Moreover, during a six-month pilot project (starting January 2006), more than 800 city officials had been lectured on how to treat the public with a modicum of respect. Reportedly, they were encouraged to view President Putin as a model of how to address members of the public (Osborn 2006).

2 Estimations of Moscow's number of inhabitants vary enormously, with many sources referring to the 10.4 million resulting from the 2002 census (cf. *Statistika Moskvy*, at: www.mosstat.ru (accessed 11/08/2006)). People living in Moscow tend to assume 12 million, considering the obvious mass of people not officially registered.

3 For example, a project 'For adequate and accessible housing' conducted by the Artists and Architects Union (presented in the documentary series on anti-corruption projects supported by the Eurasia Foundation, Eastern Siberian department of the Russian Union of Cameramen,

2001). See also Voltchkova and Zvetcova (2005) on foreign-funded anti-corruption trainings. Exchanges for investigative journalists were primarily supported by the US government and US private foundations and often implemented via US academic institutions. The Russian Union of Journalists was a main Russian partner.

4 See RSPP, at: www.rspp.ru (accessed 13/02/2009).

5 For example, the Association of the German Economy in the Russian Federation, by then the largest business community in Moscow with about 2,700 representations, stated by 2004 that almost half of all foreign investment would flow into Moscow (VDW 2004: 27). However, according to *Sotsial'ny atlas rossiiskikh regionov* (Social atlas of Russian regions), one needs to differentiate between Moscow city and Moscow oblast as well as between different periods of time: in 1996–99 about half of all investments went to Moscow city (43.8%), but considerably less to Moscow oblast (9.8%); the percentages went down for 2000–5 (city 25.3%, oblast 8.8%) and only increased again by 2006–7 (city 48.7%, oblast 8.4%) (see http://atlas.socpol.ru/overviews/econ_condition /index.shtml#globalization (accessed 20/01/2009)).

6 Kaliningrad became a Russian exclave surrounded by EU territory with the 2004 EU enlargement. The preceding negotiations thus included particular agreements between Russia and the EU, at first concerning a number of issues (including environmental protection) but then focusing on the transit regime and Kaliningrad's socio-economic development (European Commission 2001a, 2002). In 2002, the regional Duma in Kaliningrad passed a law 'On the procedure of disclosing information by the organs of the state authority in Kaliningrad oblast' (see *Pravo i sredstva massovoi informatsii*, at: www.medialaw.ru (accessed 23/11/2008)).

7 When I spent some days doing research at the office of TI-Russia in the summers of 2003 and 2004, the resource centre consisted of a shelf which contained some randomly selected booklets and papers. There were case studies, position papers, and project reports, mainly printed from the Internet and not dealing with Russia.

8 See TI-Russia, Proekty, at: www.transparency.org.ru/about_projects.asp (accessed 13/01/2009).

9 Since the launch of the Global Corruption Report in 2001, TI-Russia affiliates, other Russian and Western scholars and journalists had published chapters on Russia. In 2006, Russia remained absent from the report and in 2007/2008, contributions on Russia were written by Western authors only. See www.transparency.org/publications/gcr (accessed 05/02/2009).

10 See TI-Russia, Proekty, at: www.transparency.org.ru/about_projects.asp (accessed 13/01/2009).

11 The Youth Human Rights Movement is an international network of Russian origin (founded in 1998) with its administrative centre in Voronezh and its membership mainly within Eastern Europe (see www.yhrm.org/).

12 See *Antikorruptsionnyi setevoi kabinet*, at: http://askjournal.ru/ (accessed 28/01/2009).

13 The establishment of ALACs under the auspices of TI Chapters began in Eastern Europe and Central Asia in 2003 (see TI, ALACs, at: www.transparency.org/global_priorities/other_thematic_issues/alacs (accessed 28/01/2009)).

14 Interviews with representatives of TI-Russia, INDEM and NAK, 2004.

15 Other publications include, for example, an early article 'Russia and corruption: who wins?' (INDEM 1998) and a range of contributions on corruption and anti-corruption in relation to themes like elections, income levels, Internet usage, the business sector (see list of projects and publications at: www.anti-corr.ru/projects.htm#1998 (accessed 12/09/2008)).

16 Interview with a representative of INDEM, 2004.

17 The *Protiv Korruptsii* website kept referring to the 88 regions that officially existed by 2005 (regardless of subsequent mergers).

18 Interviews with representatives of *Protiv Korruptsii*, 2006, and of the CoE, 2007.

19 Interview with a representative of *Protiv Korruptsii*, 2006.

20 Putin spent much of his career in St. Petersburg, in the KGB and as assistant to the city's first post-Communist, reformist mayor, Anatoly Sobchak, who counts as one of Putin's former mentors. Accordingly, many officials in the president's administration and government had professional and personal ties to Putin dating back to the early 1990s (Duka and Rutland 2004: 56; Timtschenko 2003; Willerton 2005: 33–6).

21 St. Petersburg observers described the 2003 campaign as unprecedented with regard to the overwhelming use of administrative resources and media take-over (interview with two journalists, St. Petersburg, 2004/2005). At the domestic level, St. Petersburg was thus among the first regions where a Kremlin-friendly candidate had been successfully inserted during the governor election (see Coalson 2003), i.e. before the legislation was changed so that regional governors were to be appointed by the president (see Petrov 2005).

22 After Yakovlev had decided to oppose reformist mayor Sobchak in 1996, Putin considered him a personal enemy, even calling him 'Judas' (Slider 2005: 177).

23 Personal conversations with Moscow and St. Petersburg activists and journalists 2005, 2006.

24 Personal conversations during field research in St. Petersburg in 2003–5.

25 During field research in St. Petersburg in 2003 and 2005, I participated in various local press conferences, roundtables, seminars, and international conferences organised by different sub-networks. When asking other relevant (I assumed) local activists to join, they usually refused with comments like, 'We do not go to conferences in St. Petersburg', 'We were not invited', 'I have never been there', 'I know them and see them frequently, so I don't have to go to this event'.

26 These observations were confirmed for the civic scene in St. Petersburg in general; interview with a representative of a local NGO umbrella organisation, 2004.

27 Interviews with numerous local groups and individuals, 2003–5. This observation has been confirmed in interviews with local anti-corruption groups conducted by CISR in 2004 (CISR 2004).

28 See *Leontief Centre*, at: www.leontief.ru (accessed 07/09/2008).

29 Interviews with three representatives of Strategia, 2003 and 2005.

30 See Strategia, *Programmy i proekty*, at: www.strategy-spb.ru/?do=prog (accessed 12/09/2008).

31 For example: *Indeks vospriiatiia korruptsii 2002* and *Indeks vziatko-datelei* (in Strategia 2003: 435–448).

32 See *Grazhdanskii Kontrol'*, at: www.wplus.net/pp/citwatch/index.htm (accessed 07/01/2007).

33 Interview with a representative of *Grazhdanskii Kontrol'*, 2005.

34 After these two guide books (2004) had been distributed to police precincts, municipalities, NGOs, lawyers and libraries, the first edition (500 for police officers, 5,000 for crime victims) was soon exhausted while several hundred additional copies were requested, especially from St. Petersburg district administrations and the police administration (see *Graszhdanskii Kontrol'*, Protection of crime victims' rights, at: www.wplus.net/pp/citwatch/all_e.htm (accessed 07/08/2006)).

35 Interview with a representative of PRI, 2005.

36 See CISR, at: http://cisr.ru/ (accessed 11/12/2008).

37 In February/March 2008, the activities of the European University were suspended by a jurdical decision, officially because of 'violations of the fire safety code'. This incidence caused exceptional uproar in the Russian media and mobilised support among many foreign alumni and several American foundations (see www.eu.spb.ru (accessed 11/12/2008)).

38 Interviews and conversations with various representatives of CISR (during longer research stays at the institute in 2003, 2004 and 2005).

39 Participation in International Conference *Korporativnoe upravlenie, sotsial'naia otvetstvennost' i delovaia etika. Rol' biznesa v sovremen-nom obshchestve* (Corporate governance, social responsibility and business ethics: the role of business in present-day community life), and interviews with representatives of Strategia, CISR, and the UN Global Compact, 2005.

40 E.g. OECD Workshop 'Investment and Business Climate in the Russian Federation: A Regional Perspective', St. Petersburg, 9–10 November 2005 (financed by the European Commission).

41 See 10th St. Petersburg International Economic Forum, 13–15 June 2006, at: http://spbef.mk-studio.ru/en/ (accessed 23/07/2006).

42 Interview with a representative of The Institute for Information Freedom Development, 2005. See also the institute's website at www.svobodainfo.org (accessed 04/02/2009).

43 The lake holds 20% of the world's drinking water resources. It is further-more unique because it is the deepest lake (1,637m) on the globe, among the oldest (about 8 million years) and a habitat of various endemic species.

44 Social Atlas of Russian regions, Irkutsk Oblast, at: http://atlas.socpol.ru/portraits/irk.shtml (accessed 05/04/2006).

45 In general, the centralisation of financial resources to level-off crucial differences among the regions was perceived as a controversial method. In Irkutsk, salaries of officials in the regional administration were 2.2 times higher than the regional income average by 2004 (see Social Atlas of Russian regions, Irkutsk Oblast, at: http://atlas.socpol.ru/portraits/irk.shtml (accessed 05/04/2006)).

46 The management of the lake is thus also framed by an international convention which was adopted at the UN level in 1972: 'Convention concerning the Protection of the World Cultural and Natural Heritage'

(World Heritage, Convention), see UNESCO, World Heritage, at: http://whc.unesco.org/en/about/). For more details on international environmental advocacy in the Baikal region in this context, and local-level responses to it, see Schmidt (2002).

47 Severe socio-economic problems of Irkutsk oblast included very low income rates, high poverty levels, low quality of life, drug and street crime, teenage criminality, difficult access to medical services, increasing alcoholism, HIV/AIDS, and high mortality rates, which were even more pronounced in the highly subsidised but otherwise neglected agrarian hinterlands (local press, analysed 2003 and 2005).

48 On the socio-economic and cultural disparities between Irkutsk oblast and the Republic of Buryatia, and how these fed into environmental policy-making, see Schmidt (2002: 52–4).

49 That the mobilisation against the construction of the Transneft pipeline had proved successful within less than two months came as a surprise to the activists themselves: on 6 March 2006, a positive environmental assessment was issued. On 9 March, the Supreme Court rejected an appeal from environmentalists. On 20 April, Transneft still proclaimed that the project was 'safe'. On 26 April, Putin ordered the re-routing of the pipeline, referring to the ecological risk (Polotskii 2006).

50 According to the local press, the call of international organisations upon their clients to sell Transneft shares and reject Transneft's investment requests caused a dramatic slump in Transneft stocks from $US2,662 to $US580 (Polotskii 2006). According to the stock exchange data, however, Transneft shares gradually went down by about $US450 between January and April (cf. Russian Trading System, at: www.rts.ru (accessed 07/09/2006)).

51 Viktor Khristenko, Minister of Industry and Energy, was also sitting on the directorial board of Transneft.

52 The so-called 'civic ecological expertise' is a formally required independent assessment of ecological risks contained in grand construction and industrial projects. In the largely environmentally protected Baikal area, it was a frequent problem that false assessments provided by fake civil society institutions legalised highly questionable or even illegal construction projects (interviews and conversations with Russian environmentalists 2001–6).

53 *Otkrytaia Rossiia* granted $US67,000 to a USAID-supported resource centre in Samara (USAID 2004). Also personal participation in a round-table of local journalists under the banner of *Otkrytaia Rossiia* and interviews with a representative of RPI, both 2005.

54 On the range of the Wave's activities, including campaigns against illegal logging and pipeline constructions around Baikal, see www.baikalwave.eu.org (accessed 08/08/2008).

55 See TI's Forest Integrity Network (FIN), at: http://legacy.transparency .org/fin/index.html (accessed 16/06/2006).

56 Interviews with three local entrepreneurs who were locally known as anti-corruption advocates, 2005.

57 Participation in a meeting of the regional 'Association of Entrepreneurs', 2005.

58 The initiator underlined that only 5% of the shareholders voted against the financing of anti-corruption action. Reportedly, the fund was based on 33,000 shareholders and a volume of 700 million roubles of shares.

The competition was concluded by assigning the 2nd and 3rd places twice, since no article seemed worth the first place. 100,000 roubles were equivalent to about €3,000 at that time (interview with a representative of Third Millenium Fund, 2005).

59 Interviews with two local journalists, 2005.

60 One of the interviewees who had been seeking to expose crime and corruption in the region since the early 1990s had been frequently confronted with appeals to court, which usually ended in unreasonable financial fines. Once his car was burnt. Nevertheless, he was highly committed to continuing this investigative reporting.

61 Interviews with three local journalists and two editors of privately-owned newspapers, 2005.

62 See *Konkurs Proektov po preduprezhdeniiu korruptsii silami institutov grazhdanskogo obshchestva 15 noiabria 2000 – 1 iunia 2001*, at: www.eurasia.msk.ru/programs/corruption/grantees.html   (accessed 06/06/2006)).

63 Interviews with two representatives of the East Siberian Regional Branch of the Filmmakers Union of the Russian Federation, 2005.

64 If not otherwise indicated, the following paragraphs about the Coalition for Counteracting Corruption in Irkutsk Oblast are based on interviews with 11 Coalition members and personal participation in the council of the Coalition, 2005.

65 A total sum of US$206,000 was provided for the 15 projects (each lasting about 12 months); see www.eurasia.msk.ru/programs /corruption/default.html (accessed 06/06/2006).

66 See USAID, Public–Private Partnerships Against Corruption, at: www.usaid.gov/cgi-bin/documents/show_text.cgi?id=789&print =1&lang=en (accessed 30/10/2005).

67 See *Spisok Chlenov Koalitsii po protivodeistviiu korruptsii v Irkutskoi oblasti*, at: http://a-corruption.irkutsk.ru/files/members.doc (accessed 30/06/2005).

68 A list of over 60 downloadable brochures and booklets, together with draft laws and codes, survey results, and activity reports of all regional coalitions, was posted at http://rap-anticorruption.ru/?library (accessed 08/08/2006).

69 See Baikal Environmental Wave, at: www.baikalwave.eu.org/Eng /reports/rep060501.html (accessed 22/11/2008).

70 Also interview with two representatives of MSI, DC, 2007.

71 The RAP was nevertheless established in 2005, see RAP web-portal at: http://rap.stopcor.ru/ (accessed 28/01/2009).

72 Interview with a representative of TI-Russia, 2006.

73 See 'Anti-Corruption Coalition Proposes Amendments to Draft Federal Anti-Corruption Law,' at: http://vladivostok.usconsulate.gov/archive/rap .html (accessed 25/11/2005).

7

Lessons from a multi-contextual and procedural perspective

The empirical chapters in this book have traced anti-corruption activities at the international level (Chapters 3 and 4), at the domestic level in terms of governmental engagement (Chapter 5), and at the local level in terms of civil society engagement (Chapter 6). The reader may have gained the impression that Chapter 6 in particular presents a different world, or at least that the two worlds presented earlier (international actors and the government) were much more closely interrelated. It was important, however, to thoroughly map the developments in each of these dimensions in order to address the question of the involvement of civil society. With the following discussion it is now possible to zoom out again and consider the full picture of transnational anti-corruption advocacy in Russia. The following section elaborates on the nature, scope and impacts of the relationships between the actors at all three levels of analysis with regard to the core question of civil society involvement. It discusses how foreign funding opportunities were actually used by CSOs in the three cities studied and how the wealth of information generated with foreign funding was put to use. The next section then turns to the question of the success of international and domestic anti-corruption promoters in pushing the state towards accepting and implementing international standards. Building on the thorough multi-level process-tracing undertaken, it elaborates on the causalities and contingencies that contributed to changing state behaviour. Finally, the last section puts the case of anti-corruption advocacy (in Russia and beyond) into a wider perspective by outlining how it differed from earlier global movements.

Civil society involvement: three cities compared

The previous chapter has portrayed certainly not all, but the most relevant civic anti-corruption actors and activities in three Russian cities: Moscow, St. Petersburg and Irkutsk. Although theoretically local Russian activists were embedded into the same international and domestic contexts, as mapped in the preceding chapters, different features of these two contextual dimensions actually reached into the localities studied. Each local case study thus reveals a particular combination of linkages with the international and domestic domains, supplemented by particular local circumstances. When comparing civic anti-corruption activities in the three cities, and in the light of the findings about civil society involvement at the international and national levels, the most striking differences in the interrelations between international actors, local groups and the state can be found between Moscow and the rest of Russia. The main factors accounting for these differences are local governance patterns, the presence of (or access to) international organisations and foreign donors, and the specific, historically rooted characteristics of the local civil society scenes.

Outside Moscow: anti-corruption as an add-on

In Russian cities such as St. Petersburg and Irkutsk, something that may be called an anti-corruption activist scene was a rather temporary phenomenon, emerging and vanishing with foreign funding. Certainly, the anti-corruption idea as such did not merely present an imported idea. In all cities, some organisations and individuals had been concerned about corruption before the arrival of specific foreign grants. For many Russian groups in various fields, the interest in corruption and corruption prevention presented a natural by-product of their other more major concerns. When foreign grants specifically related to these issues arrived from the late 1990s, they thus met many resonance points. Without doubt, many highly motivated and also relevant corruption-related projects were conducted.

However, interactions between Russian CSOs and their foreign partners remained largely limited to sporadic grant-based projects. As outlined in Chapter 4, assistance to civil society presented a relatively minor share of the overall anti-corruption assistance provided to Russia, mainly through the government. Moreover, civil society assistance came from different sources and under separate programmes and mostly had a strong local or regional focus. Altogether this entailed a constriction of the perspective of local actors towards the overall anti-corruption venture. While focusing on the implementation of their various projects, CSOs inevitably lost sight of the simultaneously unfolding relations between the Russian government and international agents. Most of the international activities outlined in Chapter 3 proved to be hardly known and of little importance to local groups that had been conducting anti-corruption projects.[1] This isolating effect was reinforced by other external as well as domestic conditions.

On the part of the donor organisations, it is important to notice that financial assistance for civic anti-corruption projects was offered by donors who had been in the country before. This implied that anti-corruption assistance heavily built on pre-existing donor–recipient structures and relations, including commonly acknowledged practices such as the confinement of a project to a fixed time frame and rather concrete, predetermined outputs. Beyond that, it was clear to both donors and project leaders that there would not be any further interaction on this issue, unless there was another grant agreement. Even if there was an interest in continuing a particularly fruitful donor–recipient relationship, the existing structures and practices of foreign assistance usually prohibited longer-term interaction and exchange. Moreover, groups that had adopted anti-corruption projects were usually not the kind of activist organisations that were actively seeking an opportunity to initiate or hook up to campaigns in this field that would have involved other international actors than donors (a few environmental or human rights groups that had led sporadic corruption-related projects preferred to concentrate on wider campaigning on these core issues).

Many Russian groups, being overly dependent on foreign funding and having become accustomed to flexibly adjusting their medium-term planning to the changing programmes and preferences of relevant donors, had adopted anti-corruption projects as a temporary side-task. Not surprisingly, thus, many of these projects had remained half-hearted and unsustainable ventures. For many Russian leaders of anti-corruption projects it was clear that, if there was no foreign support for another corruption-related project, their organisation would not conduct any further work in this area.[2] The outcomes of once-finalised projects, in most cases information presented in the form of brochures, books, or other kinds of publications, were piling up in their offices. Project-related websites were abandoned. While an organisation sought to move on with what it considered their main mission, its members had neither the time nor the relevant networks for further distributing previously produced materials, however valuable they would have been for others. Moreover, with corruption-related projects merely presenting an add-on, the local circles of CSOs remained clustered along traditional patterns and showed little interest in searching for possible synergies with other groups within or beyond their cities. This may also have been a main reason for the tendency that anti-corruption projects, which had been designed as regional projects by the donors, were actually only implemented on the municipal level.

An extreme case of adopting anti-corruption advocacy as an add-on to their main missions was presented by the effort of building regional Anti-Corruption Coalitions through external funding (see Irkutsk). This had confronted a variety of existing Russian organisations, including oppositional activists, social-service and education-oriented groups and business associations as much as groups close to the government, with the task of coordinating themselves around the issue of corruption prevention. The various groups had to pursue this task in addition to their ongoing work and networking in other fields, and for those Coalition member organisations that had won a small grant, also in addition to realising a concrete anti-corruption project under the roof of the Calition. In Irkutsk, a place with a strong history of civic engagement, the Coalition venture eventually failed not least because many of the participants decided to return to what they perceived to be their main mission and to acquiring funding more closely related to the latter.

The domestic context of increasingly authoritarian governance also affected CSOs in the regions differently than in the core Moscow-based circle of anti-corruption groups. By the mid-2000s local CSOs encountered new difficulties when authoritarianisation reached into regional governance with the insertion of Kremlin-loyal regional leaders (as in St. Petersburg in 2004 and in Irkutsk in 2005). In Moscow, there was not such a change with Luzhkov staying on as the Mayor and Governor throughout the whole period studied (in fact since 1992 and until the time of writing). In terms of anti-corruption efforts, this mainly affected those groups who had actively sought interaction with their local or regional administrations since previously established relationships with the latter were disturbed. Examples are the Irkutsk Anti-Corruption Coalition or pro-reform, elitist St. Petersburg groups such as the Leontief Centre or *Grazhdanskii Kontrol'*. The anti-corruption projects of Strategia (St. Petersburg), in turn, were less impaired since this organisation was primarily oriented towards CSOs in other regions. Only this organisation further maintained a focus on anti-corruption, not least through collaborative projects with TI-Russia. Also journalists in both regions experienced new challenges under the new governors, although this was more related to their work in general. Investigative journalism concerned with corruption had been problematic already before this centralisation of regional governance since such work was inevitably affronting somebody among the local politico-economic elites. Finally, research groups or business consultancy organisations that had been dealing with corruption-related issues were less affected in this work by the more restrictive governance contexts since they had usually distanced themselves from politics, however critical their individual members may have been of the Putin administration in general.

The changing governance course under the Putin administration as well as the government's changing anti-corruption commitment were perceived differently by domestic and international actors. Among Russian CSOs themselves there was a general disbelief in the governmental anti-corruption efforts, yet this was rarely grounded on precise insights into these efforts. As mentioned, even in the framework of concrete civic anti-corruption projects, federal politics had hardly been an issue. Among the international actors, donor organisations that were oriented towards Russian CSOs as recipients tended to make more general judgements about the course of governance reforms under the Putin administration. Throughout the period studied, some of them had experienced outright conflicts with the government and sought to adapt to the changing context in different ways from the mid-2000s. Among the main private foundations in the anti-corruption field, some had again excluded corruption-related issues from their portfolio. The Soros Foundation, which had backed out of Russia in 2003, had nevertheless continued to indirectly provide pertinent assistance to anti-corruption projects in Russia, for example through its Budapest office. In contrast, the major international organisations or, more precisely, the particular units of those organisations concerned with anti-corruption promotion in Russia, had been interacting primarily with the government. While the latter appeared quite committed to international collaboration against corruption, these international actors had maintained a rather optimistic stance throughout the whole period under consideration. International protest against Putin's authoritarian turn came more from other international organisations or from other departments within organisations such as the CoE, the UN, the EU, the World Bank or USAID that were primarily concerned with democracy promotion in Russia.

Moscow: bundling anti-corruption advocacy

In principle, Moscow-based organisations were equally affected by the tendencies outlined above, and indeed this city had seen many sporadic and fragmented anti-corruption projects led by a variety of organisations as well. However, in addition, Moscow presented a unique locus of more substantial and sustainable interaction between Russian CSOs and international agents other than merely grant-providing donors. Throughout the period studied, the involvement of Russian CSOs in the anti-corruption promotion of external agents and respective efforts of the government had been intensifying. Knowledge that had once been generated – with or without foreign funding – was further continued and put to use. This was due to a variety of respects in which Moscow differed from the other cities studied.

First of all, specific anti-corruption organisations which could devote the bulk of their efforts to these issues existed only in Moscow. Although the three most specialised Moscow-based organisations – TI-Russia, NAK and *Protiv*

Korruptsii – differed from each other in their organisational make-up and agendas, their emergence and their subsequent activities were closely interrelated. In fact, these organisations presented quite contrary organisational models: TI-Russia was from the very beginning the most internationally linked and supported Russian anti-corruption organisation. Its close affiliation with the global TI network, which was very different from a donor–recipient relationship, had proved of considerable advantage and had clearly sparked the most far-reaching and sustainable civic anti-corruption engagement. Even if project-based in terms of funding, the fact that all the foreign-funded projects were somehow related to corruption prevention allowed TI-Russia more flexibility in using its different budgets for an overall mission.[3] Moreover, the location in Moscow entailed easier access to funds, necessary juridical help, and to the nodal points of other networks, both domestic and international. NAK, established at about the same time as TI-Russia (on the initiative of INDEM) presented a large elitist circle of people close to the government, had never used foreign grants, and actually remained unknown to the international community. It actively lobbied governmental anti-corruption reforms at the federal level. TI-Russia, NAK and INDEM (the 'head' behind most corruption-related studies actively used by the former two) were collaborating closely. Beyond that, TI-Russia was not as actively involved in networks across the Russian regions as the TI-S believed. However, the stark concentration on Moscow, and on federal rather than municipal policy-making even proved to be a major bonus. *Protiv Korruptsii*, in turn, emerged in 2005 as a government-supported organisation and mainly in reaction to the survey-based knowledge about corruption in Russia which was produced by INDEM and actively disseminated by the latter and TI-Russia.

Furthermore, collaboration between the Duma Anti-Corruption Commission and the CoE had been intensifying at that time and the latter paid strong attention to including Russian CSOs and civic expertise in official anti-corruption projects. TI-Russia, or more precisely its director, had become the main addressee for the CoE. INDEM's surveys that provided the most comprehensive, methodologically sound, and up-to-date evidence about corruption across

Russia were thus also presented directly to the CoE and gained more leverage as similar trends about growing corruption levels were also attested by the CPI and the World Bank's BEEPS in 2005. This inspired the establishment of a counter-organisation working more closely with the Duma. By that time, while the Putin administration was about to curtail the relationships between domestic CSOs and foreign donors in general, through various means, it could not afford to act with direct repressive measures against these particular Moscow anti-corruption groups. The government's own relationships with external anti-corruption promoters had been unfolding in a positive way and it seemed a more promising strategy to supplement and co-opt existing expertise by inserting *Protiv Korruptsii* as a new, allegedly nongovernmental player into the anti-corruption field. Indeed, representatives of the CoE and GRECO seemed not to be bothered by the quasi-governmental character of this organisation.[4] There were no controversies about its participation as a Russian NGO in the RUCOLA-II assistance project of the CoE and during the onsite visit of the GRECO evaluation team.

Importantly, also in the case of these Moscow organisations that had been devoted to anti-corruption efforts over a longer time period (more than just one grant-based project), an ongoing process could be observed that involved testing, learning and persistence. It was an incremental process and for some organisations it took almost a decade before viable strategies were found or substantial results could be seen. In the case of TI, this process further entailed ongoing mutual reconciliation between the TI-S and the Russian Chapter.

A process involving causalities and contingencies

From the preceding analysis, further conclusions can be drawn about a core question that students of transnational advocacy are concerned with, that is, the question about the successfulness of that advocacy in increasing a target state's commitment to subscribe to and implement international norms. In this regard, anti-corruption advocacy in Russia may be considered as a successful case: the government started with more rhetorical rather than substantial commitment towards the international community and with prosecutorial rather then preventive anti-corruption action; it had been vulnerable to international and domestic information politics; and it had eventually actively furthered the ratification and implementation of key international anti-corruption conventions (including legalistic measures, judicial and administrative reforms, subjection to external monitoring, and inclusion of civil society actors). However, when reconsidering the processes traced at the international, national and local levels more thoroughly, it becomes clear that this has not been the result of neatly interlocking forces or synergies between consistent norm promotion from above and below. Only a few Moscow-based, specialised organisations were able to persistently engage in anti-corruption advocacy throughout the whole period under consideration, and only those organisations could eventually play an influential role in the interaction between international organisations and the state. Still, the Russian state's intensifying commitment to international anti-corruption standards came as a protracted and at times indirect reaction to various contingent developments rather than as part of a generalisable causal chain.

When seeking to identify more general causalities, one has to first of all acknowledge that the analysed advocacy process had started with an inverse take-off from the very beginning. In contrast to prominent concepts that ascribe the first initiative to domestic NGOs seeking the help of more powerful external actors (Keck and Sikkink 1998; Risse and Sikkink 1999), transnational anti-corruption advocacy in general had started from the international level in the first place. Although civil society presented a main driving force in this case as well, it was represented not by some domestic organisations that were concerned about their particular country, but by TI as a rather influential international NGO (INGO) that had been expanding globally in search of domestic member organisations. This advocacy further came with unexceptional force since IFIs, other intergovernmental organisations, INGOs, Western national aid agencies and private foundations, which had taken up on the issue, had been targeting not only one particular state but several states at once. These actors, in turn, were committed to foster the participation of civil society, both international and domestic, as a supporting force. The Russian state was part of the

Eastern European region, which presented a particular focus for international anti-corruption promoters. Moreover, when Putin came to power, such anti-corruption promotion had already been established for some years. He thus took up on a pre-existing discourse, not least in order to distance himself from his predecessor with the promise to tackle one major problem that had become rampant in Russia during the 1990s. In a similar fashion, Putin's successor Medvedev soon after his appointment proceeded to realise one of the main remaining failures in Putin's anti-corruption efforts, namely the adoption of a specific national anti-corruption strategy and respective legislation. That Medvedev also went on to change essential aspects of the overall official approach to anti-corruption, such as a further strengthening of presidential institutions and of the investigative powers of the PGO and the FSB while abolishing previously active and influential agents such as the Duma Anti-Corruption Commission, may be part of the general pattern that a change in government presents a major moment in the course of international norm promotion.

Furthermore, to a substantial degree the intensifying commitment of the Russian state was reinforced by various contingent developments – and cumulative synergies between them. As underlined above, a core impetus was given in 2005 by the dissemination of comprehensive survey data about corruption in different sectors and across Russia gathered by INDEM. As INDEM could refer to a similar survey dating from 2001, it provided evidence for an alarming rise in corruption levels during Putin's presidency. Still, this information may not have been that influential, had it not been accompanied by similar international evidence as well as an increased emphasis on the part of the CoE in incorporating civic expertise in a major technical assistance project started in cooperation with the Duma Anti-Corruption Commission during that same year. TI's 2005 CPI suddenly interrupted a seemingly steady and positive trend of decreasing corruption in Russia since Putin had assumed office. This trend seemed further confirmed by the World Bank/EBRD's BEEPS, the first two of which had portrayed corruption as a decreasing problem for firms between 1999 and 2002, whereas the third one in 2005 also pointed to rising corruption.

In principle, the general assumption that information presents a main asset for domestic and international and domestic norm promoters and for them a main means of exerting pressure would be confirmed in the Russian context as well. However, the observed process was not an example of the conventional definition of 'information politics' as 'the ability to quickly and credibly generate politically usable information and move it to where it will have the most impact' (Keck and Sikkink 1998: 16). As outlined, lots of information had been generated in the given case that was rarely circulated among the domestic civic community, had never been taken seriously by local or federal administrations, and had never been fed back into external anti-corruption promotion. Instead, in 2005, it proved crucial what kind of information was provided and by whom. Importantly, it was not evidence about corruption in Russia that mattered, but evidence about growing corruption. This in turn had required constant and systematic information-gathering over a longer period of time. As mentioned in Chapter 4, it seemed not to matter that, methodologically, the CPI in particular was not a reliable indicator for trends over time. The effect of these data was strengthened by the double fact that several influential actors, both domestic and international, simultaneously came up with data supporting this claim *and* that the Russian government found itself unable to present any systematically gathered data about corruption in Russia. Moreover, by then INDEM could count as an influential actor since its data were frequently cited by TI-Russia, which had turned into the main provider of civic expertise about corruption in Russia to external actors (e.g. since 2005 directly to the CoE). This effect also had ambivalent implications, such as the government's struggles for the monopoly on information about corruption in Russia and its own strategic provision of much information about this issue. Not least, this resulted in an overflow of less relevant information.

Finally, that all this happened at the eve of Russia's first G8 presidency in 2006, added considerable momentum to the subsequent developments. When the 2006 G8 Summit in St. Petersburg was used by TI for another international anti-corruption campaign, Russia could seize this as an opportunity to distinguish itself not only from the post-

Communist world in terms of the level and format of inter-action; it could also demonstrate that it was ahead of most of the other G8 countries which had not ratified the UNCAC by that time (Canada, Germany, Italy, Japan, the United States). In contrast to most approaches to anti-corruption promotion that had grouped Russia with other Eastern European countries, this event was more attractive for an ex-superpower to distinguish itself among equals. By ratifying both the UNCAC and the CoE Criminal Law Convention on Corruption in the context of that G8 presidency and summit, Russia simply had to proceed with additional steps, such as another technical assistance project with the CoE and the CoE monitoring procedure (both of which further strengthened the inclusion of civic expertise) and a new engagement with legal reforms.

It also has to be noted that the growing commitment of the Russian government to international collaboration in this field, and the strengthening links between the government and the international community which largely bypassed civil society, had unfolded against the background of other country-specific contingencies. First, crucial anti-corruption assistance had only been offered to Russia since the early 2000s, thus increasing the external leverage in this field during the Putin era. For example, EIB lending and UNDP assistance, provided since 2001, had been expanded in 2003/2004 and the latter especially had moved from implicitly to explicitly supporting anti-corruption measures. Second, under the Putin administration, Russia could document some early successes. Incidents such as the country's fast removal from the FATF blacklist of non-cooperative countries (2002), its comparatively strong commitment to international anti-corruption conventions in contrast to other ACN countries, or Russia's bettering CPI during the early years under Putin had contributed to a growing confidence in this president's anti-corruption commitment on the part of the international community and to an increasing self-confidence on the part of the Russian state. Furthermore, other minor contingencies further influenced the direction of the government's changing anti-corruption course while equally contributing to a positive image of the Russian government. For example, that corruption in the judiciary had become a major issue in Russia had been a longer-term development that had started with a respective focus contained in the first RUCOLA project conducted by the CoE and the Duma Anti-Corruption Commission (2005). The latter then proposed this issue to UNODC as a priority theme for further collaboration (2006). Also in 2006, after the sudden dismissal of prosecutor general Ustinov, a comprehensive reform of the PGO and of the judiciary was started under the new prosecutor general Chaika. In 2007, Russia's ministry of economics, MERiT, started a multimillion Judicial Reform Programme with the World Bank. When the GRECO evaluation was conducted in 2008, which again encountered the problem of corruption in the judiciary, the government could thus credibly underline that there was a political will to tackle this problem.

Anti-corruption advocacy: not a classic global movement

This book has presented a thorough analysis of transnational anti-corruption advocacy on the ground in one particular country, Russia. By illuminating the involvement of Russian CSOs in three cities within this country, it has revealed a dynamic and complex process that eventually led to a bundling of civic expertise in the Russian capital and to the integration of that particular expertise into both international and governmental anti-corruption efforts. The analysis has further shown that, although the analysed anti-corruption advocacy process considered contained its own internal dynamics, it was embedded into wider contexts such as the transformation of Russian domestic and foreign politics under the Putin administration as well as wider structural changes affecting transnational norm promotion in general. When considering the full picture, the problem of insufficient civil society involvement may thus only partly be explained by developments in the particular Russian context at the time of study. In addition, the very roles of CSOs and international actors in this particular issue area were different from those observed in earlier global campaigns or movements.

Domestically, increasing authoritarianism and a clampdown on independent – especially oppositional and foreign-funded – CSOs certainly had a major impact on a number of Russian organisations that had, amongst others, been conducting anti-corruption projects. One should notice, however, that foreign funding for these particular projects had already vanished before the government started more strategic measures of co-opting or restricting Russian civil society. This decrease in funding was due to a number of reasons, including the retreat of a major donor from the country (Soros Foundation) and the return of other Western private foundations to less political and more social service-oriented issues, but also the acknowledgement of donors that Russian CSOs were better networked and more influential in other issue areas, or the coinciding revision of a major donor's overall portfolio (Ford Foundation). Moreover, detrimental side-effects of tensions between the government and foreign donors supporting civil society and structural changes pervading transnational assistance in general (see below) may have been exceptionally strong in the Russian context, where civic organisations and activists had remained overly dependent on foreign financial assistance. Finally also, the eventually successful integration of some core civic groups into anti-corruption efforts at the highest political level may have been fostered by the strategy of many Russian groups at that time to work closer to a more authoritarian state rather than against it, thus partly returning to Soviet-style practices of advocating political change through channels within the political system.[5]

But also the global anti-corruption movement in general has been very different from earlier global movements, such as those in human rights or in environmental protection, in many respects. Many general assumptions based on the analysis of those classic movements thus cannot be upheld. First of all, except for TI, its National Chapters, and very few domestic CSOs, there had hardly been any specialised anti-corruption organisations that would be comparable to the flocks of human rights or environmental organisations. The latter existed in Russia as well, and they indeed experienced more repression than organisations in the anti-corruption field during the Putin era. Struggles against corruption involved a wide and at times controversial set of issues and accordingly attracted a large variety of pre-existing agents, both at the international and domestic levels, who had taken on these themes as a side-task. Thereby, 'diverse actors normally at odds with each other' (Sampson 2005: 110), who simultaneously pursued a wide variety of approaches related to the multifaceted concerns about corruption, were brought together. In this case the premise no longer holds true that transnational campaigns 'are sets of strategically linked activities in which members of a diffuse principled network ... develop explicit, visible ties and mutually recognized roles in pursuit of a common goal (and generally against a common target)' (Keck and Sikkink 1998: 6). The many anti-corruption promoters had rarely linked their various activities. At the international level, general efforts to arrive at a more strategic division of labour have occurred only most recently and as part of a learning process stretching across two decades. Within a particular target state, as the Russian case demonstrates, coordination may remain at a minimum even up to the point where different anti-corruption promoters worked with the same beneficiaries on similar issues in the context of implementing the international conventions. Moreover, the local case studies presented here show how the adoption of anti-corruption measures as a side-task by domestic organisations may overstrain their capacities.

Second, by the time the anti-corruption cause had been taken up by existing international agents, these agents had already become major linchpins of a highly structured and rather technical system of transnational collaboration, aid and advocacy. The emergence of the anti-corruption regime could thus heavily build on pre-existing agents, structures and discourses through which resources, information and services could be exchanged. International financial institutions, including the World Bank, the IMF, or the EBRD, international organisations such as the UN, the OECD, the CoE, or the EU as well as many national foundations and private donor agencies have taken the issue on board. Especially in Eastern Europe, it could link with a comprehensive system of democracy-promoting structures and discourses that had emerged since the early 1990s. On this basis, the subsequent anti-corruption venture was not only an extremely comprehensive one, supplied with enormous human and financial resources. It was also an exceptionally professional venture. Although the debates about corruption in Eastern Europe were often not less value-laden than human rights or environmental discourses, the problem of corruption was also linked to a number of issues related to economic or security aspects. More importantly perhaps, having incorporated 'anti-corruption' as a cross-cutting issue in most pre-existing or ongoing intergovernmental arrangements, it has been dealt with on a rather technical basis and as a matter to be addressed in direct interaction between international organisations and governments.

The Russian case illustrates that very few CSOs became involved in these interactions on the basis of concrete contracts and via the government; they were delivering services and additional information rather than playing an oppositional role. This was not only a result of increasing centralisation in this particular country. From the perspective of most Russian CSOs, in turn, donor organisations presented the main contacts. The latter however, played only a minor role in the whole venture. The grants provided to CSOs for corruption-related projects were negligible compared to the assistance provided to the government. In addition, these grants commonly supported projects without any focus on federal politics. Moreover, from the donor side, budgets were commonly tied to particular programmes that served changing issues in the course of shifting international preferences or country strategies. The analysis of the Russian case shows that, thereby, considerable volumes of anti-corruption assistance had been devoted to many sporadic, indirect, and short-term activities in the civic sphere which proved of minor relevance to a prolonged process of transnational advocacy. Obviously, this entailed the duplication of much work and many products – which actually did not feed back into the overall anti-corruption venture – as well as a distraction of time and resources from other areas of civic engagement.

This chapter has pointed to some aspects relating to the character of external anti-corruption advocacy in general. These are highly relevant not only with regard to the Russian case. Overall, the global anti-corruption venture thus has to be conceptualised in a way that is rather different from earlier concepts of transnational advocacy as combined pressure from above and below, exerted onto certain target states by domestic civil society and international actors. Instead, it is a highly structuralised and professionalised venture building on a comprehensive system of international actors and structures that are experienced in and primarily oriented to interacting with governments directly. These interactions may build on considerable financial and human resources (assistance programmes; specialised departments or agencies), are framed by international treaties, and involve an increasing share of information directly exchanged between the governments and international agents (monitoring regimes). As Figure 1 illustrates, interaction between domestic CSOs and their governments and other relevant public bodies have to unfold in the shadow of these existing and relatively strong routines of interaction.

Civil society organisations 'on the ground' have become involved in this venture largely on the basis of contracts and other formal arrangements, mainly in the form of formally accredited National Chapters of TI or through grants provided for concrete projects. Moreover, civic anti-corruption projects have tended to remain isolated from government-oriented efforts where small grants were provided to CSOs through separate programmes offered by bilateral donor organisations and private foundations. The latter programmes tended to bear a stronger focus on local coalition-building and reform and to involve a wide variety of nongovernmental actors who are not necessarily specialised in anti-corruption matters. Via subcontracting arrangements, domestic CSOs may at times also become involved in programmes implemented by IFIs and intergovernmental organisations (as providers of additional information and services). While much emphasis is currently being placed on the implementation of international anti-corruption conventions, and on the accompanying monitoring regimes and assistance programmes, it remains unclear whether this will contribute to opening up new avenues or to further narrowing down the already meagre potential for civil society involvement in the future. On the one hand, there might be a tendency to provide more room for the integration of civic expertise in official projects and evaluations, as exemplified in the context of CoE assistance strategies and GRECO evaluations. On the other hand, highly structured evaluation procedures envisage civic participation to be arranged via the government and tend to rely on TI Chapters as representatives of domestic civil society. In addition, implementing the

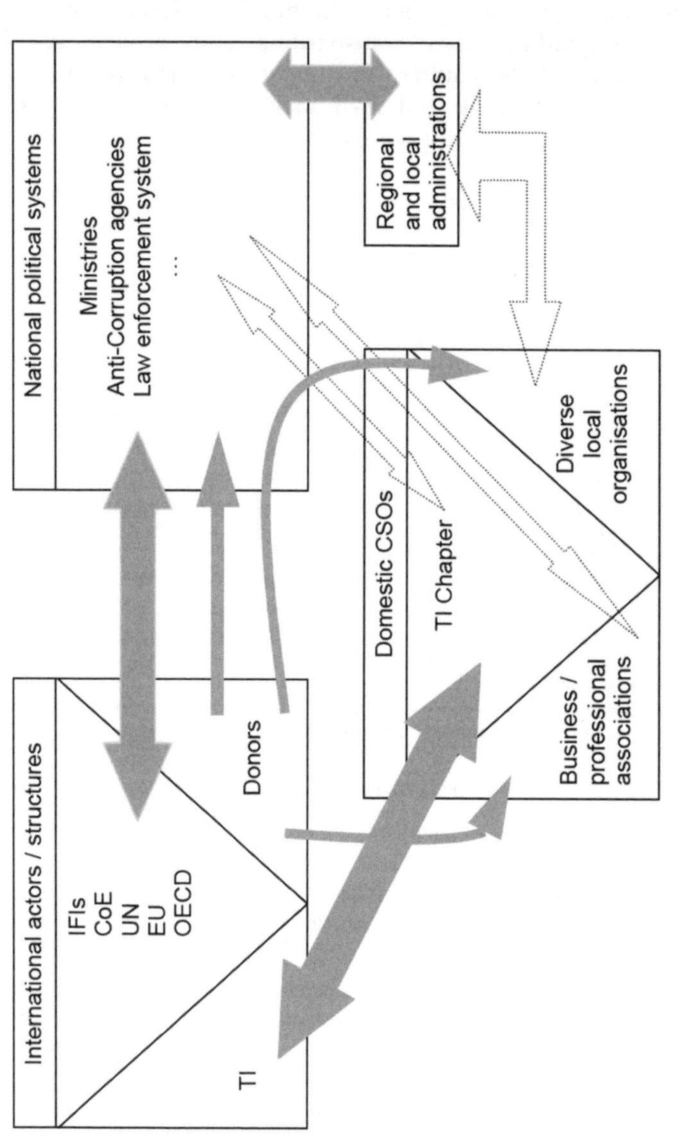

Figure 1   *Transnational anti-corruption advocacy: domestic CSOs in the shadow of established routines of interaction*

anti-corruption conventions implies mainly legal and administrative reforms in order to criminalise corruption and to provide for preventive measures as well as international cooperation in order to tackle the problem of transnational corruption and the task of transnational asset recovery. What this means for the patterns of interaction between international, governmental, and civil society actors remains an important issue for future research.

Notes

1 Although this was primarily true for groups in the regions, even TI-Russia could not manage to keep on track with the developments regarding all relevant international instruments. For example, the 2004 report on Russia, which was set up by members of TI-Russia as part of the TI Global Corruption Report (Kupchinsky, Chirkova and Savintseva 2004), did not list more than the signatures of the CoE Criminal Law Convention (1999) and the UN Convention on Organised Crime (2000). Other issues went unnoticed, such as Russia's involvement in the ACN, its desire for membership in and its rapprochement towards the OECD Working Group on Bribery, or its signature and ratification of the CoE Anti-Money-Laundering Convention and technical assistance projects in this area, which were important stepping stones for initiating closer relations between the CoE and Russia also in the anti-corruption field.

2 In all three cities (with the exception of the specialised Moscow anti-corruption groups discussed below) a common and outright response to my question on whether the interviewees planned to continue their corruption-related engagement was, 'If we get funding for it, yes. But if we do not get any funding, we will not do anything related to corruption any more.'

3 In an interview, one representative of TI-Russia also stated: 'We do not see our work in terms of projects. Although maybe jumping on from project to project, we keep a general focus' (2004).

4 Interview with a representative of the CoE, 2007.

5 For example, leading Russian human rights organisations such as the Soldiers' Mothers or parts of the Russian environmental movement sought to set up political parties (on the latter, see Vorobyev 2005). Leading individual activists also participated in the quasi-nongovernmental structures erected by the state, such as Liudmila Alekseeva in the Civic Chamber that received much criticism on the part of Western practitioners and scholars. Alekseeva was in fact also a member of the expert council to the quasi-governmental anti-corruption movement *Protiv Korruptsii*. People working in (state) universities presented another particularly influential group. On civic engagement from within the state during Soviet times, see Lewin (1991).

References

Abramo, Claudio Weber. 2005. *How Far Go Perceptions*, Working Paper: Transparência Brasil.

ACN. 2003. *Anti-Corruption Action Plan for Armenia, Azerbaijan, Georgia, the Russian Federation, Tajikistan and Ukraine*, 5th Annual Meeting of the Anti-Corruption Network for Transition Economies, 10 September 2003, Istanbul, Turkey.

———. 2005. *Glossary of International Anti-Corruption Standards with Examples of National Legal Practice*, Draft. The Anti-Corruption Network for Transition Economies, 6th General Meeting, 30–31 May 2005, Istanbul, Turkey. Paris: Anti-Corruption Network for Transition Economies/ OECD.

ACN/OECD. 2005. *The Anti-Corruption Network for Transition Economies. 6th General Meeting, Meeting Report*, 30–31 May 2005, OECD Centre for Private Sector Development, Istanbul, Turkey. Paris: ACN/OECD.

ADB et al. 2006. *International Financial Institutions Anti-Corruption Task Force.* www.ebrd.com/about/integrity /task.pdf.

AFP. 2006. Putin ratifies UN Corruption Convention. *Agence France Presse*, online edition, 20 March.

Agar, Michael H. 1980. *The Professional Stranger. An Informal Introduction to Ethnography*. London/New York: Academic Press.

Agreement on Partnership and Cooperation 1997. L/CE/RU/en 1.

Anderson, James H. and Cheryl W. Gray. 2006. *Anticorruption in Transition 3. Who Is Succeeding ... and Why?* Washington, DC: The International Bank for

Reconstruction and Development / World Bank.

Anechiarico, Frank and James B. Jacobs. 1996. *The Pursuit of Absolute Integrity. How Corruption Control Makes Government Ineffective*. Chicago/London: The University of Chicago Press.

Arbatova, Nadezhda. 2007. Russia-EU Quandary 2007. *Russia in Global Affairs* (2).

Argumenty i fakty. 2005. Press Conference with INDEM Fund President Georgy Satarov on corruption Index Studies in Russia. *AIF Press Center*, 20 July.

Athanassopoulou, Ekavi, ed. 2005. *Fighting Organized Crime in Southeast Europe*. London/New York: Routledge.

Bel'skaia, Ol'ga. 2003. *Preduprezhdenie*, Dokumental'nyi film: IROO Baikal'skaia Ekologicheskaia Volna.

Bondarenko, Sergey. 2002. *Korrumpirovannye Obshchestva*. Rostov on Don: Westminster Foundation for Democracy/ Centre for Applied Research on Intellectual Property.

Borko, Yuri. 2004. Rethinking Russia-EU Relations. *Russia in Global Affairs* (3).

Börzel, Tanja A., Andreas Stahn and Yasemin Pamuk. 2010. The European Union and the fight against Corruption in its near abroad. Can it make a difference? In *Anti-Corruption for Eastern Europe*, Global Crime, special issue, 11(2), D. Schmidt-Pfister and H. Moroff (eds).

Brewer, John D. 2000. *Ethnography*. Buckingham/ Philadelphia: Open University Press.

Burawoy, Michael, ed. 2000. *Global Ethnography. Forces, Connections, and Imaginations in a Postmodern World*. Berkeley: University of California Press.

Chelovek i Zakon. 2006. Sobytiia: detali antikorruptsionno-go konkursa. *Zhelovek i Zakon. Ministerstvo Iustitsii Rossiiskoi Federatsii*, 28 April.

Chudodeev, Aleksandr. 2006. Indeks revolutsii (Interview with Elena Panfilova, TI-Russia). *Itogi.ru*, No. 45/491, 5 November.

CISR. 2004. *Anti-Corruption Field in St. Petersburg. Actors and Activities*, Final report. Prepared within the frame of Think Tank Partnership project 'Mobilising social support to fight corruption in postsocialist countries: cases of Russia and Hungary'. St. Petersburg: Centre for Independent Social Research, unpublished document.

Coalson, Robert. 2003. Can the Kremlin Really Fight

Corruption? *RFE/RL Russian Political Weekly* 3 (28).

Coulloudon, Virginie. 2002. Russia's distorted anticorruption campaigns. In *Political Corruption in Transition. A Sceptic's Handbook*, S. Kotkin and A. Sajó (eds). Budapest/New York: CEU Press, 187–206.

Council of Europe. 1996. *Programme of Action Against Corruption*, GMC (96) 95. Strasbourg.

——. 1999a. *Civil Law Convention on Corruption*, European Treaty Series No. 174. Strasbourg.

—— 1999b. *Criminal Law Convention on Corruption*, European Treaty Series No. 173. Strasbourg.

—— 2000. *Country Report – Russian Federation*, Octopus (2000) 54 final. Strasbourg.

——. 2002. *Crime Analysis*, Organised crime – Best practice survey no. 4, PC-S-CO (2002) 2E, Strasbourg, 22 July 2002. Strasbourg.

——. 2005. *Organised Crime Situation Report 2005. Focus on the Threat of Economic Crime*, Council of Europe Octopus Programme. Strasbourg: CoE, Department of Crime Problems, Directorate General of Legal Affairs.

——. 2006. *Project 'Harmonisation of Russian Anti-Corruption Legislation with International Standards' (RUCOLA)*. Final Report (internal document). Strasbourg: European Commission/Council of Europe.

——. 2008. *Project 'Russian Federation – Development of Legislative and Other Measures for the Prevention of Corruption' (RUCOLA-2)*, Final Report. Strasbourg: Council of Europe/European Commission.

Creswell, John W. 2003. *Research Design. Qualitative, Quantitative, and Mixed Methods Approaches*. 2nd edn. Thousand Oaks/London/New Delhi: Sage.

DCD/DAC. 2003. *Synthesis of Lessons Learned of Donor Practices in Fighting Corruption*, DCD/DAC/GOVNET (2003) 1, Report prepared for the DAC Network on Governance by a team of consultants led by Mr Bruce B. Bailey, commissioned by the OECD: DAC Network on Governance.

De Sousa, Luis. 2009. TI in search of a constituency: the institutionalization and franchising of the global anti-corruption doctrine. In *Governments, NGOs and Anti-Corruption. The New Integrity Warriors*, L. de Sousa, B. Hindess and P. Larmour (eds). London/New York:

Routledge, 186–208.

De Sousa, Luis, Barry Hindess and Peter Larmour, eds. 2009. *Governments, NGOs and Anti-Corruption. The New Integrity Warriors*. London/New York: Routledge.

Demidov, Boris. 2005. Corruption in Russia, 2000–2003: The role of the federal okrugs and presidential envoys. In *The Dynamics of Russian Politics. Putin's Reform of Federal-Regional Relations, Volume II*, P. Reddaway and R.W. Orttung (eds). Lanham: Rowman and Littlefield, 319–39.

Duka, Alexander, and Peter Rutland. 2004. North-west federal okrug. In *The Dynamics of Russian Politics. Putin's Reform of Federal-Regional Relations, Volume I*, P. Reddaway and R.W. Orttung (eds). Lanham: Rowman and Littlefield, 53–86.

EBRD. 2002. *Strategy for the Russian Federation*: European Bank for Reconstruction and Development.

——. 2004. *Strategy for the Russian Federation*: European Bank for Reconstruction and Development.

——. 2006. *Anti-Corruption Report*: European Bank for Reconstruction and Development.

Economist. 2005. Corruption in Russia. Blood money. Online edition, 20 October.

EU–Russia Summit. 2005. *Road Map for the Common Space of Freedom, Security and Justice*, Moscow, 10 May 2005, press release, Annex 2.

EUMAP. 2003. *Is Civil Society a Cause or Cure for Corruption in Central and Eastern Europe?*, EUMAP: EU Monitoring and Advocacy Program. Online journal, Feature.

European Commission. 2000. *Commission Regulation (EC) No 2584/2000 of 24 November 2000 establishing a system for the communication of information on certain supplies of beef, veal and pigmeat to the territory of the Russian Federation*.

——. 2001a. *Communication from the Commission to the Council – The EU and Kaliningrad*, COM (2001) 26 final.

——. 2001b. *Country Strategy Paper 2002–2006. National Indicative Programme 2002–2003. Russian Federation*, adopted by the Commission on 27 December 2001.

——. 2002. *Communication from the Commission to the Council – Kaliningrad. Transit*, COM (2002) 510 final.

—— 2003. *On a Comprehensive EU Policy Against Corruption*, Communication from the Commission to the Council, the European Parliament and the European Economic and Social Committee, COM (2003) 0317 final.

——. 2004. *Communication from the Commission. European Neighbourhood Policy. Strategy Paper*, COM (2004) 373 final.

European Commission and Council of Europe. 2006a. *Project 'Harmonisation of Russian Anti-Corruption Legislation with International Standards' (RUCOLA). Final Report*. Strasbourg: Council of Europe.

——. 2006b. *Russian Federation – Development of Legislative and Other Measures for the Prevention of Corruption (RUCOLA-2). Project Summary*.

Evans, Alfred B. 2006. Civil society in the Soviet Union? In *Russian Civil Society: A Critical Assessment*, Alfred B. Evans, Laura A. Henry and Lisa McIntosh Sundstrom (eds). Armonk, US: M.E. Sharpe, 28–54.

Evans, Alfred B., Laura A. Henry and Lisa McIntosh Sundstrom, eds. 2006. *Russian Civil Society. A Critical Assessment*. Armonk, US: M.E. Sharpe.

FATF/OECD. 2002. *Russia, Dominica, Niue, and Marshall Islands Removed from FATF's List of Non-cooperative Countries and Territories. Summary of the First Plenary Meeting of FATF-XIV*. Paris.

——. 2007. *Annual Review of Non-Cooperative Countries and Territories 2006–2007. Eigth NCCT Review*. Paris.

Fein, Elke. 2002. Zivilgesellschaftlicher Paradigmenwechsel oder PR-Aktion? Zum ersten allrussischen 'Bürgerforum' im Kreml. *Osteuropa-Spezial* 52 (April), 19–40.

Finnemore, Martha and Kathryn Sikkink. 1998. International norm dynamics and political change. *International Organisation* 52 (4), 887–917.

Fish, Steven. 2005. *Democracy Derailed in Russia. The Failure of Open Politics*. Cambridge/New York: Cambridge University Press.

Forum Donorov. 2005. *Donorskie i Nekommercheskie Organizatsii. Chto My o Nikh Znaem. Obzor Materialov Issledovanii*. Moskva: Forum Donorov.

G8 Centre. 2006. *Fighting High-Level Corruption*, St. Petersburg Summit Documents, St Petersburg, 16 July 2006.

Galtung, Fredrik. 2006. Measuring the immeasurable: boundaries and functions of (macro) corruption indices. In *Measuring Corruption*, C. Sampford et al. (eds). Aldershot/Burlington: Ashgate, 101–30.

GC. 2004. *Guidance Document. Implementation of the 10th Principle Against Corruption*: The Global Compact.

George, Alexander L. and Andrew Bennett. 2005. *Case Studies and Theory Development in the Social Sciences*. Cambridge, MA/London: MIT Press.

Gilmore, William C. 2004. *Dirty Money – The Evolution of International Measures to Counter Money Laundering and the Financing of Terrorism*. 3rd edn. Strasbourg: Council of Europe Publishing.

Glaser, B.G., and A.L. Strauss. 1967. *The Discovery of Grounded Theory: Strategies for Qualitative Research*. Chicago: Aldine Publishing Company.

Glynn, Patrick, Stephen J. Kobrin and Moises Naim. 1997. The globalization of corruption. In *Corruption and the Global Economy*, K.A. Elliott (ed.). Washington, DC: Institute for International Economics, 7–27.

Goffman, Erving. 1989. On fieldwork. *Journal of Contemporary Ethnography* 18 (2): 123–33.

Gole, Juliet S. 1999. *The Role of Civil Society in Containing Corruption at the Municipal Level*, Proceedings from the Regional Conference of Transparency International Representatives, 29–30 April 1999, Bratislava, Slovakia. Discussion Papers, No. 10. Budapest: Local Government and Public Service Reform Initiative/Open Society Institute.

Golishnikova, Olga. 2002. St. Petersburg roundtable focuses on venture capital. *Eurasia Foundation*. Online edition, 25 March.

Gornyi, Mikhail, ed. 2002. *Obshchestvennoe Uchastie v Buidzhetnom Protsesse na Severo-Zapade Rossii*. Sankt-Peterburg: Norma.

Gosudarstvennaia Duma. 2005. *Otchet ob Itogakh Raboty Komissii Gosudarstvennoi Dumy po Protivodeistviiu Korruptsii v 2004 Godu*.

—— 2006. *Otchet ob Itogakh Raboty Komissii Gosudarstvennoi Dumy po Protivodeistviiu Korruptsii za 2005 God*.

——. 2007a. *Otchet o Deiatel'nosti Komissii*

Gosudarstvennoi Dumy Federal'nogo Sobraniia Rossiiskoi Federatsii po Protivodeistviiu Korruptsii za 2006 God.

—— 2007b. *Otchet o Deiatel'nosti Komissii Gosudarstvennoi Dumy Federal'nogo Sobraniia Rossiiskoi Federatsii v Chetvertom Sozyve Gosudarstvennoi Dumy (2004–2007gg.).*

Gray, Cheryl, Joel Hellman and Randi Ryterman. 2004. *Anticorruption in Transition 2. Corruption in Enterprise-State Interactions in Europe and Central Asia 1999–2002.* Washington, DC: The International Bank for Reconstruction and Development/World Bank.

GRECO. 2008a. *38th Plenary Meeting of GRECO (Strasbourg, 9–13 June 2008)*, Summary Report, Greco (2008) 13E revised. Strasbourg: GRECO/Council of Europe.

——. 2008b. *Evaluation Report on the Russian Federation. Joint First and Second Evaluation Rounds*, Greco Eval I-II Rep (2008) 2E, adopted by GRECO at its 40th Plenary Meeting (Strasbourg, 1–5 December 2008). Strasbourg: Group of States Against Corruption/Council of Europe.

Greenhouse, Carol J. 2002. Introduction: altered states, altered lives. In *Ethnography in Unstable Places. Everyday Lives in Contexts of Dramatic Political Change*, C.J. Greenhouse, E. Mertz and K.B. Warren (eds). Durham/London: Duke University Press, 1–34.

GTZ. 2004. *Mainstreaming Anti-Corruption. Chapeau-Papier*, Division 42 Sector Project: Development and Testing of Strategies and Instruments for the Prevention of Corruption. Eschborn: Deutsche Gesellschaft für Technische Zusammenarbeit (GTZ) GmbH.

Hamm, Brigitte. 2006. *Anti-Corruption Policy Concepts of Three Bilateral Donors – Commonalities and Differences*, Paper presented at ECPR Joint Sessions of Workshops, Nicosia, Cyprus, 25–30 April 2006.

Hammersley, Martyn. 1990. What's wrong with ethnography? The myth of theoretical description. *Sociology* 24: 597–615.

Heinrich, Volkhart Finn. 2003. Transparency and corruption within civil society organisations. In *Global Corruption Report*, Transparency International (ed). London: Pluto Press, 271–73.

Henderson, Sarah L. 2003. *Building Democracy in*

Contemporary Russia. Western Support for Grassroots Organisations. Ithaca and London: Cornell University Press.

Holm, Kerstin. 2006. Korruption in Russland. Des Beamten neue Kleider. *Frankfurter Allgemeine Zeitung*, 3 July, 37.

Holmes, Leslie. 1993. *The End of Communist Power. Anti Corruption Campaigns and Legitimation Crisis*. Cambridge: Polity.

Hornsby-Smith, Michael. 1993. Gaining access. In *Researching Social Life*, N. Gilbert (ed.). London/ Thousand Oaks/New Delhi: Sage, 52–67.

Hotchkiss, Carolyn. 1998. The sleeping dog stirs: new signs of life in efforts to end corruption in international business. *Journal of Public Policy & Marketing* 17 (1): 108–15.

IBRD/World Bank. 2003. *The World Bank and Anticorruption in Europe and Central Asia. Enhancing Transparency, Voice and Accountability*. Washington, D.C.: IBRD/World Bank.

Il'yin, Mikhail V. 2005. Studies of globalization and equity in post-Soviet Russia. In *New Directions in Russian International Studies*, A.P. Tsygankov and P.A. Tsygankov (eds). Stuttgart: ibidem, 107–25.

IMF. 1997. *Good Governance. The IMF's Role*. Washington, DC: International Monetary Fund.

INDEM. 1998. *Rossiia i Korruptsia: Kto Kogo*. Moskva: Informatika dlia Demokratii (Fond INDEM).

——. 2005. *Vo Skol'ko Raz Uvelichilas' Korruptsia za 4 Goda: Resul'taty Novogo Issledovaniia Fonda INDEM*. Moskva.

Itar-Tass. 2006. LDPR Leader Comes out with Anti-Corruption Offer. *Itar-Tass*, 10 January.

Ivanov, Kalin. 2010. The 2007 accession of Bulgaria and Romania: ritual and reality. In *Anti-Corruption for Eastern Europe*, Global Crime, special issue, 11(2), D. Schmidt-Pfister and H. Moroff (eds).

Johnson, Debra and Paul Robinson, eds. 2008. *Perspectives on EU-Russia Relations*. London/New York: Routledge.

Johnston, Michael. 2005. Participation, institutions, and syndromes of corruption. In *Syndromes of Corruption: Wealth, Power, and Democracy*, M. Johnston (ed.). Cambridge: Cambridge University Press, 36–59.

JRL RAS. 2004. Beslan and corruption. *JRL Research &*

Analytical Supplement (No. 25) October 2004, Johnson's Russia List #8290.

Kaufmann, Daniel, Aart Kraay and Massimo Mastruzzi. 2007a. *Governance Matters VII. Aggregate and Individual Governance Indicators 1996–2007*, World Bank Policy Research Working Paper No. 4654. Washington, DC: The World Bank.

——. 2007b. Growth and governance: a rejoinder. *Journal of Politics* 69 (2): 570–2.

——. 2007c. Growth and governance: a reply. *Journal of Politics* 69 (2): 555–62.

——. 2007d. *The Worldwide Governance Indicators Project. Answering the Critics*, World Bank Policy Research Working Paper No. 4149. Washington, DC: The World Bank.

Keck, Margaret E. and Kathryn Sikkink. 1998. *Activists Beyond Borders. Advocacy Networks in International Politics*. Ithaca/London: Cornell University Press.

Kliamkin, Igor' and Lev Timofeev. 2000. *Tenavaia Rossiia. Ekonomiko-Sotsiologicheskoe Issledovanie*. Moskva: Rossiiskii gosudarstvennyi gumanitarnyi universitet.

Kopecký, Petr. 2003. Civil society, uncivil society and contentious politics in post-communist Europe. In *Uncivil Society? Contentious Politics in Post-Communist Europe*, P. Kopecký and C. Mudde (eds). London/New York: Routledge, 1–18.

Krastev, Ivan. 2004. *Shifting Obsessions. Three Essays on the Politics of Anticorruption*. Budapest/New York: CEU Press.

Kupchinsky, Roman, Elena Chirkova and Marina Savintseva. 2004. Russia. In *Global Corruption Report 2004*, Transparency International (ed.). London/Sterling, VA: Transparency International, 246–50.

Lambsdorff, Johann Graf. 2001. *How Precise are Perceived Levels of Corruption? Background Paper to the 2001 Corruption Perceptions Index*. Transparency International and Göttingen University.

——. 2005. *The Methodology of the 2005 Corruption Perceptions Index*, Transparency International (TI) and University of Passau.

Lebedev, Anastasiya. 2006. Kremlin Warns Against 'Different Russia'. *The St. Petersburg Times*, Issue 1183 (49), Tuesday, 4 July 2006.

Ledeneva, Alena V. 1998. *Russia's Economy of Favours. Blat, Networking and Informal Exchange*, Cambridge Russia, Soviet and Post-Soviet Studies. Cambridge: Cambridge University Press.

——. 2001. *Unwritten Rules. How Russia Really Works*. CER Essay May 2001: Center for European Reform.

—— 2003. Non-transparency and globalization: Russia's unwritten rules. In *Resistance to Globalization. Political Struggle and Cultural Resilience in the Middle East, Russia, and Latin America*, H. Barrios et al. (eds). Münster/Hamburg/London: LIT Verlag, 86–94.

Lee, Raymond. 1995. *Dangerous Fieldwork*. Thousand Oaks/London/New Delhi: Sage.

Lee, Raymond M. 1999. *Doing Research on Sensitive Topics*. London/Thousand Oaks/New Delhi: Sage.

Levada-Center. 2006. *From Opinion Toward Understanding. Russian Public Opinion 2005*. Moscow: Levada-Center.

Levada Analitycal Center. 2008. *From Opinion Toward Understanding. Russian Public Opinion 2007*. Moscow: Levada-Center.

Lewin, Moshe. 1991. *The Gorbachev Phenomenon. A Historical Interpretation*. Expanded edition. Berkeley/Los Angeles: University of California Press.

Lofland, John and Lyn H. Lofland. 1995. *Analyzing Social Settings. A Guide to Qualitative Observation and Analysis*. 3rd edn. Belmont: Wadsworth.

Marcus, George E. 1995. Ethnography in/of the world system: the emergence of multi-sited ethnography. *Annual Review of Anthropology* 24: 95–117.

Marquette, Heather. 2004. The creeping politicisation of the World Bank: the case of corruption. *Political Studies* 52 (3): 413–30.

Martirossian, Jasmine. 2004. Russia and her ghosts of the past. In *The Struggle Against Corruption. A Comparative Study*, R.A. Johnson (ed.). New York/Houndmills: Palgrave Macmillan, 81–108.

McAdam, Doug and Dieter Rucht. 1993. The cross-national diffusion of movement ideas. *Annals of the American Academy of Political and Social Science* (528): 56–74.

McCoy, Jennifer and Heather Heckel. 2001. The emergence of a global anti-corruption norm. *International Politics* 38 (1): 65–90.

McIntosh Sundstrom, Lisa. 2006. *Funding Civil Society. Foreign Assistance and NGO Development in Russia*. Stanford: Stanford University Press.

Medetsky, Anatoly. 2006. Judges Coming under Scrutiny. *The Moscow Times*. Online edition, 23 June.

Mendelson, Sarah E. and John K. Glenn. 2002. Introduction: Transnational networks and NGOs in postcommunist societies. In *The Power and Limits of NGOs. A Critical Look at Building Democracy in Eastern Europe and Eurasia*, S.E. Mendelson and J.K. Glenn (eds). New York Chichester, West Sussex: Columbia University Press, 1–28.

Michael, Bryane. 2004a. The rapid rise of the anticorruption industry. *Local Governance Brief* (Spring): 17–25.

——. 2004b. *Some Reflections on Donor Sponsored Anti-Corruption*. http://users.ox.ac.uk/~scat1663/Publications /Presentations/Donor%20Sponsored%20Anti-Corruption.ppt (accessed 18/08/05).

Moore, Barrington Jr. 1951. *Soviet Politics – The Dilemma of Power. The Role of Ideas in Social Change*. Cambridge, MA: Harvard University Press.

Moroff, Holger. 2005. Internationalisierung von Anti-Korruptionsregimen. In *Dimensionen politischer Korruption. Beiträge zum Stand der internationalen Forschung, DVPW Sonderheft 35/2005*, U. v. Alemann (ed.). Wiesbaden: VS Verlag, 444–76.

MSI. 2002a. *Korruptsia v Samarskoi Oblasti. Resul'aty Oprosa Obshchestvennogo Mneniia, Oktiabr' 2001 g.* Washington: Management Systems International.

——. 2002b. *Korruptsia v Tomskoi Oblasti. Resul'aty Oprosa Obshchestvennogo Mneniia, Oktiabr' 2001 g.* Washington: Management Systems International.

——. 2004. *Obshchestvennoe Mnenie o Korruptsii v Irkutskoi Oblasti. Rezul'taty Sotsiologicheskogo Issledovaniia Naseleniia g. Irkutska, Mai-iiun' 2004.* Washington: Management Systems International.

Mulin, Sergei. 2006. The Sleepy Bureaucrats. *Novaya Gazeta weekly*. Online edition, 12 January.

Murphy, Kim. 2004. Russia May Pay for Bribes in Lives. *Los Angeles Times*. Online edition, 8 November.

Murray, Matthew and Elena Panfilova. 2003. How to root out Russian corruption. *The Russia Journal* (17 April): 15.

Nadelmann, Ethan A. 1990. Global prohibition regimes. The evolution of norms in international society. *International Organization* 44 (4): 479–526.

Naim, Moises. 1995. The corruption eruption. *The Brown Journal of World Affairs* II (2/Summer): 245–61.

NAK. 2001. *Osnovnye Napravleniia Antikorruptsionnoi Politiki Rossii. Proekt.*

——. 2004. *Korruptsiia – ugroza nomer odin dlia Rossii.*

Oates, Sarah. 2006. Media, civil society, and the failure of the fourth estate in Russia. In *Russian Civil Society. A Critical Assessment*, A.B. Evans, L.A. Henry and L.M. Sundstrom (eds). Armonk, US: M.E. Sharpe, 57–72.

OECD. 1997. *Revised Recommendation of the Council on Combating Bribery in International Business Transactions.*

—— 1998. *Convention on Combating Bribery of Foreign Public Officials in International Business Transactions.* Working Group on Bribery in International Business Transactions (CIME) (ed.). DAFFE/IME/BR(97)20: Organisation for Economic Co-operation and Development.

—— 2002a. *Co-operating with the Private Sector and Civil Society in the Fight Against Corruption.*

——, ed. 2002b. *Anti-corruption Measures in South Eastern Europe. Civil Society's Involvement.* Paris: Organisation for Economic Co-operation and Development.

——. 2003. *Fighting Corruption. What Role for Civil Society? The Experience of the OECD.* Paris: Organisation for Economic Co-operation and Development.

——. 2004a. Progress and prospects. In *OECD Investment Policy Reviews. Russian Federation – Progress and Reform Challenges.* Paris: Organisation for Economic Co-operation and Development, 9–19.

——. 2004b. *Questionnaire to Countries Seeking Participation in the Working Group on Bribery in International Business Transactions and Accession to the OECD Convention on Combatting Bribery of Foreign Public Officials in International Business Transactions,* DAFFE/IME/BR/WD (2004) 9.

——. 2005. *Russia. Building Rules for the Market,* OECD Reviews of Regulatory Reform. Paris: OECD Publishing.

Olimpieva, Irina and Oleg Pachenkov, eds. 2003. *Neformal'naia Ekonomika v Postsovetskom Prostranstve.* Sankt Petersburg: Tsentr nesavisimyx sotsiologicheskix issledovanii.

Olimpieva, Irina, Oleg Pachenkov and Elena Nikiforova. 2004. *Fighting Corruption in State-Business Relations. Small and Medium Business in St. Petersburg*, unpublished manuscript. St. Petersburg: Center for Independent Social Research.

Osborn, Andrew. 2006. Moscow Says 'Nyet' to Rudeness of Civil Servants. *The Independent*. Online edition, 18 January 2006.

Petrov, Nikolai. 2005. The security dimension of the federal reforms. In *The Dynamics of Russian Politics. Putin's Reform of Federal-Regional Relations, Volume II*, P. Reddaway and R.W. Orttung (eds). Lanham: Rowman and Littlefield, 7–32.

Polotskii, Semen. 2006. Narod i Transneft: kto kogo? *Baikal'skie Vesti*, 25 Aprelia.

Protiv Korruptsii. 2006. Skol'ko Vsiatok Platit Rossiia? Korruptsiia – slishkom ser'eznaia problema, chtoby iskat' ee preyvelicheniami . . . *Protiv Korruptsii*, 18 May.

Putin, Vladimir. 2000. *Annual Address to the Federal Assembly of the Russian Federation*, 8 July. Moscow, the Kremlin.

——. 2001. *Annual Address to the Federal Assembly of the Russian Federation*, 3 April. Moscow, the Kremlin.

——. 2002. *Annual Address to the Federal Assembly of the Russian Federation*, 18 April. Moscow, the Kremlin.

——. 2006. *Annual Address to the Federal Assembly of the Russian Federation*, 10 May. Moscow, the Kremlin.

Radio Maiak. 2006. *2006 God Stanet Perelomnym v Bor'be s Korruptsiei*, Grishankov in interview with radio Maiak, 16 May 2006.

Rawlinson, Patricia. 2003. Bad boys in the Baltics. In *Transnational Organised Crime. Perspectives on Global Security*, A. Edwards and P. Gill (eds). London: Routledge, 131–233.

Reznik, Boris. 2001. Russia's unhappy image. *Vremya*, 18 July 2001.

RFE/RL. 2005a. Jailed Russian UN Official Freed on Bail. 21 November.

——. 2005b. Police Search Khodorkovskii's NGO. *RFE/RL Newsline*, 9 (190), 7 October.

——. 2005c. Yukos-Connected Foundation Being Audited

Again. *RFE/RL Newsline*, 6 (36) 24 February.

RIAN. 2006a. L'approche Des Élections Favorise la Révélation des Cas de Corruption. *Ria Novosti*. Online edition, 19 June.

——. 2006b. Wrap: Lawmakers Back Chaika as Candidate for Top Prosecutor. *Ria Novosti*. Online edition, 19 June.

Risse, Thomas. 2000. The power of norms versus the norms of power: transnational civil society and human rights. In *The Third Force. The Rise of Transnational Civil Society*, A.M. Florini (ed.). Washington, DC: Carnegie Endowment for International Peace, 177–209.

Risse, Thomas and Stephen C. Ropp. 1999. International human rights norms and domestic change: conclusions. In *The Power of Human Rights. International Norms and Domestic Change*, T. Risse, S.C. Ropp and K. Sikkink (eds). Cambridge: Cambridge University Press, 234–78.

Risse, Thomas and Kathryn Sikkink. 1999. The socialization of international human rights norms into domestic practices: introduction. In *The Power of Human Rights. International Norms and Domestic Change*, T. Risse, S.C. Ropp and K. Sikkink (eds). Cambridge: Cambridge University Press, 1–38.

Russia Profile. 2006. Russia becomes competitive. Interview with Dmitry Peskov, First Deputy Press Secretary for Russian President Vladimir Putin. *Russia Profile* 3 (5): 28–30.

Rutland, Peter. 2006. Business and civil society in russia. In *Russian Civil Society: A Critical Assessment*, A.B. Evans, L.A. Henry and L.M. Sundstrom (eds). Armonk, US: M.E. Sharpe, 73–94.

Rutland, Peter and Natasha Kogan. 2001. The Russian mafia: between hype and reality. In *Contemporary Russian Politics*, A. Brown (ed.). Oxford: Oxford University Press, 139–47.

Sakwa, Richard. 2008. *Russian Politics and Society*. 4th edn. London/New York: Routledge.

Sampson, Steven. 2005. Integrity warriors: global morality and the anti-corruption movement in the Balkans. In *Corruption. Anthropological Perspectives*, D. Haller and C. Shore (eds). London/Ann Arbor, MI: Pluto Press Ltd, 103–30.

——. 2009. Corruption and anti-corruption in Southeast

Europe. Landscapes and sites. In *Governments, NGOs and Anti-Corruption. The New Integrity Warriors*, L. de Sousa, B. Hindess and P. Larmour (eds). London/New York: Routledge, 168–85.

Sandul, Irina. 2004. The Return of Public Order Squads. *Transitions Online*, 15 July.

Satarov, Georgii A., ed. 2004. *Antikorruptsionnaia Politika. Uchebnoe Posobie*. Moskva: INDEM.

Savintseva, Marina and Petra Stykow. 2005. Country report. Russia. In *Global Corruption Report 2005*, Transparency International (ed.). London/Ann Arbor, MI: Pluto Press, Transparency International, 199–202.

Schmidt, Diana. 2002. *Weltnaturerbe Baikalsee. Lokale Resonanzen auf eine globale Umweltkonvention*, Diploma thesis, University of Cologne, unpublished.

——. 2006a. *Anti-Corruption Advocacy in Contemporary Russia. Local Civil Society Actors, Transnational Networks and the State*, PhD thesis, Queen's University Belfast.

——. 2006b. Russia's NGO Legislation: New (and Old) Developments. *Russian Analytical Digest* (3): 2–6.

——. 2007a. Anti-corruption advocacy in Russia? Local civil society actors between international and domestic contexts. In *Movements, Migrants, Marginalisation. Challenges of Societal and Political Participation in Eastern Europe and the Enlarged EU*, S. Fischer, H. Pleines and H. Schröder (eds). Stuttgart: ibidem, 83–98.

——. 2007b. Anti-corruption: what do we know? Research on preventing corruption in the post-Communist world. *Political Studies Review* 5 (2): 202–32.

Schmidt-Pfister, Diana. 2008. What kind of civil society in Russia? In *Media, Culture and Society in Putin's Russia*, S. White (ed.). Houndmills: Palgrave Macmillan, 37–71.

Shkolnikov, Aleksandr. 2006. Russian Parliament Ratifies the U.N. Convention Against Corruption. *CIPE Development Blog*, 17 February.

Shore, Chris and Dieter Haller. 2005. Introduction – sharp practice: anthropology and the study of corruption. In *Corruption. Anthropological Perspectives*, D. Haller and C. Shore (eds). London/Ann Arbor, MI: Pluto Press Ltd, 1–28.

Sikkink, Kathryn. 2005. Patterns of dynamic multilevel governance and the insider-outsider coalition. In

Transnational Protest and Global Activism, D. Della Porta (ed.). Lanham: Rowman and Littlefield, 151–73.

Slider, Darrel. 2005. Politics in the regions. In *Developments in Russian Politics 6*, S. White, Z. Gitelman and R. Sakwa (eds). Houndmills: Palgrave Macmillan, 168–85.

Spector, Bertram I. and Svetlana Winbourne. 2002. Anti-corruption citizen advocacy offices: from idea to success. In *Antikorruptsionnyie Grazhdanskie Advokatury. Opyt Raboty i Razvitie Setevo Vzaimodeistviia*, MSI (ed.), Samara: Samarskii Tsentr Prava and Povolzhskii gumani-tarnyi fond, 44–6.

Strategia, ed. 2003. *Preduprezhdenie Korruptsii. Chto Mozhet Obshchestvo.* Sankt Peterburg: Sankt-Peterburgskii gumanitarno-politologicheskii tsentr 'Strategiia'/Norma.

Strauss, Anselm and Juliet Corbin, eds. 1998. *Grounded Theory in Practice*. Thousand Oaks: Sage.

Sungurov, A.I., ed. 2002. *'Fabriki Mysli' i tsentry publichnoi politiki: mezhdunarodnyi i pervyi rossiiskii opyt, Tsentry publichnoi politiki*. Sankt-Peterburg: Norma.

Szilágyi, Ákos. 2002. Kompromat and corruption in Russia. In *Political Corruption in Transition. A Sceptic's Handbook*, S. Kotkin and A. Sajó (eds). Budapest/New York: CEU Press, 207–31.

The Center for Public Integrity. 2004. *Global Integrity. An Investigative Report Tracking Corruption, Openness and Accountability in 25 Countries. Russia.*

Thomson, Brian, et al. 2007. *Evaluation of DFID's Country Programmes: Russia 2001 to 2005*, EVSUM 677, June 2007: DFID, Department for International Development.

TI. 1997. *Transparency International Publishes 1997 Corruption Perceptions Index*. Berlin: Transparency International.

——. 2000. Chapter 29: Lessons learned – a progress report. In *TI Source Book 2000*, Transparency International (ed.). Berlin: Transparency International.

——. 2003. *Comments on the European Commission Communication on 'A Comprehensive EU Policy Against Corruption'*. Brussels, 30 July 2003 (REV.1): Submitted by Transparency International – Brussels.

——. 2005a. *Corruption Still Rampant in 70 Countries, Says Corruption Perceptions Index 2005*, Press Release,

London/Berlin, 18 October 2005.

——. 2005b. *Report on the Transparency International Global Corruption Barometer 2005*. Berlin: Policy and Research Department, Transparency International – International Secretariat.

———, ed. 2005c. *Global Corruption Report 2005. Special Focus. Corruption in Construction and Post-conflict Reconstruction*. London/Ann Arbor, MI: Pluto Press, Transparency International.

TI, and UN-Habitat. 2004. *Tools to Support Transparency in Local Governance*, Urban Governance Toolkit Series. Nairobi/Berlin: Transparency International/United Nations Human Settlement Programme.

TI-Russia. 2002. *Corruption Indices for Russian Regions. Project Description*. Moscow: Transparency International Russia.

Timtschenko, Viktor. 2003. *Putin und das Neue Russland*. Muenchen: Diederichs.

Tisne, Martin and Daniel Smilov. 2004. *From the Ground Up. Assessing the Record of Anticorruption Assistance in Southeastern Europe*. Budapest: Central European University Press.

UNA-USA. 2005. *Independent Inquiry Committee Final Report on the Oil-for-Food Investigation*: United Nations Association of the USA and the Business Council for the UN.

UNDP. 1997. *Corruption and Good Governance. Discussion Paper 3*. New York: United Nations Development Programme.

——. 2003. *Country Programme Otline for the Russian Federation (2004–2007)*, DP/CPO/RUS/1. New York: United Nations Development Programme.

——. 2004. *Anti-Corruption. Practice Note*. New York: United Nations Development Programme.

——. 2007. *UNDP Country Programme for the Russian Federation (2008–2010)*, 27 July 2007: United Nations Development Programme.

United Nations. 2004. *United Nations Convention against Corruption*. New York: UN/UNODC.

——. 2005. *Corruption: Threats and Trends in the Twenty-First Century*, Working paper prepared by the Secretariat. A/CONF.203/6. 16 March 2005. Bangkok, 18–25 April

2005. Eleventh United Nations Congress on Crime Prevention and Criminal Justice.

UNODC. 2004. *UN Anti-Corruption Toolkit. The Global Programme Against Corruption*. 3rd edn. Vienna: United Nations Office on Drugs and Crime.

——. 2005. *Compendium of International Legal Instruments on Corruption*, United Nations Office on Drugs and Crime. Vienna/New York: United Nations.

UNODCCP. 2001. *United Nations Manual on Anti-Corruption Policy*, Global Programme against Corruption. UN Anti-Corruption Policy. CICP-16. Vienna: United Nations Office of Drug Control and Crime Prevention.

USAID. 2004. *The Development Challenge. Russia*.

——. 2005a. *Russia: Corruption and Transparency in Business Registration and Regulation*: IRIS Center.

——. 2005b. *USAID Anticorruption Strategy*. Washington: US Agency for International Development.

USAID and MSI. 2003. *Civil Society Successes in Fighting Corruption in Russia's Regions*. Washington: Center for Governmental Integrity Management Systems International/United States Agency for International Development.

Vasiliev, Dmitry. 2002. Kodeks povedenia gosudarstvennykh sluzhashchikh: evropeiskoi opyt i rossiiskaia deistvitel'nost', *Brifingi Moskovskogo Tsentra Karnegi* 4 (7): 1–4.

VDW. 2004. *Wachstumsmarkt Russland. Die Zukunft hat begonnen*, Jahresbericht 2004 des Verbandes der Deutschen Wirtschaft in der Russischen Föderation. Moskau: Verband der Deutschen Wirtschaft.

Vernidoub, Artyom. 2002. Ustinov Holds Back on Anti-Corruption Campaign. *gazeta.ru*. Online edition, 16 May.

Volkov, Vadim. 2002. *Violent Entrepreneurs. The Use of Force in the Making of Russian Capitalism*. Ithaca/London: Cornell University Press.

Vol'skaia-Vinborn, Svetlana et al. 2004. *Protivodeistvie Korruptsii Organizatsiami Grazhdanskogo Obshchestva. Iz Opyta Realizatsii Programmy Partnerstvo v Protivodeistvii Korruptsii*. Samara/Tomsk: Koalitsiia 'Partnerstvo po protivodeistviiu korruptsii' v Samarskoi oblasti/Koalitsiia protiv korruptsii v Tomskoi oblasti.

Voltchkova, Ludmila and Tatiana Zvetcova. 2005. The

Russian Federation. In *Anti-Corruption Training Programmes in Central and Eastern Europe*, B. Michael (ed.). Strasbourg: Council of Europe Publishing, 79–89.

Vorobyev, Dmitry. 2005. *Strengthening Green Ideology in Russia under the Pressure of Globalisation and Authoritarianism*, Paper presented at the 3rd ECPR Conference, Section 19/7, Budapest, 8–10 September 2005.

Warren, Kay B. 2002. Toward an anthropology of fragments, instabilities, and incomplete transitions. In *Ethnography in Unstable Places. Everyday Lives in Contexts of Dramatic Political Change*, C.J. Greenhouse, E. Mertz and K.B. Warren (eds). Durham/London: Duke University Press, 379–92.

Willerton, John P. 2005. Putin and the hegemonic presidency. In *Developments in Russian Politics 6*, S. White, Z. Gitelman and R. Sakwa (eds). Houndmills: Palgrave Macmillan, 18–39.

Williams, Robert. 2000. Introduction. In *Controlling Corruption*, R. Williams and A. Doig (eds). Cheltenham/Northampton: Edward Elgar, xi–xiii.

Williams, Robert and Robin Theobald, eds. 2000. *Corruption in the Developing World*. Vol. 2, *The Politics of Corruption*. Cheltenham/Northampton: Edward Elgar.

Wolf, Sebastian. 2010. How the Council of Europe, OECD and Transparency International view corruption in Eastern Europe. In *Anti-Corruption for Eastern Europe*, Global Crime, special issue, 11(2), D. Schmidt-Pfister and H. Moroff (eds).

World Bank. 1997. *Helping Countries Combat Corruption. The Role of the World Bank*, Poverty Reduction and Economic Management Network. Washington, DC: World Bank.

——. 2000a. *Anticorruption in Transition. A Contribution to the Policy Debate*. Washington, DC: The World Bank.

——. 2000b. *Helping Countries Combat Corruption. Progress at the World Bank Since 1997*, Poverty Reduction and Economic Management (PREM) Network. Washington, DC: World Bank.

——. 2003. *Multi-pronged Strategies for Combating Corruption. Civil Society Participation*, Anticorruption Project of The Wold Bank Group.

———. 2006. *Strengthening Bank Group Engagement on Governance and Anticorruption*, Development Committee DC2006–0017, 8 September: IMF and World Bank.

———. 2008. *Streghtening World Bank Group Engagement On Governance and Anticorruption. One-Year Progress Report*. Washington, DC.

Yablokova, Oksana. 2004. Putin Tells Diplomats to Do PR for Russia. *The Moscow Times*. Online edition, 13 July.

———. 2006. Bureaucrats are Facing Pressure to Work Faster. *The Moscow Times*, 31 July, 3.

Yablokova, Oksana and Nabi Abdullaev. 2006. New Chief Prosecutor Sacks Six Of His Deputies. *The St. Petersburg Times*, 7 July.

Index

Note: 'n.' after a page reference indicates the number of a note on that page